The Setting Sun

The Setting Sun

*A Memoir of Empire
and Family Secrets*

Bart Moore-Gilbert

VERSO
London • New York

First published by Verso 2014
© Bart Moore-Gilbert 2014

1 3 5 7 9 10 8 6 4 2

Verso
UK: 6 Meard Street, London W1F 0EG
US: 20 Jay Street, Suite 1010, Brooklyn, NY 11201
www.versobooks.com

Verso is the imprint of New Left Books

ISBN-13: 978-1-78168-268-5
eISBN-13: 978-1-78168-269-2 (US)
eISBN-13: 978-1-78168-646-1 (UK)

British Library Cataloguing in Publication Data
A catalogue record for this book is available from the British Library

Library of Congress Cataloging-in-Publication Data

Moore-Gilbert, B. J., 1952–
The setting sun : a memoir of empire and family secrets / Bart Moore-Gilbert.
  pages cm
  ISBN 978-1-78168-268-5 (hardback) – ISBN 978-1-78168-269-2 (ebook)
1. Police misconduct – India – Satara (District) – History – 20th century. 2. Police
– India – Satara (District) – History – 20th century. 3. Terrorism – India – Satara
(District) – History – 20th century. 4. India – History – Autonomy and
independence movements. 5. India – History – British occupation, 1765–1947.
6. Moore-Gilbert, B. J., 1952 – Travel – India. I. Title.
HV8249.S37M66 2014
954.03'59092 – dc23
[B]
                                   2013037732

Typeset in Sabon by MJ & N Gavan, Truro, Cornwall
Printed in the UK by CPI Group (UK) Ltd, Croydon, CR0 4YY

This book is for you, Madeleine. It's no substitute for your grandfather, but it will help you to know him better.

'We have to create our lives, create memory.'

Doris Lessing, *Under My Skin*

'So while, when I travel, I can move only according to what I find, I also live, as it were, in a novel of my own making, moving from not knowing to knowing, with person interweaving with person and incident opening out to incident.'

V.S. Naipaul, *Finding the Centre*

Contents

Acknowledgements

Writing this book, I've accrued debts to many people. First I would like to thank everyone I met in India who facilitated my journey and the researches on which it is based. Several are mentioned in the text, one or two with their names changed – at their request. Without their friendship and help, there would be no narrative.

In the UK and elsewhere, many family members and friends helped by reading drafts and making comments, by providing information and photographs, or otherwise facilitating the progress of the text from uncertain beginnings. These include: Anthony and Pat Bicknell; Janice Biskin-Stanton; Bernadette Buckley; Patrick Gilbert-Hopkins; Keith Goldsmith; Anna Hartnell; Manali Jagtap-Nyheim (who provided invaluable help with translations from Mahratti); Ames and Lindsay Moore-Gilbert; Blake Morrison; Susheila Nasta (who published one extract from an earlier draft in *Wasafiri*); and Sanjay Seth (who published another in *Postcolonial Studies*).

My most important debts are to Francis Spufford, who provided huge support throughout and brilliant editorial interventions in early drafts. His sure feel for what was really at stake in the text and gimlet eye for what was redundant played a huge part in its final shape. And Leo Hollis at Verso responded with wonderful enthusiasm from the moment he received the unsolicited script.

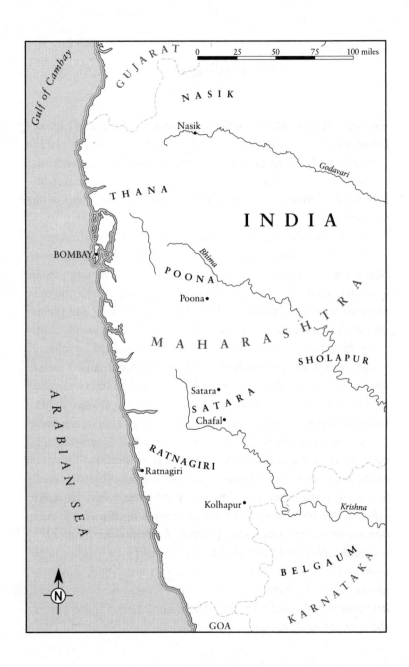

Prologue

'Get up, Nigger, quick,' Wilson's whisper rasps, 'don't wake the others.'

The boy stirs reluctantly, flinching at the icy draught from the window above his bed. Next to him, he can just make out the beached bulk of Greenwell, the largest pupil in his year, snoring softly.

'The Colonel wants to see you.'

The boy's instantly alert. Wilson, the head prefect, who sleeps on the floor below with the senior boys, has never acknowledged his existence before. His housemaster? Why? He jerks back the blankets and reaches for the dressing gown on his chair. It feels like the middle of the night.

'In his study.'

The boy's too intimidated to ask questions. His mind churns over recent misdemeanors. No, he's already been called to account for those. Perhaps another prefect overheard him tonight, telling his tale, long after lights out. They often take turns. The boy's generally reluctant to participate, even though he loves stories and there's no set formula to follow. It can be made-up, a summary of a film, anecdotes about their fathers' work, or a commentary on a recent sporting event. He can't rehearse the plots of television programmes because his family has never owned one. They've only had electricity since he was eight. He loves football, but hasn't been here long enough to have mastered recent developments in the league. Hearing about Herbert Chapman, or Highbury's record crowd, things his father has passed on from when he lived in England before the war, interests no one.

PROLOGUE

So when his turn comes, the boy usually talks of Africa, because that's what he knows. Often he speaks about the minder he's had since the age of four. Kimwaga can uncap a fizzing bottle of Pepsi with his back teeth, feather the boy's arrows and locate wild hives by following the honeybird, which he answers with a special whistle. It's Kimwaga who gave him the elephant-hair bangle to keep him safe in England and which the boy never removes, even in the shower. Some of his schoolmates insisted it was plastic, until one day he put a match to one of the ebony-coloured filaments and the stink convinced them.

As the boy talks, he can almost smell the woodsmoke on Kimwaga's warm black skin, see the dark eyes glinting above knobbly cheekbones, trace the crisped hair so different from his own. It's his favourite way of insulating himself against this freezing country where there's been no sun to speak of for half a year, where the birds all seem to be grey, brown or black and where he's had to learn endless rules, most of which make no sense.

Generally his classmates listen politely; but what he speaks of is so alien – rescuing stricken hens from safari ants, greasing tranquillised hippos to stop their hides cracking when the pools dry up, having his Wellingtons scoffed by a hyena. Sometimes, sensing their resistance, he tones it down to make it more like what they know, to make himself more acceptable. Tonight two of them had talked about their pets' mishaps. So he decided to tell of how one of the boxers got into a fight with a leopard.

Tunney had disappeared one afternoon, and came hobbling back at dusk from the direction of the nearby hill, gabled with great bald rocks and thicketed with thorn and cactus. Much of his right shoulder was missing, skin, muscle and sinew ripped away. The shiny grey cartilage and glistening bone beneath had made the boy want to vomit. It looked like one of the cheaper cuts hung outside the butcher's stall in the village in central

Tanganyika where they live. Tunney's joint, too, was already attracting the fat green flies that buzzed round the wedges of crimson flesh hanging from hooks above the counter or settling on the plates of marbled brains along it. The dog's blood smelled like warm brass. At first the boy's father frowned, his brow knitting in the expression which withers the boy when it's turned on him.

'He'll be alright,' he suddenly smiled, pinching his son's cheek. 'Don't cry, now. It won't help. Go and get some water.'

When the boy returned at a run, bowl slopping, his father was fiddling in the green canvas medicine bag. As the dog lapped and lapped, he took out a squat steel hypodermic, attached the long needle and punched it into a phial. Clamping the boxer's back legs between his thighs, his father squirted some liquid from the needle, before stabbing it briskly into the dog's haunch. Then, refilling from a different phial, he repeated the process. Both times Tunney yelped, but didn't struggle. His long tongue drooped, showing damp squiggles of gold and black fur wedged round his canines. While his father was gently cleaning the wound, the boy held Tunney's chest in his hands, willing the panting slower. When the dog at last flopped down on one side, the boy began to pick grey ticks from between his pet's toes, rolling them like blobs of plasticine under the sole of his takkie *and setting them aside to burn later.*

His father's face was close to him. By this time of day the shadow deepened round the chin, as if the thick dark growth on his head, convict-short at the sides and lightly Brylcreemed on top, needed to find somewhere else to emerge.

'At least it's not a snake. It's that damned chui. *Look at the claw-marks down his back.'*

For several nights, since they'd first heard the leopard's growling cough from the hill, Tunney and Dempsey had been shut indoors. Leopards like dogs almost as much as goats. His father put an arm round the boy's shoulder.

'*He'll be fine. I promise.*'

The boy sighed with relief, laying Tunney on a blanket on the floor of the veranda. He couldn't go through the grief of losing another dog. His father must know; he is Bwana Nyama, *the game ranger. And he never breaks promises.*

'*I've given him something to sleep. Come on, get your bat. We can keep an eye on him while we work on your sweep.*'

That story had been the boy's contribution to the evening's dormitory entertainment. He'd realised it didn't have a plot like the stories they read in English. There'd been the usual silence when he finished. Eventually a voice piped up from the far end of the dormitory.

'Boxers are brave,' Jones conceded, 'but a bit ugly, don't you think?'

The boy had bitten his lip, aggrieved.

He tries to borrow Tunney's courage now as he follows Wilson down the flights of wooden stairs. In slippers they can be deadly; but that's not why the boy takes his time. The Colonel usually dispenses justice straight after prep. The boy racks his brain again. He's learned there's nothing worse than being unprepared. Even if he's done nothing wrong, his lower lip has a tendency to wobble betrayingly when he's caught off guard. Surely no one's sneaked about the fight in the shoe-room? Fighting's a beating offence, but the prefects almost always turn a blind eye. In any case, he didn't have a choice, once Congleton challenged him. The boy had shaken his pudding-bowl fringe as if to confirm that he was indeed the blondest boy in the school, after Congleton called him Nigger. *There are no niggers in Tanganyika,* he'd insisted after further provocation, *only Africans. In any case, if he's a nigger, the Africans certainly can't be.* Congleton reddened, before smirking triumphantly and demanding satisfaction for being cheeked.

At the brown drape dividing off the housemaster's quarters from the stairs, Wilson pauses.

4

'Go on. He's expecting you.' Then the prefect does something extraordinary, intimate. He squeezes the boy's bicep. 'I'll be waiting here.'

Thoroughly perplexed, the boy pulls the curtain back and knocks timidly. There are sounds of movement, as if people are taking up position.

'Come.' The Colonel's usual bark is somewhat muted.

The room's overheated by the log fire snapping in the grate. A crumpet-fork lies on the mantelpiece beside a gilded clock, which confirms that the boy's only been asleep an hour or so. He glances fearfully at the bag of golf clubs in one corner, amongst which the housemaster keeps his canes. Has he never pulled one out by mistake on the golf course? The Colonel's in his usual uniform, navy blazer with silver buttons, grey trousers, narrow-striped tie. To the boy's increasing confusion, the housemaster's wife is also there, flopped in a maroon leather armchair with cushions as saggy as her upper arms. Her orange dress jars with the green lampshades. She must have been pretty once; now her blonde hair has rusted and her eyes are puffy. It's an article of faith among the boys that she's mad, though one of the gardeners says the problem is drink. The most important thing in her life is Oswald, a liver-and-white Blenheim. It's the only dog the boy has ever disliked. It shepherds the junior boys on their pre-breakfast run around the walled gardens to the prefabricated refectory. The threat of Oswald prompts all but the sleepiest to maintain at least a trot. He's been known to grab slowcoaches with his front paws, bouncing behind on his hind legs, like a hairy shrimp, groin pumping furiously against an unwary calf.

The housemaster and his wife are flushed and breathing heavily. Once the boy came into his parents' bedroom and found them like that. The boy dismisses the thought instantaneously. Everyone knows that this couple doesn't have sex. Otherwise they'd have children themselves, wouldn't they, instead of looking after other people's? Still, the Colonel *seems strangely embarrassed, his wary left eye more narrowed than usual, as though training his other one on a particularly elusive target.*

'Come and sit down.'

The Colonel motions him to an upright chair, before pulling up another for himself. The boy is agonisingly aware that their knees are almost touching. He sits rigidly, afraid to breathe in case they do. The Colonel glances at his wife, perhaps hoping she'll speak first; but she continues to study the engraving on Oswald's collar, as if she's seeing it for the first time. The dog makes to jump down to welcome the visitor, but she restrains him and he begins to whine. With a sigh of frustration, the Colonel turns back to the boy.

'The thing is ...' he ventures. He scowls again at Oswald's protesting yap.

His wife blushes and places one beringed hand over the dog's mouth.

'The thing is ... thing is ...'

The boy stares. His housemaster is supposed to have been among the first English contingents ashore on D-Day; but now his hands are trembling. Purpling, the Colonel squints beseechingly, before cocking himself like a gun.

'I'm very sorry to have to tell you your father's been killed in a plane crash.'

For a moment the boy's simply nonplussed. Why's the Colonel saying this? He knows his father is a brilliant pilot. He's flown innumerable anti-poaching missions. Then there's a blood-chilling wail. At first he thinks it's the Colonel, but his housemaster is gazing at him, aghast, lips pursed again. Oswald buries his nose in his mistress's lap, ears flopping over his eyes. It's as if the boy is shaking to bits. Fluid leaks every-where, tears and snot and saliva, from his eyes, his nose, his mouth. It goes on so long that he starts to feel like he's drown-ing. His chest is red-hot, his throat raw. As the tears boil in his eyes, the housemaster's wife changes shape, bulging and shrinking, like in a crazy fairground mirror, until she eventually pushes Oswald off her lap and waddles forward, tugging a hanky from her pocket. When the boy doesn't take it, she dabs clumsily at his face, holding herself apart as though fearful she'll be splashed. The Colonel, too, is on his feet now, performing an agonised minuet.

'We're so very sorry.'

A look passes between the housemaster and his wife, who retreats through the door leading to their private rooms. Courage recovered, Oswald jumps playfully at the visitor.

'Where's my mum?' the boy stammers, feebly fending the dog off. He's used a word which is banned among his schoolmates and some reflex makes him wonder if it's been noticed. His housemaster looks down unhappily.

'Apparently there's no telephone at the chalet. We're trying to contact her through an old boy who lives in Lausanne.'

He can't take it in. As the sobs break out again, the Colonel's wife returns, bearing a caramel éclair on a white plate. Condensation sweats on the icing. She presents it to the boy formally, as if he's won a prize. Oswald leaps prodigiously. She just manages to whisk the éclair out of reach, catching the icing clumsily under her thumb.

'You bad thing, it's not for you,' she admonishes indulgently. The visitor gazes dumbly at the plate in his lap, cold through his pyjama bottoms. The glazing has buckled and cream oozes out. The dog is frenzied with disappointment.

'Your aunt phoned the headmaster from Nairobi,' his housemaster announces. 'She thought it best you were told straight away. We don't know how long it'll take to get through to your mother.'

'And Ames?'

His older brother is in one of the senior houses, a mile away.

'You can see him in the morning. I've spoken with Mr Tring. We think it's too late now.'

The boy feels helpless. He knows that if it isn't a lie, it's an absurd mistake. But he doesn't know how to challenge these adults. He just wants to get away. He's thankful when the Colonel eventually bends stiffly, palms on knees, like an umpire with a tricky adjudication to make.

'Do you think you'd better go back to bed?'

He in turn seems grateful when the boy nods. His wife coughs asthmatically. She looks like she wants to hug him but doesn't know how. The boy is strangely relieved.

'Are you sure you don't want the éclair?' she pleads. 'It's from Amps.'

The boy's spent many a breaktime gazing covetously at the pastries in the grocer's in the village square, wondering whether it's worth the risk of expulsion to steal one. He shakes his head.

'I'll just pop it back in the fridge, then,' his hostess responds, taking the plate.

'I'll fetch Wilson,' the Colonel says nervously.

The boy gets up slowly and follows. His head is spinning, so that only when his housemaster calls from the passage does he register that Oswald's pinioned his leg. Before he can react, the dog has ejaculated.

'See you in the morning, then,' the Colonel says in a hollow voice.

Oswald barks appreciatively. The boy's afraid he'll start crying again in front of Wilson. If he can just hold out until he gets back to bed. But he feels so leaden that he can barely lift his feet. Wilson takes him by the arm again.

'I'm sorry, Nigger,' he mutters.

The boy senses the prefect casting for something else to say, but there's only the creak of the interminable stairs. Through a window, a sliver of pewter moon is frozen in its tracks above the bell tower of St Peter's church. On the landing outside the dormitory, Wilson pauses.

'I hear you looked after yourself against Congleton the other day. Good man,' he mutters encouragingly.

PROLOGUE

The boy slithers back between the frosty sheets. Everyone else is fast asleep. He wants to cry again. But it's as if, during the short time in the Colonel's study, he's expressed every drop of water in him. If he starts sobbing, blood will run down his face. The cold scorches his raw lungs. One calf of his pyjamas is damp, but now his brain is working again and he barely notices. What is it, not to have a father? Does this mean no more safaris like the one to the Ugalla River basin the previous Easter, just the two of them, camping under the stars and eating fire-burnt sausages, chalking stumps on the towering anthills? But his father wrote to him only ten days ago, promising tickets for Peter Parfitt and Co. at Lord's when he comes on leave in June. He knows how disappointed the boy was to have missed out when the MCC came to Dar es Salaam because of cramming for his entrance exams. Not even the scorecard, signed by all the tourists, had consoled him. Promise. The boy rolls the word round and round his mouth. Tunney recovered, didn't he? So it will be alright. It will. His father will come and the whole family go to Lord's and they'll talk about Kimwaga and the dogs and the boy's trip home later in the summer.

CHAPTER I

The Father I Did Not Know

One midsummer afternoon, forty-three years after that terrible night, I'm at the computer. Five o'clock. I'm expected in the pub soon, but I just have time to check my emails. On Friday afternoons, nothing much comes in except offers to enhance my breasts or invitations to share the booty of some recently deceased dictator. Hurrying to purge the dross, I almost delete the message from an Indian university. This time it's not a request for a reference or information about an author. A colleague is researching the nationalist movement during the 1940s in the Mumbai archives. 'One finds several references to the significant role of a senior police officer named Moore Gilbert.' What? A hot flush pulses over me. It's not me but my long-dead father he's interested in. I can hardly believe my eyes. 'He had been especially brought to Satara District to deal with the powerful political agitation then going on. This officer had the distinction of having successfully suppressed the revolt of the Hoor tribes in the Sindh province (Pakistan).' Do I have any family papers which might shed light on those events?

It's a while before the ringing in my ears dies down. This is the first independent reminder in ages that I once had a father; that the man who castled me so often on his shoulders, found me a porcupine for a pet, taught me football, was a real person. Yet his influence still pervades so much of my life. Even the fact I was writing a lecture about African autobiography when the email arrived can probably be traced back to his accident, and the consequent trauma of expulsion from my childhood paradise. It wasn't just losing my father, but

Kimwaga, my beloved minder, the exotic pets and wildlife – and Tanganyika, too, its peoples and landscapes – everything that constituted Self and Home. Well into my thirties, I continued to consider myself an exile here in the UK. Those distant events – and my difficulty in coming to terms with them – underlie the unlikely transformation of a sports-mad, animal-obsessed, white African kid who wanted to be a game ranger like his father into what I am today, a professor of Postcolonial Studies at London University. These days I specialise less than I used to in colonial literature, and more in the literatures in English which have emerged from the formerly colonised nations, especially autobiography.

I reread Professor Bhosle's message several times, trembling with excitement but also a little anxious. The email opens up dimensions of my father's life I know little or nothing about. I knew he worked in the Indian Police before I was born, but this is the first I've heard that he'd been in what later became Pakistan. Or that he was involved in counter-insurgency. I've always had difficulty imagining my father as a policeman. He seemed most himself in the informal setting of safari life, clothes dishevelled, sometimes not shaving for days. So why did he join the Indian Police, with its rigid hierarchies and complex protocols? My paternal grandfather was in the colonial agricultural service. But there's a world of difference between tropical crop research and imperial law and order. My father would've spent school holidays in places like Nigeria and Trinidad. Perhaps that gave him a yen to work somewhere in the empire. That and his love of adventure, wild nature and sport, must have made the IP a far more appealing prospect than some industrial enterprise or life assurance office in England. Still.

My gaze swivels to the bookshelf, where a black-and-white photo of my childhood hero stares back with a half-smile, as if he's about to play one of his practical jokes. I feel an aftershock of the avalanche of grief and yearning which engulfed

Bill in 1964, the year before his death

my early adolescence. Taken a few months before he died, it shows a handsome man in his mid-forties, with the strong nose I've inherited, a hint of heaviness settling round dark jowls, a second line starting to score his brow and wide-set, mischievous eyes. It's an out-of-doors face, lean and tanned, a touch of mid-century film-star glamour in the immaculately groomed dark hair. Since overtaking him in age more than a decade ago, I've come to think of him as 'Bill', the nickname his peers used. It suits much better than his old-fashioned given names. I can't imagine a Samuel Malcolm wearing that puckish expression.

It's barely dawn and he's still in pyjamas, at once excited and fearful, racing along the edge of the sandy shamba *where Kimwaga and the cook grow maize. He's been strictly forbidden to follow, but the boy can't help himself, his curiosity's too strong. Besides, he knows he's completely safe with his father there. But why are adults so contradictory? His parents have told him a thousand times that if he meets a snake, he*

13

must back off slowly, keeping his eyes riveted on it. How can he forget poor Shotty the spaniel, coughing his guts out after the green mamba bit him? Yet here's his father now, still in his maroon slippers, loping after the cobra through the skinny shadows of the young maize-stalks. One hand grasps the panga, a long strip of beaten metal, curved at the bottom and wickedly sharp, which Kimwaga cuts the grass with. The other's raised defensively, palm forward, at chest height. Yet there's a half-smile on his father's face, as if it's just another game.

Occasionally the boy glimpses the oily black wriggle in front, hurdling the furrows with surprising speed. On the far side of the shamba, *Kimwaga and the cook wait, banging saucepans and shouting 'nyoka, nyoka, hatari,' as if no one knows that snakes are dangerous. Mainly, though, they're laughing, the boy can't understand why.*

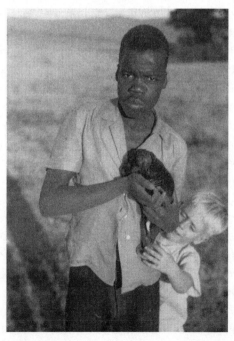

The author, with his minder, Kimwaga, and hyena cub c. 1957

Frightened by the commotion, perhaps, the snake pauses, turns, rears its hooded head and sways, as if on a puppeteer's string. When his pursuer's about four paces away, the cobra whips forward, spitting a long needle of liquid. The boy's father flinches but doesn't break his stride. The child averts his eyes, only to see the shadow of the panga *in its awful rise and fall. For a while there's complete silence, as Kimwaga, the cook and the boy approach warily. But his father's soon laughing the tension away, setting the others off again.*

'That's the last time this bugger has the chicken eggs,' he proclaims. 'I told you to stay back,' he adds sharply, as the boy goes to take his hand. His son pauses, uncertain. But the face softens.

'Curiosity killed the cat.' His father shakes his head and puts an arm round the child's shoulder.

The boy loves that feeling. It's as if his father's skin and his melt together, making them one. He smells sweat and Old Spice and severed flesh. The snake's head lies upside down, the bobbing target cleanly cut with a single blow. Its body, six feet long and thicker than the boy's arm, with beautiful rust and black markings, continues to thrash blindly in a circle, a few paces away.

'Look,' his father says, showing the palm of his left hand, sticky with milky spittle. 'If that got in your eyes, you'd be in big trouble.'

Nonchalantly, he flicks the snake's head over with the toe of his slipper. The tongue still flickers between white fangs. Sand clogs the eyes. The boy turns to see Kimwaga guffawing as he tries to steer the serpent's body into the sack he's holding. With the help of the cook, who exhales breath stale with last night's beer, he eventually traps it. Then the boy's father glances at his watch, grins and beckons them all to follow.

'Bring the bag,' he tells his son.

The boy does so unwillingly, glancing at Kimwaga for reassurance. His minder grins back, eyes wet with laughter. The sack pulsates alarmingly as the rope of muscle continues to work inside. It's much heavier than the boy imagined and his biceps are soon red hot with effort.

He follows the adults up the drive, to where the evergreen manyara *hedge meets the ditch beside the road into the village. His father signals Kimwaga and the cook to wait where they can't be seen. He motions the boy to get down in the ditch with him and they squat next to the culvert. The boy's confused again. Isn't this just the kind of cool, dark place snakes love to hide? Soon they hear the messenger's bicycle wheezing up the sandy track, and the boy's father puts one forefinger to his lips. Through the tall spring grass growing up from the ditch, the man comes into sight. When he's a few yards away, the boy's father opens the sack and the snake flails out into the road as if being confined has given it new energy. There's a cry and the clanking sound of the bicycle falling. When the boy stands up, he sees the messenger running back the way he came, while the snake writhes sinuously into the verge on the other side. His father's eyes brim with the effort of keeping quiet. But Kimwaga's snorting giggle is uncontainable, setting off the cook's bass gurgle. The boy laughs along, he doesn't know why. Adults are such a mystery. More than anything he's relieved to be rid of the snake. Once he's sure the coast is clear, his father hauls him out of the ditch and they begin gathering up the manila envelopes.*

How vague, by contrast, is my sense of Bill's life in India between 1938 and 1947. I've no memories, and even relics are few and far between. My younger brother has the police uniform he wore on his wedding day, his medals, a fearsome braided leather riding-crop, a Sam Browne belt and the red pennant from the front wing of his car. In an album compiled by his sister Pat, who phoned my school from Nairobi with news of the air crash, are some black-and-white photos from that phase of his life. Two show an eighteen-year-old

Bill uncomfortably stuffed into what looks like mess dress, black tails, wing collar and cummerbund. There's one of a tiger hunt, the head of the unfortunate creature propped on an improvised tripod. The snarling trophy was part of the furniture of my African childhood, its glass eyes swivelling uncannily as one passed, as though calculating the moment for revenge. At the time, it never occurred to me that this was an odd thing to find in a game ranger's house.

Another photo shows him in riding boots and spurs, astride a white horse, concentrating hard. There are others of men in various uniforms, presumably his comrades, and one page is captioned 'Bill's girl-friends in India'. Most are of someone called Beryl Grey. In the first, looking like an aviator in her bathing cap, she smiles coquettishly, toned forearms folded on the lip of a swimming pool. In an adjacent picture, she's holding an infant with her own ash-blonde locks. Somebody's wife? Below her is a brunette identified as 'Maria, Bill's fiancée'. She wears a forage cap and on one cropped shoulder of her uniform are three letters: 'W.A.O.'. Women's Army Ordinance Corps? She has a pretty, open face, with full lips and a slightly startled expression. Why didn't they get married? I was disappointed that there wasn't a picture of the Gaekwad of Baroda's sister. Aunt Pat had once told me that Bill knew her 'very well', and scandalised the members of the Bombay Yacht Club by taking her in for a drink. It seemed an unlikely story. Surely the Indian princes and their families were exempt from the racial distinctions of the Raj?

'He adored women, your father,' Pat insisted, 'they made him thrilled skinny to be alive. It didn't matter who they were or where they came from, young or old as God. Before the war, he did social work in Wales one school holidays. He got on like a house on fire with the miners' wives and daughters. One of them used to write for years afterwards. He was always so ga*llant*.'

The old-fashioned stress on the last syllable made Bill seem even more part of a bygone era.

Not for the first time, the cook's wife has fled her quarters to take refuge in their house. She's crying and, jiggling her baby on one hip, shows the boy's mother the weal on her arm. One eye's already closing. The indignant voice outside grows louder.

'Send Eunice out or I will come in and get her.'

The boy's never heard the cook talk like this. He rushes to the bathroom window which looks onto the yard. His father's already on the kitchen steps, threatening to sack the man if he doesn't go home at once. The cook makes to lunge past his employer and regain Eunice, who begins wailing. The boy's father shoves him back. In a trice the two men are locked in a wrestling hold. The cook's the same height but considerably broader than the boy's father, though much of him is beer belly. Time is suspended, the two men completely motionless, heads resting on each others' shoulders, as if companionably supporting one another. But through the cook's torn shirt and below his father's shorts, the boy can see muscle quivering with effort. It's like when male buffaloes lock horns. Sometimes minutes pass as they push at each other, sinews standing out like cables, even through the thick hide, before one concedes. There's no snorting and stamping now, but both men are breathing heavily and the boy has the same sensation of the earth trembling. He senses his whole world will be shaken to bits if the cook wins. The boy can't bear to look any longer and runs to his room. But he can't stay still. He has to go and help his father.

By the time he's evaded his mother's snatch and got into the kitchen, however, his father's walking back up the steps, tossing a piece of torn cloth towards the grate beneath the 44-gallon drum which heats their bathwater. There's a graze on his neck and his face flushes with an expression of disgust as he wipes some drool off his shirt-front. The boy throws his arms round his father's waist in sheer relief and won't let go. Behind, he sees the cook stumbling towards his quarters. The rip in the back of his shirt is wider and the black skin beneath dusty. Otherwise everything's eerily normal.

'We can't sack him,' he hears his mother say later. 'He'll take it out on Eunice.'

'He should bloody well learn to appreciate her,' the boy's father complains. 'Do you know, the bugger tried to touch me for an advance yesterday so he can get himself a second wife.'

'It's just the way they are,' his mother rejoins, 'we shouldn't interfere more than we have to. Besides, where are we going to find someone who cooks like him out here in the bush?'

'He's a bloody bully when he's had a drink.'

'Tell him how quickly he could get his second wife if he stopped the booze.'

But Bill hardly ever mentioned India. He once demonstrated some unarmed combat moves he said he'd learned at police training school. They worked beautifully on me, but when my turn came, Bill was too stocky, my muscles too feeble, to unbalance him. Another time he explained that his poor hearing in one ear was the result of a perforated tympanum.

'I was lured to a house by terrorists, who threw a home-made grenade into the room where I was waiting.'

'What does terrorist mean?' The word was cropping up increasingly on the radio in connection with the Mau Mau uprising in neighbouring Kenya, where Pat had married into a settler family, their farmhouse increasingly resembling a fortress.

There was a second wound, which used to fascinate and scare me, a lumpy patch of hard yellowish skin above his right knee. Another improvised bomb had done the damage, this one hurled during a communalist riot. When it particularly troubled him, my father would sometimes call us to his bedroom and my brothers and I would take turns massaging the ache away, watching almost sorrowfully as the pain slowly evaporated from an expression grey as his eyes. It was an incomparable feeling when he needed us like that.

Looking back, I realise that, even if rarely mentioned, his previous life marked my African childhood in other ways. A few Indian words found their way into our vocabulary, including *tatee*, Bill's word for pooh, whether ours or the dogs'. Another was desk-wallah. 'I'm turning into a bloody desk-wallah,' he'd moan, when paperwork kept him too long from safari.

Besides the threatening tiger-head, there were bronze figurines in the display cabinet, Shiva, Kali and – my favourite – the pot-bellied Ganesh with his elephant head. Once a ring-tailed mongoose set up camp in our garden. It was soon christened 'Rikki-Tikki-Tavi'.

'Why?'

'Gosh, you're just like the elephant's child in the *Just So Stories*,' Bill grinned, tweaking my nose gently in his knuckles, 'such a one for questions. I'll ask Gran to send you the *Jungle Books* when I next write. Then you can find out all about Rikki-Tikki-Tavi.'

Two months later, they arrived from England. Perhaps that was the germ of my lifelong interest in Kipling, who became the subject of my first book.

There was an Indian flavour, too, in what we ate and drank. Bill's favourite tipple was freshly squeezed lime-and-soda, a taste he'd acquired in the subcontinent. Except during our posting to chilly Ngorongoro in northern Tanganyika, he'd usually have one as soon as he got in from the office. I loved to aim the soda siphon into his chunky glass tankard, scattering the pips and betting which dimple they'd settle under. Racing my brothers to jump on his lap as the strains of 'Lillibullero' heralded the news from London, followed on Saturdays by the football scores, I'd triumphantly nurse his saucer of nuts, lightly fried with chilli, while we anticipated the results from the announcer's intonation. Sundays, we usually had curry with chapattis, dal, mango pickle so strong it stripped the lining from your mouth and – when it could be ordered from the coast – Bombay Duck. The moment the tin was opened, the fetid stink betrayed it as fish, however, dark and stringy as a chocolate flake.

'Why's it called duck, then?' I inevitably asked.

Bill shrugged with an amused look. 'Things aren't always what they seem in India.'

'Why?'

'You'll have to go and see for yourself.'

I'd stare, heart racing, as he speared a fragment into the pot of pickle, manoeuvred out a chunk of mango and crunched it all together in his mouth. No one, surely, could consume such a combination and survive. But Bill simply laughed, ha-ha breath fiery as a flame-thrower. His maroon slippers also came from Bombay, the leather uppers conserved through periodic re-solings, instruments of terror when we children misbehaved.

~

The obvious source of information about Bill's life in India was my mother. How could he have resisted seducing her with tales of the gorgeous East during their courtship in Blitzed-out, monochrome London, to which he returned after Indian Independence in 1947? But she became ever more remote after his death. Barely forty, her hair was dappled-grey with shock by the time she finally returned from Switzerland. She seemed dazed, unreachable, when she first visited us at school. Despite my own bewildered grief, I was painfully struck by how unwilling she was to discuss what had happened. She had so many difficult practical issues to address, I suppose: where we'd live now, how she was going to manage with three of us still to educate.

Perhaps her unwillingness to talk about Bill was because she was trying to protect us. More likely, she was barely coping herself, now that history had repeated itself. My father was the second husband she'd lost to a violent death. The first was an impoverished Irishman she defied her outraged parents to marry, who drowned in the oil spill of his torpedoed destroyer. While she was pregnant. She'd never mentioned him much, so I was scandalised when his photo appeared one day next to Bill's on her bedside table in the red-brick terrace house she bought us in Gorleston-on-Sea – a decaying Norfolk seaside resort where her father had practised law and my frail grand-mother still lived, in a flat on the cliffs.

'What's he doing there?' I once asked with adolescent resentfulness.

My mother smiled uncertainly. But I began to connect Sub-Lieutenant Hopkins with the misty inner world into which she increasingly retreated.

That first encounter after Bill's death established the pattern. Even years later, her face would cloud if anyone asked about Africa. Outwardly, at least, I observed her wish that we accept that England was home now, though I hated the huddle of dreary, fog-prone streets facing the brown North Sea wastes which was Gorleston. In such circumstances, Bill's life in India seemed as remote as Mars on the few occasions I gave it any thought. Once a letter came from a former police colleague, now stationed in Assam, covered with crossed-out addresses and stamps from three continents, which my brothers and I fought over for our collections. But whether my mother even answered it, I don't know.

The other person who could have told me about Bill's previ-ous life was his sister Pat, who followed us back from Africa some years after his death, settling in an equally cheerless seaside town in Kent. We met only once or twice, however, during my adolescence, because of the bitterness my mother felt towards her. The feud had begun during their time on my paternal grandparents' coffee farm in southern Tanganyika. Bill's father bought it as a retirement hobby, after stepping down as director of the government Coffee Research Station in the foothills of Kilimanjaro. Following decades as an agricultural officer in Nigeria, Trinidad and Tanganyika, he had no immediate wish to return to England. Bill, his bride and four-year-old son from her first marriage emigrated to the farm immediately after their wedding in December 1947. But it was a struggle for two families to make a living, and soon there was such friction between my mother and her female in-laws that my father escaped as soon as he could to a job in the Game Department. Bill's death, however, brought the old vendetta to a climax. Unable to contact my mother, Pat had – very reasonably, I thought, even at the time – flown his broken body up to Nairobi to be buried. For my mother it was the last straw. Not only had she been deprived of the opportunity of seeing Bill off, she once complained, but Pat had taken him out of Tanganyika, away from the national parks which were his life.

'He always wanted his ashes scattered in the Ngorongoro Crater if something happened,' my mother sniffled into her tissue.

Instead he'd been plonked in a suburban cemetery, hemmed in by desk-wallahs who'd died of drink and boredom.

'Can't we move him?' I couldn't bear the thought he was lying somewhere he might be unhappy.

My mother shrugged helplessly.

Only once I'd left home did I feel free to contact Pat. A flamboyant extrovert, with a colourful life of her own, her stories about Bill seemed too melodramatic, or gilded by time, to take very seriously. As far as India was concerned, she claimed he'd worked undercover for a while, dressed in a kaftan and passing as a Pathan in the border region abutting Afghanistan. Had she mixed up the North-West Frontier with Sindh? Once, apparently, Bill and an Indian subordinate chased some malefactors into a ravine. Turning a dog-leg in the chasm, the Indian suddenly barged my father from his saddle, cushioning him in his arms as they fell. Only as he dusted himself down did Bill notice the wire ahead, stretched taut and sharp as a blade at neck height across the defile.

Another time she talked of riots he'd distinguished himself in handling, as Partition approached. But there were never any specific places, dates, or names to anchor these daredevil tales. Like my mother, Pat had never been to India, which she seemed to conceive in terms of Orientalist romances like *Beau Geste* or *The Four Feathers*, so unaccountably popular with moviegoers in the 1930s. She was nine years younger than Bill, still at school when he left for the subcontinent; and when she described his exploits there, it was with the starry-eyed look of someone describing a matinee idol.

'Do you know he was the youngest-ever winner of the Indian Police Medal?' she'd enthuse. 'You should be incredibly proud of him.'

But Bill had been in the subcontinent well before I was born, and if I occasionally wondered about his experiences there, other questions were much more pressing. Why had my father been on that plane in February 1965? Why had he joined the UN-funded mission to the mountainous south-west of what by then had become Tanzania, scouting for suitable areas to settle Tutsis fleeing from the Hutu terror in neighbouring Rwanda – events repeated with such catastrophic results thirty years later? Why were too many passengers aboard? Why had no one factored in the extra distance required for take-off at that altitude? Why had the plane broken in two when, according to witnesses, it barely brushed the tree-tops at the end of the dirt runway? Why had only the front part burst into flames when it hit the ground, so that Bill and the pilot were probably burned alive? Why Bill, why us?

It was no consolation that he'd died trying to help refugees, the line so many people took after his death. As a young adult I returned to Tanzania on several occasions, hoping to settle the ghosts of the past. The new African owners of the houses we'd lived in looked at me kindly but blankly, as if the times I talked about were already as remote as the Triassic era. The bitterest disappointment was that Kimwaga had vanished. After Bill's death, he'd apparently worked briefly for another European family, before joining the Game Department himself. But no one could tell me where he'd been posted, or name the village he originally came from.

~

In the pub, Anna leans across the table. 'Maybe this email's a sign? That you should go yourself. Find out about the Hoors and Sindh and what your father got up to in Satara.'

I shrug.

'You've never been to India, have you?'

I feel a little foolish, as I always do when people ask me that. The subcontinent's always loomed large in my research. Why haven't I gone? Partly because for many years I used what time and money I had to head back to Africa. Since then, there's been the rest of the world to see. In any case, I'd always assumed that the India I'd been most interested in, the India of the Raj, has vanished even more definitively than the Tanganyika of my childhood. The summer, when I have most time to travel, is one long monsoon downpour in western India, making it difficult to get around. By Easter, it's an oven again, the thermometer at forty degrees or more. Christmas, which everyone agrees is the best period to visit, has been spoken for as long as I can remember. Professor Bhosle's email hasn't made me any keener to go. I'm sure I can now find out all there is to know about Bill's time in India from him.

My confidence is misplaced, however. Following his request, I contact my brothers, asking if any of them found papers about Bill's time in India after our mother's death a few years ago. In the meantime, my historian colleague informs me that he's written books on the Independence Movement in Bombay Province and has recently begun to focus on Satara District more specifically. He's especially interested in a secret Memorandum Bill's supposed to have written about the Parallel

Government. Google reveals that Satara is a remote country district several hundred miles south of Mumbai, and that the Parallel Government was an armed underground movement formed after Gandhi's imprisonment in August 1942. I'm now burning to know more about Bill's involvement.

Frustratingly, Bhosle doesn't add much to what he said about him in his first email. He does, however, tell me where the relevant archives are located, offers some pointers about histories of Sindh and directs me to what he describes as the best book so far on the Parallel Government, by one A.B. Shinde. Unfortunately, it's not in the British Library; nor can I find a copy for sale on the internet. When I report back from my brothers in the negative, Bhosle starts taking longer and longer to return my emails. Eventually, he says he'll collate everything he's got on Bill after his next research trip to Mumbai. He's planning two weeks there in December. It's only intuition, but I can't help feeling he's increasingly reluctant to answer my questions. Why?

By the end of summer, the idea's taken root. For the first time in years I'll be free this Christmas. I could spend part of the vacation in the archives, alongside Bhosle himself, perhaps. Maybe, after all, something of the India of my father's time has survived the tsunami of globalisation driving this latest tiger economy? It's a golden opportunity to add to my knowledge of Bill. I only knew him for my first eleven years; that's just two years more than the period he spent in India, which was no doubt crucial in making the man I remember. On the other hand, I wonder how much personal material there's likely to be in public archives. Will I really learn much about what he was like as a young man from administrative reports?

Still undecided, I contact Bhosle again in mid-October, asking if we can meet over Christmas. In his reply, the professor tells me he won't be going to Mumbai in December after all. Nor can he receive me in his home city of Kolhapur, where I've offered to travel to meet him. However, he promises to advise Dr Dhavatkar, the director of the Elphinstone Archives and a friend of his, to smooth my passage should I decide to go. His apparent evasiveness is disconcerting. But even if Bhosle's so inexplicably unavailable all of a sudden, he's given me enough to get started. If I don't seize the chance, I know I'll regret it. Before I can change my mind, I book the flight.

On 26 November, ten days after getting my visa, and barely two weeks before my intended departure date, Mumbai is attacked by a dozen heavily armed Islamists, who apparently arrived by sea from Pakistan. Scores of civilians are killed in and around sites favoured by Westerners in the city, as well as in the main railway station. The Foreign Office immediately advises against all non-essential travel. Shocked by graphic pictures of the still-burning Taj hotel, the bloodied platforms of Victoria Terminus and the heart-rending story of the Israeli infant saved by his Indian ayah from the mayhem in Nariman House, I question the wisdom of my trip. The assassination of Benazir Bhutto in December 2007 provoked serious sabre-rattling between Pakistan and India and only a few years earlier the subcontinental neighbours were on the brink of nuclear war. The current rhetoric between the two sides is reaching an alarming pitch.

'I wouldn't go, if I were you,' Anna advises when we meet again at the beginning of December in a Waterloo pub. 'It's not the right time.'

'If something else kicks off, maybe not. But Mumbai will be swarming with security, there's probably never been a safer time. Besides, it's cost me a packet and I can't claim on insurance if I cancel, because it's a terrorist incident. Anyway, I'm too curious now about Bill's life in India.'

As she's getting us another round, I overhear a woman at an adjoining table declaiming drunkenly about the Muslim plot to take over Britain.

'It's all been planned, you'll see!' she shrieks. 'Mumbai's a warning to us all.'

CHAPTER 2

Picking Up the Trail

First impressions of Mumbai blur chaotically. I'm badly disoriented by a delayed night flight during which noisy neighbours and expectation kept pricking me awake. Once off the plane, I'm too excited, too bewildered by a rip tide of jet lag and sleeplessness, to be able to order my perceptions. Every Indian man seems to have a moustache; there's a guard in the airport men's room, with what looks like a musket nipped between his knees, his eyes half-closed, as if stupefied by the acid stench. But outside the terminal, the jacarandas are in full purple bloom, reminding me joyously of coastal Tanganyika, though the palms are cankered by pollution. It's claustrophobic inside the bubble of the taxi; as the drive into the city becomes extended by one snarling jam after another, sweat slithers me from side to side across the plastic rear seat.

Stupidly, I didn't buy water at the airport and soon I'm parched. Coming from an English winter, the light's squint-bright, and I can only snatch glimpses of slums which seem to stretch to the horizon, where distant skyscrapers thrust up like something out of *Dallas*. Suddenly, we're too close to a gorgeously painted lorry, 'Horn OK Please' emblazoned on its tailgate. I'm thrown forward violently as the brakes bite. The Ganesh statuette reclining on the rear-window shelf tumbles over my shoulder and catches in my shirt. Before the driver's finished apologising, we graze a stick-like woman, dark as the tarmac she's repairing, faded sari clamped between her teeth, basket of shingle on folded head-cloth, infant slung gracefully on one hip like a counterweight. At every junction, bandy-legged boys with beatific smiles jog beside my window, proffering crimson candyfloss trapped in dusty cellophane, newspapers, snacks so salty-looking the mere sight of them leaches any remaining moisture from my gullet. The sickly jasmine air freshener is sometimes overwhelmed by the smell of fried food, melting bitumen and human waste sucked in through the fan. For what seems like hours, the skyscrapers float far away as ever in the milky haze. Are we driving round in circles? Scorched by dehydration now, I slip into an uncomfortable trance. The aching anticipation of finding out more about Bill alternates with stabs of apprehension. People say several terrorists are still on the run, all these days after the attacks. Perhaps the centre will be locked down, preventing me getting to the material I need? Have I been over-impulsive?

~

Forty-eight hours later, the answer seems to be yes. In fact I'm ready to abandon my trip. Bleary-eyed despite my early night, I report to Elphinstone Archives first thing the morning after I arrive. To my huge relief, there's no sign of disruption. A twig-limbed man in khaki, who disconcertingly introduces himself with enormous pride as 'the peon', takes me from office to office, where successively more important officials smile and waggle their heads ambiguously. Eventually I reach the director's suite, where a plump, bronze-coloured man with gold-rimmed glasses and silvery hair invites me to sit. I show my London University card and pronounce Professor Bhosle's name, confident they'll prove my open sesame. Dr Dhavatkar nods when I mention the historian, but clearly knows nothing about me. I'm baffled that Bhosle hasn't kept his promise. The director returns my card.

'You need an attestation from your embassy,' he wheezes, scratching one smooth dewlap with the tip of his pencil. Sounds like he's got a sore throat. I'm stunned. Why didn't Bhosle mention this requirement? Or has it been introduced since the attacks?

'My embassy? But if I have to go to Delhi, it could take days.'

He shrugs. 'Sorry. That is the rule, only. Perhaps the consulate can have one faxed? It's at Makers' Chambers in Nariman Point.'

I sense the ghost of the young Bill, hovering just out of reach. It's hard to contain my frustration.

Despite evoking the aura of the East India Company, Makers' Chambers turns out to be a weather-stained 1960s concrete tower. Security is tight and the queues long. It's getting to lunchtime before my turn comes. The young woman at the window is polite but firm. No, they can't fax Delhi, I'll need to go in person with my documents. I'm evidently looking disconsolate, because her expression suddenly softens.

'Well, if Elphinstone will take an attestation from us,' she eventually says conciliatingly, 'I'll see what we can do. You'll have to leave your passport.'

The fee she demands is exorbitant. Still, much more convenient than going all the way to the capital. With Christmas and New Year approaching, I'm acutely aware of the need to be efficient with my time. But will Dhavatkar accept the letter? I need to find out at once. If not, I have to book for Delhi before the holiday rush begins. But first I need to see if Bhosle's responded to the email I sent just before leaving London, asking if we can at least speak on the phone once I get to India.

Heading back to the archives, my tuk-tuk passes a scorched park where numerous cricket matches are underway. A huge banner hangs on the railings: 'I cannot teach you violence. But I can teach you not to bow your head.' Behind is a statue of the author, Gandhi dressed in a dhoti, his expression determined but benign. I wonder if it's been put up as a riposte to the terrorists. The driver drops me at an internet café he recommends, the other side of Elphinstone. Accessing the internet involves checks, and the proprietor is suspicious that I don't have my passport. Fortunately he knows my hotel and after letting him use my mobile to make a confirmatory call, he nods.

'Why all the questions?'

He shrugs amiably, his smile popping in and out beneath his moustache like a nervous mouse. 'This terrorism.'

Over his shoulder a notice announces: 'Phonography and Other Adult Material Not Allowed'. Phonography? I can't help smiling. But to my intense disappointment, there's no answer from my mysterious historian colleague. For the time being, I'm on my own.

I walk back to the Archives. So soon on from the atrocities, early morning Mumbai seems amazingly recovered. At each intersection up what used to be Hornby Road, the main thoroughfare of British Bombay, I have to perform a St Vitus's dance to negotiate the torrents of people and hurtling traffic. Hornby's a canyon of imposing buildings, storey piled on storey of monsoon-patterned brick, the pavement arcades now clogged with hawkers' stalls. High on one edifice, a bush grows precariously from the crumbly facade. Nonetheless, I quickly realise I'm in one of the great Victorian cities, grand as the centre of Glasgow or Manchester, but subtly orientalised with ironwork jalousies, miniature domes and lancet windows. Wondering how his first impressions of the city compared, I excitedly try to identify the buildings Bill would have known: the Army and Navy Stores, which doubtless supplied his uniform, the Sassoon Memorial Library, and Watson's, the infamous Raj hotel. It looks like a slum tenement now, part of one wing collapsed, the revolutionary ironwork frame an exposed and rusty skeleton.

As I reach Elphinstone, my mobile goes. It's the consulate. There appears to be a problem with my passport. Have I ever lost one? I struggle to remember. Yes, once in Carcassonne. But it was found and returned. Not before I'd had a new one issued, I suddenly recall. The man's voice is distinctly suspicious.

'The system's registering a problem, only. We'll have to look into it.'

To my intense frustration, he can give me no time frame. I feel marooned, the hours already ticking away uselessly, eating into what little time I have. I jog up the stairs to the archives to be told Dhavatkar's not returned from lunch. His subordinate's charming, but has an accent so thick it takes me a while to understand that he's inviting me to park myself at a desk in the archives while I wait. He leads me to a dusty room the size of a squash court, with floor-to-ceiling bookcases and perhaps a dozen carrels. The tall windows at the far end are nailed shut above piles of what look like ancient mail sacks, dusty and forlorn. A couple of ceiling fans tick listlessly, tugging the stale air up and down. Some desks are occupied, others stacked with pyramids of reserved material. I can't resist opening the ledgers on the table I'm shown to. They're written in beautiful faded copperplate, regular as print, and concern shipping in the 1790s. Perhaps some clerk in the original Maker's Chambers produced them? Ink has bled through the pages and the paper's brittle. Worried I'll cause further damage, I push them to one side and take out my pad to scribble some bullet points. What I'm after all seems hopelessly broad: Indian Police, Hoors, Satara, Parallel Government. How am I even going to get started?

Soon the supervisor approaches to say the director may not be returning at all today. He's unwell. I'm thoroughly demoralised now. I've invested so much in this trip, financially and emotionally, and seem to have come to a complete dead end before I've even begun. The feeling's made worse by awareness that right here, under my nose, are the documents which will unlock Bill's past. Dhavatkar might be off for days. What if he refuses the attestation when he returns? But without my passport, I can't book for Delhi. It takes me a moment to understand that the man's saying I'm welcome to wait, just in case, though I can't order any material. Hungry, heat-sapped and with jet lag weighing again, I ponder going back to the hotel to eat and rest. But I can't face the steamy, teeming streets just yet. I decide to read for an hour to take my mind off things, until it cools down.

How different my entire trip might have been if I'd left then. Almost as soon as I've taken Nirad Chaudhuri's *Autobiography of an Unknown Indian* out of my bag, a tall, angular man flops into the adjoining carrel. Opening a daunting-looking set of leather-bound reports, he begins writing furiously. He's around sixty, with lank salt-and-pepper hair and a walrus moustache. He glances up with droopy eyes and smiles briefly, before returning to his task. Eventually, I lay my book down and prepare to leave. My neighbour glances at the cover.

'Ah, Nirad Chaudhuri, so good on the problems facing historians in India,' he mutters approvingly. 'What brings you here? For Chaudhuri you need Calcutta.'

'Actually, I'm researching the Indian Police in Bombay in the 1930s and 40s.'

His tawny eyes light up. I give a brief account.

'Your father's name?'

I offer my visiting card. His gaze lingers a moment, then he stands up briskly, a gangling man in a white Nehru shirt, faded blue slacks and outsize trainers. A faint fragrance of flowery cologne. 'Do you have time for chai?' I warm to him.

In the Elphinstone canteen, he extends his hand a little circumspectly, as if it's an unfamiliar manouevre. 'Rajeev Divekar.'

He orders glasses of tea. When they come, a fly bobs just below the milky surface of mine. I pretend to sip while he fiddles with my card.

'Does the name mean something?'

When he nods, I almost swallow the fly.

'Can't remember where exactly. A couple of years ago I

was working on the history of the Maharashtra police force, the successor to the old Bombay IP your father worked in. So many names and dates.' He tells me a bit about his project.

'Were you in the police yourself?'

Rajeev looks up with hooded eyes. 'Let's say I'm an independent scholar with an interest in policing and security issues.' He writes my contact details in a tatty notebook.

'So your father was pukka IP?' He's clearly impressed. I explain about Bhosle's email, why I know so little about Bill's career and my problems starting my researches.

'Never mind,' Rajeev nods sympathetically. 'I have something to get you going. Lucky you caught me. This is my last day here before the holidays.'

Back in the reading-room, he pulls a slim blue volume from a stack of gazetteers on his desk. It's the *History of Services, Bombay Province*.

'This records every posting of everyone ever employed by the British government.'

I'm shivering with excitement. He checks the index, before flicking back to the relevant page.

'Look, your father was in the second-last cohort appointed from England. There were only four probationers in 1938, and two more in 1939. Once war started, recruitment from the UK was suspended.'

Bill's entry shows that after joining up in Bombay, he attended the Central Police Training School in Nasik for two years, followed by six weeks' military instruction in Colaba Barracks.

'Just down the road from here,' Rajeev explains.

Then Bill returned to Nasik as probationary Assistant District Superintendent.

'Nasik's about five hours inland by train.'

But here's a puzzle. There's a long hiatus, between March 1941 and January 1943. Was this when Bill was in what's

Bill aged eighteen at school in 1938, the year he left for India

now Pakistan, suppressing the Hoors? After another period in Nasik, I see he was transferred to Satara in January 1944, where – according to Professor Bhosle – he worked against the Parallel Government. Now his rank is Special Additional Superintendent. What does 'Special' signify? In 1946, he's posted to Ahmedabad, today in the neighbouring state of Gujarat. Then the record stops. Why?

'Is there a later edition? He was here until Independence, for sure.'

Rajeev grimaces regretfully. 'Not until 1950. And it doesn't have records for those who'd retired by then. Perhaps he stayed in Ahmedabad until he returned to the UK?'

That would corroborate Aunt Pat's instinct that Bill witnessed first-hand the horrors of Partition. Ahmedabad is the closest Indian city to what's now southern Pakistan, and many a refugee train would have left or arrived there. Was that where he received his wounds?

'What about this gap between his first and second spells in Nasik?' I repeat what Bhosle told me about the Hoor rebellion.

Rajeev shakes his head after a moment. 'No, look here.' He shows me another page, where the entry of a contemporary of Bill's reads: 'Services placed at the disposal of the Government of Sindh.' He shakes his head. 'So if your father went there, it should be recorded, too.'

It's perplexing. 'But there's no mention of his Indian Police Medal, either. It's listed for other people.'

'Maybe he got it in late '46 or '47?' The mournful look returns. 'I found discrepancies during my own research.' He's almost apologetic. 'I think the British became less meticulous about record-keeping towards the end, perhaps because of the war or because they knew they'd soon be leaving.'

Despite the frustrating incompleteness of the record, for the first time I have an outline of Bill's Indian career. What a stroke of luck to have run into Rajeev.

I ask my engaging new acquaintance how he became interested in Indian police history. He looks startled for a moment, before explaining that he lives in a building near Churchgate station, formerly inhabited by several IP officers, mostly Parsis. Their stories inspired him to research the Bombay branch of the service in his spare time.

'My upstairs neighbour was Nagarwala, the man who arrested Gandhi's assassin. Six foot four and fair as an Englishman. Nags joined the service in 1935. Your father would certainly have known him. He died a couple of years ago only.'

I feel horribly cheated. Why didn't I come to India earlier? 'Are any of his contemporaries still alive?'

Rajeev shakes his head regretfully and looks heavenwards. 'Not here in Maharashtra. They have all gone up.' He smiles encouragingly. 'Listen, I'll look through the notes I have at home. Perhaps there are some references to Moore-Gilbert. Unless you know what you're looking for here, it's like trying to find a needle in a haystack. Everything's so chaotic and disorganised now.'

I suddenly remember. 'There's a book by someone called Abasaheb Shinde, about the Parallel Government. Professor Bhosle told me it was the most authoritative account. Do you think they might have it here?'

Rajeev cocks his head doubtfully. 'Abasaheb Shinde? Just a minute.' He gets up and approaches the supervisor's desk. I'm struck by the deference my new friend is shown. The supervisor bows and nods throughout their animated conversation, following which they pore over an ancient computer terminal. Rajeev returns with a sorrowful expression.

'No sign of this Shinde. Let me make inquiries.' He glances at his watch. 'I have to go and pick up my wife. Can you come tomorrow?'

'Isn't this your last day?'

'My dear man, you've got me curious now, too. Will you be here?'

'If they let me in.'

'Any problem, send someone to get me,' he pronounces authoritatively, extending his hand. 'I'm very pleased you've come to do this research. It's important the past isn't forgotten.' He taps the ledgers on his desk. 'Before it all disintegrates.'

~

Morale partly restored, I take a quick shower back at the hotel before heading out to familiarise myself further with Mumbai. Through the half-open window of the bathroom I see an alley directly opposite. Plastic bottles, old clothes, twisted metal lie heaped between fetid-looking pools. So still does he squat that it takes me a while to notice the man crapping behind a pile of cardboard boxes. Unnervingly, he seems to be looking straight at me. By the time I'm dressed he's gone, thank God. I check the guidebook and step out of the hotel onto streets heaving with office workers heading home. I merge into the flow streaming towards a magnificent edifice, with mosque-like domes and pointy windows.

'Victoria Terminus, now Chhatrapati Shivaji station,' a stall-holder explains.

He tells me with unmistakable relish that Shivaji is the local hero who drove the Muslims out of Maharashtra in the seventeenth century. I'm reminded of St Pancras in London, but the scale is even more colossal. Outside, snub-nosed yellow-and-black taxis butt through the throng like giant bumblebees. I can't begin to imagine what it must have been like on 26 November, the panic, the terror here as the terrorist attack unfolded.

Ducking down a side street, I join a crowd outside the white-painted eighteenth-century cathedral of St Thomas to watch an organ-grinder with his monkey. I suddenly understand what Kipling wrote about Indian crowds in *Kim* – how they contrast with the indifference of English ones. Here I'm not just an anonymous atom; somehow I feel enhanced by the multitude, which seems not just to surround, but to support me. The feeling intensifies when I run into a wedding procession, led by a marching band in gold tunics, black jodhpurs and turbans with trailing tails. The brass sections blare back to wailing reeds and ear-splitting drums. Behind comes the wedding vehicle, a kind of barouche, but raised and rounded at the rear like the back end of a galleon and hauled by several pairs of horses. Every square inch of the coach is covered with what looks like beaten tin, scored with intricate patterns, madly reflecting the light of tapers, camera-flashes and street lamps. The bridal couple's gorgeous in yellow and orange and purple, garlands of jasmine and marigold draped round their shoulders, the exhilaration of their well-wishers contagious. It seems the most natural thing in the world to join in.

As I work my way closer through a swirl of incense and rose-water spray, a man bumps into me. He pauses apologetically before spitting what looks like a mouthful of blood into the dirt. As he moves on, he's already feeling among the biros clipped inside his shirt pocket for the next green twist of *paan*. I'm almost near enough now to touch the couple on the palanquin. In the blinding electric light mounted above them, they look hardly more than teenagers. The bride smiles diffidently through her tinkling nose-pendants, but the boy looks as if he's on his way to be sacrificed. He grips the handrail with both fists, staring straight ahead, oblivious to the shouts and laughter of the guests who eddy round.

After months of difficult negotiations over bride price, a posse of Kimwaga's future in-laws has arrived for the wedding in Tabora. It includes a pair of lumpy matriarchs who smoke evil-smelling clay pipes of crinkly local tumbaco, *their demeanour plainly suggesting Kimwaga isn't good enough for their girl. The young man's thoroughly intimidated, his habitually sunny eyes screwed with anxiety. He was unable to smile even when, the day before the ceremony, one of the turkeys escaped its pen and put his startled tormentors to flight.*

A goat is killed and fires lit outside Kimwaga's quarters when the big day dawns. The boy's father sends over a few cases of beer to supplement the revellers' pombe, *the curdy, musky banana or millet brew which starts to be consumed in impressive quantities as soon as breakfast is over. The boy darts in and out of the festivities, gawping at the bride, an impossibly young, shy creature, who's equally cowed by her mother and aunt.*

Early evening, as the drumming and dancing is reaching a crescendo, the boy finds himself back in the living room, where his father's reading the Tanganyika Standard. *Just as 'Lillibullero' sounds on the BBC, Kimwaga stumbles in.*

'Ninaogopa, bwana, *ninaogopa.'*

The boy's father stands up, concerned. 'What are you afraid of, young fellow?'

A flush darkens Kimwaga's face. 'Tonight, the two bibis, they will be with us.'

The boy's father nods uncertainly.

'No, I mean, her mother and aunt, they'll be in the room tonight.'

His employer takes a moment to understand before his face melts. 'I'm sorry,' he says, struggling to contain his laughter, 'you mean …'

Kimwaga can't see what's funny. He nods disconsolately as the boy's father puts an arm round his shoulder.

'Grab a couple of eggs from the fridge,' he tells his son. 'And a spoon.'

When the boy returns, his father's at the drinks cabinet, Kimwaga holding the chunky dimpled glass normally reserved for lime-and-sodas. His employer pulls out a bottle of evil-looking yellow syrup.

'From Prince Bernhard,' he assures Kimwaga, 'dawa nguvu, strong medicine. This will do the trick.'

The Prince of the Netherlands has recently come out on safari with the boy's father, leaving behind several cases of Heineken and a variety of liqueurs. Kimwaga was thoroughly awed by his contact with royalty, as well as amazed to see the boy's father defer to another man. He watches intently now as his employer pours generously from the bottle, cracks the eggs on the edge of the glass and whisks them briskly into the custardy Advocaat, before splashing in a dash of Lea and Perrins.

'Drink up,' he orders.

He stands over the trembling Kimwaga until it's drained.

'Yote itakua sawasawa. Everything will be alright. Go on, now. See you tomorrow.'

Kimwaga already looks an inch taller as he makes his way out to the kitchen. The boy's relieved. He'd been dismayed to see his minder in distress, irritated by his father's levity.

Later that night the boy's woken by triumphant ululations. In the morning, a dark-stained blanket hangs from the *window of his minder's quarters. The smell of roasted meat and* pombe *still hangs in the air. The matriarchs sprawl on the steps, puffing at their pipes, complacent smiles signifying that everyone's done their duty. The boy's father winks at him as they make their way to the Land Rover. His son affects a worldly expression. On the way back from their wonderful safari to the Ugalla River, his father decided to explain the facts of life, in interminable detail, with the aid of a cold sausage. His face had been so intent, so concerned not to shock, that, despite the boy's exquisite embarrassment, he couldn't bring himself to confess he'd already learned it all at school.*

At breakfast the next day, I get another call from the consulate. Back on course, thank God. They've established that I'm not a drug dealer or a gunrunner, and invite me to pick up my documents. Rushing back to Makers' Chambers in a tuk-tuk, I pick up the attestation and return to Elphinstone. There's more good fortune when I get there. Dhavatkar is still ill, and his deputy genially accepts the document without even mentioning Delhi. Perhaps things are really beginning to go my way. Rajeev's already at his carrel, smiling like the Cheshire Cat. This time I order a Coke in the canteen.

'Look at this,' he says, once the pleasantries are over. He removes a manila envelope from his satchel, out of which in turn he fishes a scanned photograph. The caption reads: 'Central Police Training School, Nasik, 1940'.

Despite the poor quality of the sepia reproduction, I immediately spot Bill in the front row. My heart leaps. He looks as fresh-faced as a model for Pear's soap, much blonder than I remember. Perhaps it's overexposure? One shoulder's slightly turned, as if he's cramped amongst his close-packed comrades. He gazes back at the photographer with the ghost of a smile. For some reason, he's the only one not wearing riding boots. Perhaps he was late for parade?

'These are the others from his cadre,' Rajeev explains, pointing to the front row. To my surprise, Indians outnumber whites.

'Who are the people behind?'

'The ones in black shakos are trainee sub-inspectors. Behind them, head constables. The civilians in the second row taught riding, law and languages.' He hands it to me. 'For you. I copied it.'

I'm deeply touched by his thoughtfulness. 'Can't tell you how grateful I am, Rajeev.'

Here's the first new visual evidence of Bill's Indian career, another piece in the jigsaw. I'm impatient to find out more and suggest we begin our search in the archives. My new friend detains me a moment.

'I looked at the notes I have on the Parallel Government, so called.'

'Why so-called?'

Rajeev's eyes droop. 'Terrorists mostly. Many started as petty criminals, although some of the leaders became important politicians after Independence. One such was Vasantdada Patil, commonly known as Nana Patil, who ended up chief minister of Maharashtra. Then there was Y.B. Chavan, later federal defence minister under Indira Gandhi. He helped bring in the Emergency in the 1970s when Indira Gandhi wouldn't give up power, using legislation which the British brought in during the 1940s. Nearly a million people were locked up.'

I'm surprised. 'That many?'

Rajeev's expression is bitter. 'The British only put away a hundred thousand in six years of war.'

I nod sympathetically. 'But what about the underground in Satara?'

'In Marathi, they called themselves the Prati Sarkar, the Parallel Government. But they were soon renamed the *Patri* Sarkar.'

'Meaning?'

'The Government of the Bastinado.'

I look at him blankly.

'The bastinado is a thin cane used to beat the soles of the feet. The standard punishment for anyone who opposed them.' Rajeev grimaces. 'Agonisingly painful. But they did far worse. Gandhi himself denounced them from jail in Pune. Anyway, I didn't discover anything about your father's relations with them.'

'Any luck with Shinde's book?' I ask.

Rajeev shakes his head. 'No one I know has it. There are various second-hand places. But it'll be a lot of bother, especially in this heat.'

I'm not too disappointed. Between Rajeev and the Elphinstone staff, I'm sure I'll soon have some kind of compass. I've already got a sense of the context surrounding Bill's posting in Satara. How had he dealt with these opponents and how successful had the counter-insurgency been? What did they get up to, for the Mahatma to disown them? However, I'm aware of possible complications in Rajeev's account. If they were just thugs, if they flouted Gandhi's precepts, how come Patil and Chavan reached such elevated positions in Congress-dominated India after 1947? In any case, why does Rajeev seem so sympathetic to the British?

But, as he warned, the archives are indeed chaotic, catalogues missing or incomplete, files with different numbers to the ones I ordered coming up, all effected with interminable slowness. Bill's period of service has a limited role in Rajeev's research, and he's unfamiliar with the holdings I need. With a harassed-looking member of staff, who makes increasingly less convincing suggestions, we call up file after file either side of lunch. There's little on the Hoors. Rajeev speculates that the relevant archives are in modern-day Sindh, now in Pakistan. Material on Satara's plentiful, however. At times I feel the ghost is almost within my grasp. At one point a folder arrives with documents signed by Lindsay Padden-Row, in later life godfather to my younger brother, after whom he was named. It consists of correspondence with the district magistrate in Satara during Bill's posting there, but concerns only air-raid precautions and an internment camp for foreigners. Did Bill read the letters, or was he consulted about their contents?

'Without more specific information, we could spend weeks looking,' Rajeev laments.

I'm beginning to feel discouraged again. 'Bhosle told me to come here.'

'These provincial historians,' he mutters with a deprecating expression.

'Looks like I've got to get hold of Shinde's book.'

Rajeev looks mournful for a moment. Suddenly his eyes light up. 'What about the old University library?'

'Where's that?'

~

Strolling through late-afternoon Mumbai, with its softening light and body-temperature fug, I have a feeling of extraordinary connection to Bill. In Rajeev's photo, he's so much younger than I am now that I feel almost fatherly. What would he think of the quest I'm undertaking? He always encouraged my curiosity, and took pride in my achievements at school. Perhaps this journey will prove a fitting final homage to his memory. To reach the old campus, I skirt the Oval Maidan, where a dozen cricket pitches are crammed together. Given his passion for the sport, I wonder if Bill might have exercised his talents here, during his periods of leave. Several children are playing a scratch game against a bin, arguing over whether the batsman is out.

Behind the nets at the Arusha Club, the boy watches hot-cheeked as his father puts an arm round François. His temporary foster-brother's upset.

'Come on, François, you have to learn to be a good sport.'

*The child looks up uncomprehendingly. He's the son of
the private secretary to the exiled Kigeli V of Rwanda, and
is himself distantly related to the recently overthrown king.
With civil war threatening, François's mother is trapped in the
capital Kigali and his father's gone back to try and get her
out. But what to do with their kids in the meantime? They've
been farmed out to various friends and the boy's parents
have agreed to look after the oldest, a timorous ten-year-old
with almost blue-black skin, enormous eyes and long lashes.
François has become increasingly fretful as his father's absence
stretches from week to week and no news comes from home,
leading to one or two tantrums recently.*

*Amongst their own children, the boy's parents don't toler-
ate displays of temper. Yet when François flies into a rage, they
simply look at each other knowingly and indulge him. Most
of the time, the boy gets on well with their guest. They share
a room and he loves the new stories his foster-brother tells at
night. But he's beginning to resent the different way François
is treated.*

*'When will his father be coming back?' the boy asked his
mother disingenuously only that afternoon.*

*'As soon as they stop slaughtering each other, I expect,' she
responded cheerfully. 'Until then, you carry on treating him
just like Ames and Lindsay.'*

*Still the boy's aggrieved, blaming François rather than his
parents for the confusion they've introduced. So he watches
triumphantly as his father strides over when the protesting
shouts begin.*

*'But it was out, Mr Moore-Gilbert,' Rolf Trappe appeals,
seconded by others. 'He was hit below the knee, everyone saw.'*

*Tears welling, François eventually confirms it. The boy's
father speaks softly to him in French, before reiterating it in
English.*

*'It's very important to be a good sport, François,' he con-
cludes: 'rules are rules. You can't change them as you go along.'*

He turns before his son has time to wipe the smirk from his face.

'Why are you grinning like an idiot? They don't play cricket in the French-speaking parts of Africa. How would you feel if you lived in Rwanda and people teased you because you didn't understand the laws of boules? You're old enough to know better.'

What is bool? *the boy wonders. What kind of sport has a name like that? Is it to do with bullfighting? And if French-speakers don't play the game, why is it called French cricket? But wilting beneath his father's frown, he decides to keep quiet.*

Later that evening, the boy observes François peering into the cage containing the family's pair of parrots, Congolese Greys with brilliant red tail-feathers. He's feeding peanuts to Ruanda, the female, while her mate Urundi preens himself, making ear-piercing whistles. François mutters something, a tear rolling down his cheek. It sounds like a prayer, though whether in French or Kinyarwanda, it's impossible to make out. Mortified, the boy goes to him.

The original Bombay University looks like Oxford's Keble College transplanted to the tropics: contrasting-patterned brick, grassed quadrangles, confident Gothic bell tower. The library has an Arts-and-Crafts feel, breathtaking teak barrel-vaulted ceiling, imposing issue desk, busts of Victorian benefactors surveying the handful of students at long tables. After signing me in, on the strength of my London University visiting card, a librarian sifts the ancient index with the dexterity of a card sharp. Among innumerable Shindes, she finally finds the one I'm after. I wait with increasing anticipation as it's fetched from the stacks.

When the book arrives, I settle down to read, disturbed only by an occasional pigeon sweeping disconcertingly through the open leaded windows. It's a 500-page hardback with a curious illustration on the front, an enormous wave about to overwhelm a frail-looking barque. *The Parallel Government of Satara: a Phase of the Quit India Movement*, the red lettering proclaims. According to the dust jacket, Dr A.B. Shinde is a college principal in Kolhapur with a PhD from Shivaji University – the same place Bhosle works. They must know each other. Have they collaborated in their research? I spend time getting a feel for the text, chapter headings, appendices, sources. It has every hallmark of serious historical research, relying not just on archival material but first-person testimony, including extracts from the weekly confidential reports of successive district superintendents of police.

From the opening chapters, I get a very different impression of the movement to what Rajeev suggested. It doesn't seem like a terrorist organisation. Like so many of the anticolonial nationalist movements I've studied, it seems to have emerged out of entirely justifiable and long-standing political dissatisfactions, which were aggravated when Britain declared war on Germany in India's name – without bothering to consult its peoples. The Defence of India Rules, applied in draconian

Bill on the mess steps, Nasik PTS c. 1939

fashion once hostilities broke out, further inflamed the situation. From what Shinde says, Gandhi's arrest in August 1942 was the final straw, provoking armed rebellion on the part of the Parallel Government. With my professional hat on, I can see nothing to disapprove. How then to account for Rajeev's animus against the movement?

There's not time before the library closes to read the text systematically. Turning to the index, my heart jumps to see Bill's name. I skim to the first page referenced. This is what I'm after. 'By the end of 1944 ... Satara was in turmoil.' Despite increasing pressure from the Raj, 'the movement did not break down'. 'Atrocities'. The word leaps off the page. Not ones committed by the Parallel Government. 'The police, therefore, lost self-control and perpetrated atrocities on the people.' I brace myself to read on. 'Moore-Gilbert, the Additional DSP, Satara, got wide notoriety for his ruthlessness with which he conducted these raids.' The narrative zooms in on a single day more than sixty years ago: 'Moore-Gilbert, accompanied by 100/150 policemen marched into the village Chafal on December 4, 1944, at about 4 a.m. and camped in the temple of Mahadeo situated on the banks of the river Uttarmand.' Where's Chafal exactly? 'The inhabitants going to the river, or proceeding to their farms or villages or to the forest were rounded up and herded together like cattle in the temple: they were deprived of their clothes and mercilessly beaten up.' Inside the temple? 'Cow-dung and mud were thrust in the mouths of some while others were made to lie prostrate on the ground and nearly frightened out of their life by holding bayonets to their throats; even old men were not spared.' I feel sick. 'The inhabitants of Chafal are filled with panic; even a rumour of a police raid frightens them away to the forest and shop-keepers roll down their shutters. Even the leading Congress workers from the district are afraid of visiting Chafal and consoling the people.' But there's more. 'A few days ago, a similar havoc was played among the villages Mhavshi and Tambve ...'

Something I can't yet name cracks inside me. Is it to protect me from all this that Bhosle decided to make himself unavailable? I'm so upset I can barely see to jot down the identification numbers of the archival files on which Shinde draws.

CHAPTER 3

Memory and Doubt

Leaving the library, I wander in a daze. Must be some mistake, I keep repeating. The image of my father constructed in my childhood memories, such a stable emotional anchor all these years, has fractured. Frantically I turn the pieces over, trying to fit them back together. But they won't go. I've taught auto-biography for long enough to know that memories, especially early memories, aren't necessarily trustworthy, whatever sub-jective truth they might embody. Didn't J.M. Barrie write that 'God gave us memory so that we'd have roses in December'? Michel de Leiris is similarly ambivalent: 'I do not know if what I remember of my youth is true. But I remember it truly.' Whatever, the stench of something foul is threatening to over-whelm the scent of my December blooms.

The disillusion's so excruciating, I can't think straight. Assuming I've been heading back to my hotel, I eventually realise I've gone the other way, into Colaba. Here's the Leopold Café, scene of one of the bloodiest recent terror attacks. I'm startled to see it already packed with tourists again. The group nearest the door as I come in, burly young men with pirate bandanas and angry sunburned faces, look drunk. In clashing voices they denounce the prohibition on beach parties in Goa, brought in a few days ago as a security precaution. Only one table's free. There appear to be bullet holes in the plate glass behind it. Haven't they had time to repair the damage? How neat the punctures are, the surrounding glass immaculate, as if drilled by a craftsman. On an adjacent plinth are garlanded photos of two murdered waiters, with collecting boxes for their families. No wonder the table's not occupied.

It would be too ghoulish to sit there, desperate though I am for a drink. But if I share someone else's, I'll have to talk. I shrink back into the crowded pavements, like an injured crab seeking the safety of water. There's no relief here. Everything jars; sharp-eyed hawkers' fangy grins, garishly lit shop fronts, screeching music from successive pavement stalls, incomprehensible shouting, combine to create a nightmare fairground. A street-child begs. While guiltily fumbling for change, I accidentally give him my room key, which he returns disdainfully, as if I'm a cheapskate. I come within a hair's breadth of being knocked down by a cab when I step carelessly off the kerb. In his wing mirror, the driver's face is a rictus of soundless curses. I feel entirely abandoned.

I must get away from this city of dreadful night. There's a travel agency. As I plunge in, the young woman adjusts her electric-blue sari with a startled expression. Do I have the mark of Cain?

'Goa,' I mutter. 'I'd like to make a booking.'

'Yes, sir. Where in Goa?' Bangles jangle on her wrist, skin the colour of cinnamon, as she waves me to sit. Posters extol the castled glories of Rajasthan.

'Arjuna Beach.' It should be really quiet now.

Her X-ray eyes cloud. She shows me brochures of anonymous package hotels. I haven't even considered what I want. My incoherence makes the woman increasingly uneasy. She speaks into an intercom and a short, perspiring man emerges through the flimsy partition behind. He's chewing and exhales a nauseous gust of garlic and *brinjal*.

'Looking for beach action or what?' he demands, as we go through a more promising list of small guest-houses. 'Don't worry about the so-called ban,' he adds airily. 'There'll be lots going on. This one's very popular with the younger crowd.'

I don't want to be with the kind of people I've just overheard in the Leopold.

'Are you alright, sir? You look pale.'

Doesn't everyone look grey in this merciless neon? 'Just a bit hot,' I mutter, flicking blankly through another brochure.

'Why don't you come back when you're clearer about what you're looking for?' he eventually asks, understandably impatient to get back to his meal.

This is better. At the end of a lane leading from Colaba Causeway, I come to the promenade overlooking the Arabian Sea where I sit heavily on a stone bulwark. To my left, I see the darkened Taj Hotel, spectrally impressive beyond the surrounding security barriers, where soldiers are stationed at intervals. 'Crime Scene. Do Not Cross', the plastic tape insists. Once finished at the Leopold, the terrorists must have come this way to join their colleagues attacking the Taj. In the eerie street-light it has the look of a ruined monument, windows smoke-scorched, one cupola badly burned. In front of it, the Gateway of India seems to float out of the water. The triumphal triple arch marks the spot where the King-Emperor George V became the first British monarch to visit his Indian possessions, in 1911. It represents everything Bill was defending. Incredible that within less than forty years, all the power

The Gateway of India, Bombay 1938

it symbolised had melted away. What part did the Parallel Government play in that process?

Despite the uncanny atmosphere, the lapping waves and starlight are calming and I start to order my reactions to Shinde. Does anything in what I remember as a child hint that my father was such a man as he describes? Bill certainly had a temper. Yet, despite racking my brains, I can't remember him being involved in any physical violence during my African childhood – apart from the incident with the cook.

The boy and his father are in canvas chairs, sipping tea from white enamel mugs and scoffing the first sausages of the day. Embers glow in the creamy ash of the previous night's fire. Above the tents, the dawn clouds are coral still and the birdsong deafening. The boy's tired. He was up late the previous evening while his father mapped the night sky for him, with binoculars so powerful the boy has to rest them against a tree to stop the shake. And it's hard to get to sleep in the tent they share. The bush comes alive at night, the air thick with insect noise, the calls of animals looking for a mate or prey, the greedy gulps of frogs. Even the canvas seems to come alive, stretching and contracting like a skin in the night breeze. Every so often he'll ask his father what's making a particular sniffle, whimper, hiss or cry. The answer comes immediately, whether it's a bug, bird or mammal. There's nothing about the natural world he doesn't seem to know, what a bull hippo weighs or how long the eggs of weaver birds take to hatch. The bush fits him like a glove. He's invariably right when instinct tells him they're close to an animal they can't yet see. The boy wonders if he'll ever be master of all this, too.

A scout approaches, saluting smartly, red beret with brass buffalo-head insignia pulled down to his ears against the early chill. He looks tired after being out all night, having left the previous afternoon to make inquiries amongst the fishermen. One of them's with him, a very tall, slender man with a small head and dull eyes. He looks unsteady on his legs, perhaps because of his height or because he's more at home on water.

'He says there's an elephant in a trap, bwana,' the scout announces. He gives rough co-ordinates and the fisherman answers some questions.

'Asante, Daoudi, thank you, bwana. Bring the gun case,' his father commands, standing up, scratching his stubble and gulping the remainder of his tea.

The boy goes to fetch the awkward oblong box from the back of the tent where it's buried under the pile of dirty clothes. The boy loves the freedom of safari, without his mother always telling him to tidy his things. By the time he returns, his father's organised the team. A driver, Hamisi Sekana, two game scouts – Daoudi and light-skinned Salim – the fisherman and an Ndorobo tracker, a tiny man with a wispy goatee and a right arm so muscular it looks deformed. It's because he's been drawing his bow on that side since he was a child, the boy's father explained on the first day of the trip.

Soon the Land Rover is bucking off-track towards the low hills overlooking the Ugalla River. They go slowly, because the wet-season grass is growing rapidly, concealing rocks and pot-holes. The fisherman stands next to Daoudi and the tracker, even more unsteady in the unfamiliar environment of a vehicle, gripping the metal tubing behind the cab, squinting like a ship's lookout as he scans the fever-trees. Daoudi bangs on the roof occasionally to indicate to the driver to change direction. Hamisi and Salim cradle their weapons, faces impassive. Are they anxious? the boy wonders. He is, but not so much as he's proud. It's not like with the spitting cobra, when he was told to stay behind. Now he's beginning to be treated like a man. Often these days his father asks his opinion on things. Sometimes, he even seems impressed by the answers.

A gang of warthogs suddenly appears. The mother stares reproachfully over stubby tusks, before high-stepping away; the piglets follow like pinnaces behind a top-heavy mother ship. Once in longer grass, only a rustling current betrays their passage. Along the crest of a hill, a caravan of giraffes proceeds on its stately way, coal-black twigs against the rising sun. The breeze is deliciously cool as it plays through the boy's blue Aertex shirt. This is heaven, being in the bush, for the first time just him and his father, seeing such sights. He wishes it could be the pattern for all his days. If only there weren't an elephant in a trap.

It's an hour and much hotter before Daoudi bangs and points to two o'clock. The Land Rover pulls over and they all get out. The men check their weapons. The boy holds the gun case, trying to keep his back straight, while his father takes out the double-barrelled .458, a gift from Prince Bernhard. 'Holland and Holland, Piccadilly', the gold letters read on the red velvet lining. The boy loves the peppery smell of warm gun-oil which percolates as his father fixes both barrels to the carved stock. They sit over-and-under, not side-by-side like the twelve-bore. The driver's told to wait with the fisherman. Then they set off in single file, Daoudi and the tracker first, the boy and his father, Salim and Hamisi Sekana bringing up the rear. They walk in silence, dewy grass muffling their footsteps. No one knows where the poachers are and, like buffalo, they're sometimes bold enough to ambush their pursuers.

Before long they come to the edge of a gently rising clearing, where the tracker stops. Urgent whispers pass between him and the boy's father. The boy can see the crushed grass ahead. There's elephant dung as well. Moist with dew, it looks fresh. But he can tell by the crust it's a day old, possibly more. They skirt the clearing cautiously, half crouching amongst the low acacia thorn. Halfway across they hear the first scream. The boy goose-pimples. There's nothing so blood-curdling as the sound of an elephant in pain, not even hyena howls at night, which make him almost want to be young enough still to crawl into his father's camp bed. The tracker proceeds unhurriedly. Despite his impatience, the boy knows that if they go too quickly, important evidence may be overlooked.

'Nne,' the tracker whispers, holding up four fingers.

At least they're not outnumbered, the boy reflects with relief. There's another anguished trumpet, weaker than the first.

When they reach the second clearing, the boy wishes for a moment he hadn't come. Although upwind, the elephant knows they're there and makes frantic efforts to break free. It's a young female, tusks ten or fifteen pounds apiece at most. From this distance, the wire's invisible, but each time she raises her foreleg, the boy glimpses the hideous red grin below the knee. The same haunted look appears on his father's face as when Shotty the spaniel died.

'Stay here with Salim,' he whispers.

Once he's binoculared the surrounding bush, the boy's father takes out a waxy carton of bullets from his safari jacket, breaks the .458 at the breech and loads a slug in each barrel. He slips a third in his mouth like a dummy before checking his sights. Hamisi Sekana and Daoudi lock their bolts as they slowly advance, one to each side and five yards behind the game ranger. The elephant turns head-on, trunk curling and unfurling as she sips the breeze. Above his pounding heart the boy hears the slap of her ears. Salim faces behind them, cradling his rifle, while his father approaches to about forty yards from the animal. He examines the young elephant again through his field glasses, before signalling Hamisi up beside him.

The boy sees the black spot between the target's eyes before he hears the deafening report. There's a cacophony of protest as every bird within half a mile takes wing. The elephant settles itself a moment before slipping gracefully to its knees, then keels over in slow motion. The trunk's the last thing to hit the ground, as if it wants one last draw of savannah air. The boy's awestruck.

'Keep your eyes peeled,' his father calls back, breaking the

dead silence which eventually ensues, 'the mother may still be around.'

The boy looks warily along the inscrutable scrub. But white egrets are already returning to sit amongst the thorn branches, at a respectful distance. If they all suddenly flap up again, it's time to worry. Yet he's trembling violently when they advance to examine the animal. Its foreleg's in terrible condition. In trying to free itself, the elephant has tightened the noose and the wire has cut to the bone. The iron picket to which the noose is attached is hammered down below ground level, protected by barbed wire to prevent the elephant pulling it out. Even had she succeeded, which sometimes happens, the injury would soon have finished her off. Maggots are already swarming in the raw flesh, flies settling on the clouding long-lashed eyes. In its death-throe, the elephant has expelled a last massive pat of dung, which smells sweet as cut meadow.

The boy's father gives orders to the scouts and tracker, who disappear towards the east. Hamisi follows behind. With his easy loping stride, which can swallow forty miles in a day, he can afford them a head start.

'They'll probably have heard the shot and be miles away by the time we find their camp.'

'Why did the mother leave her?' the boy asks, focused entirely on the elephant.

'Maybe they killed her first. This one's tusks are so small they perhaps couldn't be bothered, and she wandered over here. Or they're coming back later to check the trap.'

His father's subdued for the rest of the day. The episode has cast a shadow over what, for the boy, has been the happiest three weeks he can remember. On returning to camp, the game ranger dispatches more scouts with the driver, to dig up the noose as evidence, hack out the tusks and cut up the carcase to be distributed to the fishermen. It's a way of keeping them onside, they're a vital source of information. Late afternoon, they drive the Bedford truck down to the marshes. The fishermen are pleased to see them and even happier with the elephant meat, strips of raw, red, rubbery flesh which turn the boy's stomach as they slither across the tarpaulin. More and more poachers are coming across from the Congo side, the fishermen complain. They, too, suffer from the trespassers, who often demand food and sometimes take their catches by force.

While the adults discuss, the boy wanders off. He's fascinated by these temporary wet-season settlements. The fishermen make platforms of reeds to sleep on, within a scaffolding of branches, lashed together with strips of bark, on which they dry their harvest. Mainly it's catfish, with flat, wide heads and long whiskers. In the broiling sun they shrink, turning and leather-brown, like stinking sandals. Around their camps, the reeds stretch for miles in ankle-deep water from the flooding Ugalla. The boy loves to slosh through them in his new gumboots, replacements for the ones stolen from outside his tent on the floor of the Ngorongoro Crater. His father hadn't believed him when the boy claimed to have heard snuffling during the night. Only when they continued the hyena cull the following day and one gumboot was found in an elderly female's stomach did his father apologise. The next time he went to Arusha, he bought the best replacements he could find.

Later, the fishermen take them to see the latest wave of migratory birds. Crouching behind a tussocked ridge from where the flat opal surface of the seasonal lake stretches away, the boy's father gets out his decoy, a black tube like a relay baton. A few toots bring some Egyptian geese scooting over the water, brown and white with iridescent green heads and a blue wing chevron. But the boy isn't all there. He keeps having flashbacks to the elephant's dreadful gash, and smoulders with anger against those who did it.

When they get back to camp, it's growing dark. There's laughter and excitement amongst the scouts building the fires.

Strips of elephant meat have been set out to cure on frames like the ones the fishermen use. Light-skinned Salim's back, and the Land Rover's gone one last time to fetch Daoudi, the tracker and Hamisi Sekana. They've found the poachers' camp and are bringing someone in. The boy and his father barely have time to measure the tusks of the young elephant, still partly encased in a crimson honeycomb of shattered jawbone, when they see headlights bumping towards them. Soon three figures emerge from the shadows. Hamisi leads forward a small, undernourished man wearing only filthy shorts and sandals made from old tyre treads, wrists handcuffed behind his back. Despite his bare, pumping pigeon-chest and pronounced limp, the boy takes a violent dislike to him. It's the sly eyes and obsequious smile. On each shoulder, Daoudi bears a tusk. These must be forty pounds each.

'We found the camp and this man hiding in the bush nearby. There was this ivory. And traps.'

The murderous wires tinkle and glint in the firelight where Hamisi sets them down. He's smiling. It's a job well done, and the boy's father tells him so. Then he compares the first noose recovered with these ones.

'You see,' he shows the boy, 'they've got five twists around the neck. Made by the same person.'

'He's not from round here,' Hamisi interjects. 'He says he comes from the north, near Mwanza. But his Swahili is shenzi.'

The boy spotted some of the man's, too, has mistakes. His father nods and begins to ask questions. At first his tone is conversational, as if they've all just met in friendlier circumstances. What's the man's village, his tribe, his father's name, those of his relations? The man shifts from foot to foot, as if his bad leg's giving him trouble. At times he's defiant, more often ingratiating. He claims to have been travelling south and stumbled on the deserted camp. Hearing the scouts approach, he hid nearby, fearing the owners were returning. He knows nothing about the tusks or nooses.

'*Where were you travelling to? Who were you visiting and where? Why didn't you go by the road?*' Then the questions become more general.

The boy's becoming increasingly angry. Who cares what the president's wife is called? With every faltering answer, as the suspect mangles the Swahili words, he knows the man's lying. Why isn't the questioning more direct?

'*Have you ever seen an animal caught in a noose?*' his father eventually asks the man, almost as an afterthought. '*Can you imagine what it feels?*'

The suspect denies it emphatically. Hamisi's face twists into a sneer. The boy's finding it hard to control himself. He wants to beat the man, make him confess and apologise. Put his bad leg in a wire noose and see how he makes out. Then his father begins to ask the identical questions he began with, in the same matter-of-fact tone. The boy's furious. Why's his father wasting time? Adults can be so unfair sometimes. His father thrashed him once for twisting their pet monkey's tail, yet now he's smiling at this man, politely inquiring after his personal affairs when the suspect's caused the elephant intolerable suffering. Suddenly his father sits up straighter, his tone steely at last.

'*The first time you said your village was to the east of Mwanza, now it's the other side. If you came from anywhere near Mwanza you'd know Binti Nyerere's name. Do you take me for an* mpumbafu?'

Daoudi laughs derisively. It's the prisoner who's made a fool of himself. Traps don't have to be made of wire, the boy realises, with a burst of admiration. In the firelight, his father's face flickers lividly. Surely he's going to give the man a thrashing now? Perhaps the suspect fears the same thing, for his expression suddenly crumples. Looking down, he confesses to coming across Lake Tanganyika three weeks earlier, from Rwanda, where unspeakable things are happening.

'*We are poor men, bwana, we have been chased from our homes. What can we do?*'

He explains that the gang was paid by an Indian they met in Kigoma, who smuggles ivory to the Far East. The boy's father is calm again. He listens attentively.

'So many of these buggers are coming over now,' he mutters.

'What'll happen to him?' the boy asks later, tucked up under his mosquito net, still aggrieved.

His father stirs. 'We'll take him up to the police post in Mpanda. They'll do the paperwork and send him on to court in Tabora.'

'And if he denies it in front of the judge?'

'You have to collect the evidence. Then it's for other people to decide,' his father explains, as if to an apprentice. 'We need to catch the rest of the gang and persuade him to give evidence against them. If that happens, he'll be fined and they'll probably get a couple of years.'

'That's more than the poor flump will have.' The boy's face burns vengefully again.

'Well, at least she's out of her misery. Think about something else or you'll have nightmares.'

Author sitting on rogue elephant shot by Bill,
holding a rifle, c. 1961.

'I want to smash that man.'

'Yes, I understand. But we'll be needing his help.' The boy's father sits up. 'Did you leave your Wellingtons outside?'

'Should I bring them in?'

'No thanks, old chap. I doubt the Ugalla hyenas could face the smell of your toe jam. They're not as brave as up at the Crater.'

Before the rumbling laugh dies down, the boy's asleep, exhausted by the emotion of another long day.

At first I'm reassured by my recollections. Surely, if Bill had the traits that Shinde describes, he'd have sought fresh opportunities to indulge them in Africa. Yet he didn't join the police in Tanganyika, which would have been a logical step. Nonetheless, there wasn't, I now realise, such a divorce between Bill's career here and his role as a game ranger. He caught the man out using interrogation techniques he'd no doubt learned as an IP officer. Tracking poachers probably involved the same sort of skills as hunting the Parallel Government. Catching malefactors, gathering evidence, consigning them to justice, was consonant with his earlier vocation. However, if Shinde's account is true, it seems strange that Bill didn't take the opportunity to rough up the poacher. It's what I'd been hoping he'd do. Perhaps he held back because I was there. I didn't accompany him every time he was in the bush. Still, if Bill was that kind of man, word would surely have got around. Yet I never saw a glint of fear in Kimwaga's eyes, or a flicker of caution in Hamisi Sekana's. If he was a constitutionally violent man, I'd have expected them to show some reserve. Even with the cook, Bill used only enough force to protect Eunice.

But then the doubts set in. Shinde's narrative seemed unimpeachably scholarly. I'm suddenly angry and disgusted with Bill. Did he think such actions would pass unremarked at the time, or escape the subsequent searchlight of History? It's as if he's compromised me as well. In turn I'm angry with myself for my naivety. For as long as I knew so little about Bill's career in the subcontinent, I didn't waste much time thinking about it. Once decided on coming to India, however, I did follow up some of Professor Bhosle's leads. But I was too busy to do more than read a couple of books on Sindh.

The story of Britain's acquisition of the region is another dispiriting chapter in our imperial past. Ignoring long-standing friendship treaties with local chieftains, Charles Napier annexed it in 1843 to Bombay Presidency – an act of treachery for which he was later knighted. His expedition was partly mounted, it seems, to compensate for the catastrophic failure of the recent attempt to invade and subdue Afghanistan. Sindh's later history under the Raj is hardly more appetising. In the early 1940s, under the leadership of their charismatic religious leader, the Pir Pagara, certain Muslim communities in Sindh pronounced themselves *hur*, or free of imperial control. The British declared marshal law against these 'Mohammedan fanatics', herded large numbers into concentration camps and introduced a shoot-on-sight policy for those who refused to go. The Pir Pagara was hanged in March 1943, after a show trial, although the Hurs continued to agitate long afterwards.

However, I could find no reference to Bill in these texts – more to my relief than disappointment, given the story I uncovered. With time at a premium before departure, the issue of what he was doing in Satara would have to wait until I reached Mumbai. Indian friends in London reminded me that after Gandhi's 'Quit India' speech in early August 1942, there were mass arrests of nationalist activists in Bombay and other Indian cities. But they weren't aware that significant violence was involved – on either side – during the round-up and its aftermath. Nor that there was much agitation outside the urban areas.

Now I wonder if I haven't been guilty of self-deception, even bad faith. Perhaps it's been a little too convenient that Bill's Indian career remained shrouded in mystery. As a professor of

Postcolonial Studies, I'm well aware of the long tradition of negative literary representations of the British Empire. More specifically, I'm familiar with the disobliging portraits of the Indian Police drawn by writers like George Orwell and Paul Scott. In Orwell's *Burmese Days*, Flory is a pathetic and primarily self-destructive character, undone in the end by his inability to escape the straitjacket of the racial thinking of his time. By contrast, Superintendent Merrick in Scott's *Raj Quartet* is one of the most chillingly manipulative and self-serving characters in postwar British writing, someone who grossly abuses his position to advance his own interests.

When I read these works years ago, I did sometimes have uneasy feelings about Bill's career, wondering how accurate such depictions were of the declining standards of the service as the Raj sped towards dissolution, in the period when my father was in the subcontinent. But Merrick, at least, was exceptional, a rogue officer, acting out perverse private notions of justice or simply satisfying sadistic urges. Otherwise it would be hard to explain the disapproval shown him by other characters, as well as Scott's narrative voice. So I didn't ever connect someone like him with Bill, even as Scott helped me understand that the IP was British India's first line of defence and a prime instrument of its control.

It's a hot night, and I'm so restless that when I eventually get back to my hotel, I spend much of the night in the shower. As I stand under the piddling dribble, I revolt against the clashing image-repertoires I now have of Bill. Can the father I so loved and respected as a child really have been capable of the excesses Shinde describes? How could the person who gave his life trying to help refugees have committed such crimes? The figure in Rajeev's photo, with which I formed such a powerful connection earlier in the day, now feels like a repulsive interloper amongst my memories. If Shinde's allegations are true, Bill's behaviour is against the rules of any civilised society – even if these standards have been subject to still more merciless assault in the era of Blair and Bush, of Guantanamo and Abu Ghraib. Perhaps the IP was simply a vile and brutal instrument of occupation. But if so, it's strange I've been made so welcome everywhere, despite my openness about Bill's years in the force. And even odder that such a gentle and intelligent man as Rajeev Divekar seems to so admire the service.

I know from talking to friends, as well as teaching male autobiography – from Edmund Gosse and Samuel Butler to Hanif Kureishi and Nick Hornby – that there comes a moment when everyone sees through the father-figures constructed in childhood. The venality or violence, the failures and disappointed hopes one day thrust like a fist through the canvases they'd so lovingly created. Barack Obama describes this moment beautifully in *Dreams from My Father* when his half-sister, on a visit to the US, recounts what the Old Man was really like in daily life back in Kenya: 'I felt as if my world had been turned on its head; as if I'd woken up to find a blue sun in the yellow sky, or heard animals speaking like men. All my life, I had carried a single image of my father, one that I had … never questioned.'

My circumstances, however, differ from Obama's. My father didn't desert me in any conventional sense, and I have a rich collection of childhood memories of him. Moreover, he didn't live to a ripe old age. Nonetheless, perhaps precisely because Bill died before I reached adolescence, and more so because everyone spoke so well of him, the moment of disenchantment has been postponed until now. I recognise that, even at my age, I have further growing up to do.

Still, I've only read one account of his activities in India. Whatever the density of Shinde's archival material, his narrative – like any historian's – is shaped by his particular investments, personal and political. That's one of the sharpest lessons of Nirad Chaudhuri's memoir of his life as a historian, which now lies on my bedside table. Perhaps the same material could be read differently. Maybe other sources exist which cast a different light. If I can get to see the full versions of the confidential weekly reports which Shinde occasionally cites, Bill's own point of view might emerge. After all, by his own admission, the Congress worker on whose account Shinde relies so heavily wasn't able to get to Chafal himself. How, then, did he compile his report? It wouldn't be the first time a nationalist politician exaggerated events to mobilise opinion against colonial authority.

So, however tempting the prospect, I can't run away to Goa after all. Further investigations may throw up evidence to challenge Shinde's narrative, or at least put Bill's behaviour into some sort of context. On the other hand, perhaps they'll simply confirm the accusations. I feel trapped between the emotional loyalties formed during childhood and the postcolonial political ethics I've acquired as an adult. How am I going to resolve things?

CHAPTER 4

Glimpses of Bill

Over late morning tea with Rajeev in Elphinstone, I conceal how disturbed I am. I don't know him well enough to confide.

'May have a surprise later,' he twinkles, as I get out my file. 'Won't say anything more for the moment.'

I'm not in the mood for further shocks. But I force a wan smile.

'Well, did you find your Shinde?'

I nod equivocally. 'Lots of references to follow up. He says district superintendents of police had to write confidential weekly reports,' I say evasively. 'I'd give my eye teeth to get hold of my father's.' Anything to deflect attention from my wound.

Rajeev nods. 'Yes, it's the same system today. The originals are held in the station concerned, copied to the inspector-general, then to state headquarters in Mumbai. In those days, Satara reported to the inspector-general in charge of Southern Range, in Belgaum.'

'Where's that?'

'It's in Karnataka now – the next state down. It got tacked onto Kannada-speaking territory when Maharashtra and Gujarat came into being. They'll have their own archives.'

My heart sinks.

'Anyway, according to the *History of Services*, your father was a special additional district superintendent of police in Satara, a temporary position. He may not have written such reports himself; that was the job of regular DSPs.'

'But Bhosle says he produced this secret Memorandum on the Parallel Government. And according to Shinde, he was in charge of anti-insurgency operations in Satara, not the DSP in place.'

Rajeev looks askance. 'You may be right. But in any case, such reports are destroyed after thirty years. There simply isn't the space to keep them.'

'Shinde's book came out in 1989. That's forty-five years after the events.'

'He might have done the spadework earlier?'

'Is everything destroyed? Even material of such obvious historical importance?'

'It's possible that some was kept,' Rajeev concedes. 'In fact, I'm not sure exactly when the thirty-year rule was introduced. Did you make a list of Shinde's sources?'

I detach it from the rest of my notes. He looks puzzled.

'But most of these are Home Department and Special Branch reference numbers. Special Branch is now State Intelligence Bureau. Each has its own holdings.'

Why on earth did Bhosle send me here to Elphinstone? 'Then I'll try them.'

Rajeev glances at me mournfully. 'You won't get in just like that. Especially now, since the attacks.'

I try not to look discouraged. 'How do I get permission?'

'Normally you'd write. You could try in person. But they can be sticky at the best of times. Your attestation from the consulate should help.' Rajeev pats my arm. 'Look, I can't stay, the wife's poorly. Just a seasonal bug, but nasty enough. Believe it or not,' he adds, fanning himself with his folder, 'this is mid-winter here.' He bends towards me, smiling enigmatically. 'I want you to come over to my place when you've finished today. I may be onto something which could really help.'

It's an effort now to contain my curiosity. 'But your wife's unwell.'

'My dear man, it's only for a cup of tea.' He scribbles directions.

~

Mantrale, seat of the Home Department of the Government of Maharashtra, is, indeed, crawling with security. The main building's another ugly 1960s tower and someone forgot to plant any trees round the concrete apron in front, which shimmers like a grill. The queue for admission snakes far down the street. Joining it, I take out my new book, Rohinton Mistry's *A Fine Balance*, set in mid-70s Bombay during Indira Gandhi's Emergency. After Rajeev's scathing comments, I want to find out more about that period. But I'm too tired to concentrate and soon feel faint from the heat and caustic smell of melting bitumen. My spirits plummet. Am I going through all this just to defend the indefensible?

By the time I get to the front gate, I'm not just demoralised, but thirsty and sunburned. After signing in and showing my documents, I'm nearly stifled by the press in the single up lift. On the seventh floor, where I've been directed, there's another queue – this one comprised entirely of Westerners. I check with an elderly attendant, only to find I've been sent to the wrong place.

'I will take you,' he offers, once he registers my long face and the throng at the lift.

Two flights up is another bare, airless corridor with peeling veneered doors. To my huge relief, no one's waiting. The attendant knocks at a door and leads me in. The disorder reminds me of Elphinstone, with the same dusty document-sacks, crammed shelves, ancient typewriters and rickety chairs. Hard to believe this small room's the Home Department archive. The young man behind the front desk has a mole on his chin and hunched shoulders. He motions me to sit but is in no hurry with the paperwork before him. Indeed he looks ostentatiously at his brassy watch, as if to suggest I've come at an inconvenient moment. At last he yawns, scratches the chest of his greying polyester shirt and asks my business. When I explain, he looks put out. I show him Shinde's list of sources.

'Do you have permission?'

'Yes. I'm a professor at London University,' I state importantly, showing him the consul's attestation.

He studies it. 'This is for research in Elphinstone archives.'

'I need a separate letter here?'

He nods blandly.

'But I've come all the way from England, and I only have a couple of weeks.'

'Foreigners should apply from country of origin. It takes about two months.'

Desperate to locate Bill's reports, I try arguing. He's adamant.

'Can you at least tell me if these files still exist?'

'Sorry, closing in half an hour. We're short-staffed because of seasonal leave. Archives in other building.' He points out of the window to a beautiful colonial edifice, across a road so busy it'd probably take that half-hour just to cross.

'Well, thanks very much and have a nice Christmas,' I reply sarcastically, frustration getting to me. But his offhand manner has fired me up for one last throw of the dice. Will the State Intelligence Bureau keep the same hours as Mantrale? Even if they work later, they're doubtless up to their necks dealing with the aftermath of the attacks. My chances of accessing their archives are probably nil. Still, there's nothing to lose now. I'll have no peace until I see those confidential weeklies. Delaying only to buy a bottle of water from a stall, which I drain in two long gulps, I hail a taxi.

'Maharashtra State Police Headquarters.'

Close to the Gateway of India, it's another monumental Raj building, several floors of the same yellow brick and stone-faced windows as Elphinstone. The main gate's guarded by men in khaki. Beside them, the barrel of a machine gun pokes out of a makeshift pillbox constructed from sandbags. Beyond I glimpse an immaculate lawn, edged with orange lilies, dwarf fan palms and oleander bushes daubed with creamy-pink blossom. A statue of what looks like a medieval horseman with drawn sword gallops motionlessly towards the city. It's the ubiquitous Mahratta hero, Chhatrapati Shivaji, who liberated Maharashtra from the Mughals.

'What is your affair?' the duty constable asks affably.

'I need to see the commissioner of SIB, please.'

'Your affair?'

'It's hard to explain. Could you send this note up?'

I give him my university visiting card. On the back I scrawl: 'My father was in the Indian Police, 1938–47.' The constable takes it into the guardroom, where I see him conferring with a superior. The latter's sceptical expression makes me regret my cut-offs and sandals.

Half an hour later, the affable constable returns. 'Do you have other visiting card?' he asks. When I produce one, he smuggles it hastily into an inside pocket.

'One day I will visit London. Now enter.'

I can hardly believe my ears. In the guardroom I go through scanners and my bag's emptied, its contents checked. Then the constable leads me round the side of the building, through a pool of white 4×4s with red sirens, to the sandbagged main entrance. It's deliciously cool in the tiled porch. After a body search, I'm escorted up some stairs, lined with photographs of commissioners, stretching back to 1947. On the second floor, I'm shown to a tatty divan on the deep veranda, from where I can see the Taj tower, bone-white against the cloudless sky. A sickly looking crow sits brazenly on the balustrade, stropping its beak with one claw.

It's well after six when I'm eventually summoned. The attendant directs me into a box-like office, its walls entirely lined with hazel formica. There's a neon strip light and air conditioning. Three people are seated before a large glass-topped desk, behind which sits a powerful-looking individual in a beige safari jacket. He has a bullet-shaped cranium, straggly silvery hair and watery eyes. The desk's covered with dockets, intercoms, a fan and a couple of photographs. He's closely examining my card.

'Commissioner Sivanandan is away. I'm Assistant Commissioner Poel, SIB.' He waves me to a chair with a quick smile. 'So your father was Indian Police?'

I get out my copies of Aunt Pat's pictures. Poel seems fascinated, as are his visitors, to whom he passes the pictures across the table.

'He was at Nasik Police Training School, too?' he asks, examining Bill in his black-tie rig. 'The building behind is the mess. I was there in the 1960s.'

Their curiosity apparently satisfied, the three men get up, bow a *namaste* and withdraw.

'How can I help?'

I tell my story, omitting what I've discovered in Shinde's book. Poel nods and murmurs as I speak. When I've finished, he presses a buzzer.

'I'm very grateful to you for seeing me when you must be so busy dealing with these terrible attacks.'

A world-weary look settles on my host's face. 'Very busy. Doing nothing.' Catching my look of surprise, he shrugs. 'What to do? We have the surviving perpetrator. Now is up to the prosecutors and politicians.'

'Do you think the terrorists had inside help?' It's the current obsession of the newspapers.

He shakes his head. 'That's just *badmashes* trying to stir up communalist feeling.'

I wonder how he can be so sure, given the intelligence failings for which the SIB must be partly responsible. The attendant pokes his head round the door.

'Take the sahib to Records.' Poel turns back to me. 'Just to show you where they are. Come again at ten tomorrow and we'll see what we can dig up.'

The Assistant Commissioner hasn't mentioned the word

'permission'. I want to jump across the desk and kiss him. He throws me a soulful look as I get up to leave.

'It must have been very hard to lose your father so young.'

At the Records office, the desks are empty. I look round eagerly. Somewhere here, I'm sure, I'm going to find what I need. I make my way out of the building in a daze. Have I really just seen the second-in-command of the current anti-terrorist operations in Mumbai? I'm so tired, maybe I've hallucinated it all. It's hard to account for such helpfulness. Perhaps it's another sign of the continuing prestige of the IP. Or the clout of a London University professorship. Surely it can't be because I'm white? I call Rajeev to tell him the good news. He congratulates me on my persistence.

'You'd have made a good detective, just like your father,' he says hoarsely. 'Listen, I've caught this wretched thing from my wife. I don't think you'd better come this evening after all. Don't know if it's swine flu or what, but I feel like a pig.' He manages a weak chortle. 'Do you have enough to keep you busy for a couple of days? Haven't had time to work on that lead.'

I'm more relieved than anything. All I can think of is getting my aching bones to bed. I reassure him I'll have no problem passing the time at the SIB.

~

When I report to the old Special Branch building the following morning, Poel's not there. He's apparently been called away to a meeting of police chiefs in Nagpur. Afterwards, he's going on Christmas leave. To my immense relief, however, he's left instructions for me to be admitted to Records. The chief archivist, Mr Walawalkar, is charming, middle-aged, very dark, breath smelling of fried chicken. However, he doesn't seem to recognise Shinde's file numbers or know where the confidential weekly reports might be located. I'm taken aback.

'Records system changed in late 1980s,' he explains apologetically. 'Reorganisation. Some older material moved to different parts of the building.'

Walawalkar takes my list and promises to begin searching. Meanwhile, he suggests that the 'Indian National Congress' holdings might provide an overview of the contexts out of which the Parallel Government mobilisation emerged. It may even contain some of the material I'm after. He parks me at a desk in an annexe to the large room he works in. It has its own side door onto the outside corridor, past which uniformed personnel scurry. As I finish the cup of tea Mr Walawalkar offers, an attendant arrives, struggling with armfuls of dark-blue folders from the 1940s.

They have a strange odour, both acid and musty. Even more curious is the miscellany of documents they contain: crude cyclostyled anti-British cartoons, intercepted letters, Government Orders, abstracts of secret intelligence, telegrams between 'Crimbo' and 'Peeler'. CID and the ordinary police, presumably? I begin working my way through, page by disintegrating page, trying not to damage them further. Within an hour, I strike gold. Here's a document signed by Bill, reporting on two nationalists he's taken in for questioning in Nasik. It gives his rank as assistant district superintendent of police, and is dated 7 August 1943. There are no details about the outcome of the investigations. Similar documents follow at intervals, his signature unformed compared with the one I remember.

Slowly, out of the seemingly random mass of material, I start to build a profile of Bill's activities in the period before he went to Satara. He certainly had his hands full. On one occasion, he raids a photography shop suspected of supplying chemicals to nationalists to make crude explosives. Another time, he reports defusing a Mills bomb rigged up to a railway bridge. I remember the scars on Bill's legs, and begin to understand how easy it might have been to come by them in the course of dealing with an armed insurgency. It must have taken some nerve to approach this sort of device and neutralise it, doubtless without proper tools or today's protective clothing. Less dramatically, he visits schools to warn against the blandishments of 'extremists'. He investigates anonymous tip-offs about the political sympathies of government employees, most of which, to his evident satisfaction, turn out to be malicious. He seeks to discover who pasted up nationalist flyers and where they were printed. He searches bookshops for proscribed publications, and enforces cinema censorship regulations relating to the reporting of the war. He even visits US army units in nearby Deolali Camp, to ask them not to send home photos of the base in case they fall into the wrong hands.

The evidence suggests that Bill was very much a cog in the imperial machine during a particularly repressive phase of its history, as the British struggled to contain the twin threats represented by the Japanese land advance towards India and the surging tide of Indian disaffection. Several things in the folders strike me about the nature of the nationalist agitation. The first is how controversial violence was considered to be, as a mode of resistance to the Raj. I come across the very last message from the Indian National Congress executive before it was arrested and detained en masse in August 1942. The directions are unambiguous: 'Every man is at liberty to do by non-violent way, any act that will disturb the Government work completely. Make it impossible for the British to rule by observing general strikes and by any other non-violent means possible ... Do or die.' It's signed by Gandhi, the ink surprisingly fresh-looking. Congress sympathisers reiterate the thrust of these instructions, even as armed resistance begins to spread. One activist's letter, intercepted at the height of the disturbances in 1944, insists that 'it cannot be said that such acts of violence and sabotage ... have the sanction either of Gandhi or the Congress ... People should non-violently agitate against repression.' If what Rajeev hinted about the methods used by the Parallel Government is true, it's little surprise that the Mahatma denounced the movement as a betrayal of his principles. From what I had time to read, this is an issue which Shinde seems to have skated over.

The Parallel Government aside, not everyone toed the official Congress line. Letters intercepted by Special Branch often equate Britain with Hitler's Germany and call for armed rebellion, even total war, against foreign rule. There are frequent reports of sabotage; and evidence of occasional direct attacks on British personnel, notably a bomb planted in a Poona cinema which killed a number of soldiers. As one might perhaps expect, the authorities describe as 'terrorists' all those seeking to resist their rule by such means. Perhaps more surprisingly to a modern eye, the term 'terrorist' is sometimes used as a badge of honour by nationalists themselves. Here's a cyclostyle of May 1943 lamenting the death in a police raid of one Comrade Kotwal, described as 'this brilliant terrorist … the immortal martyr of Maharashtra'.

Above all I'm struck by how vulnerable the Raj seemed to its supporters, especially after the fall of supposedly impregnable 'Fortress Singapore' to the Japanese in late 1941. There's a recurrent note of panic in many of the letters opened by the censors after that event. A Hungarian Jew, recently escaped from Europe, complains that he's escaped the frying pan only to fall into the fire of civil disorder in Bombay. In September 1942, a Russian in Goa writes to his brother: 'One cannot help thinking that the world will be organized by Hitler … if he succeeds in breaking through in the Caucasus, in 2–3 months he will reach India and join the Japanese.' Foreign nationals, British citizens and Indians alike, evidently believed at various times that the Japanese had already entered India through Assam, even that Bombay had been bombarded from the sea. Air-raid precautions were hastily improvised, and lines of retreat to the hill stations planned in detail. The government was sufficiently concerned about the Province's porous coastline to set up watchtowers along the entire littoral, from Goa to Sindh, and introduced a system of licences for fishing-craft.

A bass note sounds through the authorities' response to such developments – fear of a repeat of the great Indian 'Mutiny' of 1857, which for a time threatened to bring British rule to an end. In one report, they are exercised to catch the author of a message to an Indian soldier overseas, which confidently predicts that 'on the 13 June, 1943, all of the Collectors [chief district administrators], wherever they are in India, will be killed.' In Satara, the situation was growing grave. A magistrate writes in September 1942 that 'the lives of the Government officials and property are in imminent danger ... and public safety is in general danger.' Things must have got much worse by the time Bill was posted there, more than a year later. I wonder if he was prey to such anxieties, and whether they influenced the way that Shinde alleges he behaved in villages like Chafal.

~

By the end of my first day's digging, I've amassed three pages of useful notes, but found nothing on Bill's actual dealings with the Parallel Government. Indeed there's been surprisingly little reference altogether to the movement. And although I've come across excerpts from some police officers' confidential weekly reports, there's no sign of my father's, even from the period when he officiated as DSP in Nasik, during his superior's absence on leave. Thinking about it overnight, I decide to change tack. The following morning I consult Walawalkar, who now belatedly explains how the British organised their records. I ask to see the list. The headings include 'Foreigners', 'Communal Troubles', 'Special Crimes', 'Native States' and – the word leaps out – 'Terrorism'. I suddenly intuit why the Parallel Government is barely mentioned in the Congress files. The Raj doubtless drew a distinction between 'legitimate' political opposition and organisations like the PG – or the Hoors of Sindh.

I ask for everything under 'Terrorism', starting in 1941, the year Bill graduated from the Police Training School, up to 1945, when he left Satara. Walawalkar looks uncertain. He says they may take time to locate, because they were moved to a different part of the building during the 'reorganisation' he mentioned yesterday. In the meantime, he wonders, would I like to look at anything else? Remembering Lindsay Padden-Row's correspondence about the internment camp at Satara, I decide to examine 'Foreigners', the files for which arrive quickly. They seem primarily concerned with spies and fifth columnists. To my surprise, however, they yield useful material, with reports both made to and by Bill. I also sometimes catch a heartening glimpse of his personality through the official-speak.

Here's one example; ironically, it concerns Bill being hauled before his own superior in Nasik. He's been at a dinner attended by a Frenchwoman, identified only as Madame Agnes; she describes the occasion in a letter, pounced on by the censors. According to her account, at one point during the evening she complains to Bill that the bread tastes dreadful. He takes a bite, makes a face and advises her against eating any more. When asked why, he says it's probably poisoned. While I can immediately visualise the puckish mock-solemn expression which so often accompanied his jokes, Madame Agnes takes him seriously: 'He is the Asst Supt of Police, so he should know ... funny thing, though, I've had tummy trouble for four days.' The censors demand that both Bill and Mme Agnes be formally reprimanded by the DSP for spreading demoralising rumours, prejudicial to the war effort. According to his superior's minutes, Bill insists it was, indeed, simply a joke – after all, he'd swallowed his mouthful in front of her. The DSP decides to give the Frenchwoman a mild warning and a brief introduction to the vagaries of English humour.

A second nugget which brings Bill vividly to life comes in another intercepted letter: 'The turkeys travelled down very well with the exception of one hen bird which had a swollen and lame right leg ... the ducks seemed in perfect condition

Bill on horseback

except one which had a very husky throat and is also being treated.' Again, I can easily visualise Bill's struggle to keep a straight face as he comments: 'Although I am no ornithologist, mention of a duck suffering from a husky throat sounds somewhat peculiar and indicates the use of some sort of code in the letter.' He decides to investigate the writer, though the outcome isn't recorded anywhere that I can see.

When I've finished flicking through 'Foreigners', I return to Walawalkar's desk. 'Very useful, thank you. Any news about the "Terrorism" holdings?'

He looks embarrassed. 'Missing, only.'

It takes a moment to register. 'Surely not the whole run?'

'Already not here when I arrived in 2004.'

'But Shinde must have seen them,' I splutter, 'you've got his list. Where have they been moved?'

'I don't know, sir. Sorry.' He returns my list.

I'm thrown. Instinct tells me those files would be much the best place to look for Bill's reports and for the British view of the Parallel Government and its methods. They must be here, in some dark corner of this cavernous building, tied up in musty mailbags to 'protect' them.

'I will make more inquiries. But meanwhile, you can maybe find more of the material you want under other headings? What about "Special Crimes"? I can have them ready for you after lunch.'

When I return in the early afternoon, Walawalkar's station is empty. However, a pile of files is waiting at my desk. While waiting for my friendly archivist to reappear, a man I haven't seen before passes by. I'm instinctively wary. He's about thirty, with a feeble moustache and shifty eyes. His formal white shirt, with black lacework patterning, gives him the air of a Mexican country-and-western singer. From time to time he passes through the annexe, gazing suspiciously about. Finally, he stops and asks what I'm doing. When I tell him I'm researching the Parallel Government, his face lights up.

'A glorious chapter of our history,' he enthuses.

I feel we've broken the ice, and regret judging him so hastily. Towards the end of the afternoon, however, he approaches once again.

'Who has given you permission to work here?'

I'm startled. 'Assistant Commissioner Poel.'

It's his turn to look surprised. 'When?'

'A couple of days ago.'

'He is not here today.'

'I know. He's in Nagpur. He didn't say I can only work here while he's in the building.'

The man's nonplussed for a moment. 'I cannot check your story.'

'What about asking Mr Walawalkar?'

'He leaves early on Friday. Then he is on holidays.'

Why on earth didn't Walawalkar mention his plans?

'I'm in charge in the interim.'

Oh no. I suspect no one's looking for the 'Terrorism' files now. My interrogator disappears, returning a short while later with a thick orange file. Opening it, he shows me various letters addressed to the Assistant Chief Secretary, Home Department, copied to the SIB, from researchers requesting access to the old Special Branch archives. 'Where is yours?'

'I went to Mantrale. They told me to come here and ask,' I lie.

'Who told you?'

'I didn't get his name. On the seventh floor, I think.'

'Where is the rule? Show me the rule.'

I stare at him, perplexed. 'Which rule?'

'That says you can enter without permission.'

I wonder if he's related to the obstructive man at the Home Department. 'Why not phone Mr Poel?'

The man looks outraged at the suggestion.

'Give me his number, I'll call him,' I backtrack placatingly.

'Mobile is confidential,' my tormentor says sternly. 'Without written permission, no notes are to be taken away.'

I'm flabbergasted. Who knows when Poel will be back? I'm in danger of wasting two full days of research. Exasperation generates my scheme.

'OK, whatever you say. The attendant's supposed to be bringing up "Strikes and Labour Unrest" before closing time. Can you call the stacks and tell him not to bother? I'll get my notes in order for you.'

He can't resist the invitation to order someone else around. As soon as I hear him on the internal phone next door, I arrange some of my jottings from Shinde in a neat pile on my desk. I can always go back to the University library and retrieve the information I need. I hastily gather the notes I've taken here in the SIB and stick them in my bag. Then I scarper out the side door. Haring down the staircase, I half expect to hear police whistles. But I reach the gate, where I'm waved through by the affable constable, who seems disappointed I won't be lingering for our usual chat about London. Out on the street, I congratulate myself on my quick thinking.

Then I wonder if I've been so clever after all. Perhaps I've made trouble for Poel, and he won't let me back in as a consequence.

Returning to the hotel, I feel increasingly deflated. Fascinating though my researches have been, I haven't made any progress in addressing the accusations against Bill. Nor have I found any evidence about his time in Sindh. Indeed, I've seen nothing which might account for the blank period in his *History of Services* record. The disappearance of the 'Terrorism' files is very disheartening, although it may explain why Professor Bhosle has not been able to find Bill's secret Memorandum. Until Poel gets back, there's no possibility of returning to the SIB. Given that I've largely drawn blanks at Elphinstone, Mantrale and Police HQ in turn, I seem to be completely stuck. I need to consult Rajeev.

~

The following morning I catch a cab to the address he's given me, and find myself outside a once-lovely Art Deco building off a tree-lined avenue close to railway tracks. Trains jangle in and out of Churchgate, their passengers crammed precariously on the carriage steps. My host comes out when I pull his bell, looking a little pale. Floor tiles lead in intricate abstract patterns along the communal corridor, which smells of stale cooking oil, towards a beautiful brass and hardwood lift. Rajeev opens the door of his apartment and shows me in to what he calls his day room, a study with a single, bolster-strewn bed, waist-high stacks of yellowed newspapers, haphazard bookcases, a couple of upright chairs at a desk. Incongruously, Elvis blares from something I haven't seen for years: an enormous chrome-effect ghetto blaster. Rajeev catches my startled look.

'Nothing like the King when you're feeling blue,' he affirms. 'Sit, sit,' he urges, turning it down and motioning me to a chair.

'Wife still unwell?'

Rajeev shakes his head. 'Better, thanks. No, a friend wounded in the recent attacks has just died.'

'I'm really sorry.'

'He's not the first. They killed the president of the Gymkhana Club, to which I belong. At the Taj. And my dear friend Kamte. He was one of the policemen ambushed outside Cama hospital. His grandfather was in the IP at the same time as Moore-Gilbert. They'd certainly have known each other.'

'How awful for you, Rajeev.'

His habitual gentleness evaporates in a scowl. 'Those bearded bandit bastards, what do they hope to achieve?'

'Well, one's been caught, perhaps we'll soon find out?'

He shrugs unhappily 'Here, I dug out the grandfather's book. You can borrow it.'

What? I can barely contain my curiosity. If the elder Kamte knew Bill, perhaps there'll be something about him in the work Rajeev places before me. *From Them to Us*, its battered cover proclaims. But my host's still looking upset, so I put it away in my bag for later. Rajeev sighs.

'You know, I'm glad I'm coming to the end of my career. Such bungling, you wouldn't believe. Three intercepted signals, sent at monthly intervals, warning of the attacks.'

My ears prick up. 'You saw them?'

Rajeev looks momentarily nonplussed. 'Friends, contacts,' he then says.

'But if there was intelligence, why didn't they prevent it?'

'The signals only said luxury hotels would be attacked. Not which ones or when. You can't lock down a city like Mumbai. Anyway, sometimes these messages are sent to deliberately mislead.'

'Where did they come from?'

'Pakistan, though they deny everything.'

'Is it all really about Kashmir?' Some of the media have hinted at this. As I understand it, the wound's been festering since the 1940s, when the British gave its Hindu ruler the choice of joining India or Pakistan at Independence. Defying his Muslim subjects, the overwhelming majority, the Rajah chose India. Imperial law gave him the constitutional right to do so, and this remains the basis of India's claim to the region. Its military, many assert, enforce that claim by behaving like an army of occupation, and is responsible for innumerable abuses.

Rajeev guffaws dismissively. 'Of course certain people will say so. Obfuscation. But it's partly our fault as well.'

'Why?'

My host launches a diatribe against the incompetence of the authorities. Federal and state agencies are in competition, depriving each other of crucial intelligence. The Navy blames the coastguard and the coastguard blames the inshore marine police. No one will take any responsibility.

'Mumbai will never be the same,' he concludes mournfully. 'Everyone stays at home in the evening now. How can you trust anything? I was at a wedding at the Taj myself, just days before the attacks.'

While we talk, a woman comes in with bowls of spicy-smelling tomato soup and toast. She says nothing; whether this is Rajeev's wife or a servant, I can't tell. We eat and have tea, during which my host tells me more about the IP officers who lived upstairs. We're interrupted by his mobile going off. He glances at it before letting it ring and ring.

'Don't mind me,' I murmur.

He shakes his head. 'I don't pick up unless I recognise the caller. I wait a while, then sms them to text their message.'

I'm puzzled, but Rajeev diverts my attention by asking how the research is going. He grimaces sympathetically when I describe what happened yesterday. But his face lights up when I mention Poel.

'I know him. And Commissioner Sivanandan. I'll try to find out when Poel gets back. I'm sure he can sort it all out.'

He's impressively well connected. My host leans forward with a teasing look. 'Look at this now.'

He pushes across a slab of a book. It's a coffee-table-format tome on the Maharashtra Police, produced – Rajeev says – to mark the centenary of the modern force in 2006, though its roots go back almost a century earlier. Abundantly illustrated, there are several photos from the 1930s and 40s. Some are riot scenes, one showing a young white police officer and a dozen Indian constables, wooden lathis drawn, facing an ocean of angry faces across a street strewn with bottles and stones. The European's features are indistinct, but I think immediately of Bill and his injuries. There are some recent shots of the training school in Nasik on which I also linger. Why, here's the old IP mess Bill and Poel would have frequented. Towards the back, a scrap of paper sticks out.

'Look carefully,' Rajeev urges with a smile.

The page opens at a formal portrait of a man in his fifties, with long beaky nose and hooded eyes. The caption reads: 'Emmanuel Sumitra Modak, Commissioner of Police, Maharashtra State, 1972–5.'

'I don't understand, Rajeev.' But the name's somehow familiar.

'E.S. Modak was assistant superintendent of police in Satara the whole time your father worked there.'

Of course. His name came up occasionally in the SIB archives. If only I'd known, I'd have paid more attention. I greedily examine the photograph. The face is highly intelligent but the expression's guarded, the lips pale and thin.

'And,' Rajeev grins, 'it appears he might still be alive.'

Jaw-dropping. 'But you said all my father's contemporaries had died.'

He grimaces apologetically.

'Where is he?'

'Somewhere in Pune. Now I don't want to get your hopes up. I haven't heard anything about him myself since 2001.' He glances heavenwards. 'Which is why I thought he'd gone up, like all the others. My contact says he was ill a few years ago, so bad he had to go to Rhode Island, where his son lives, for treatment. He doesn't know one way or the other what the result was. But someone thinks they sighted him a couple of months ago.'

'How old would he be?'

'Eighty-seven, eighty-eight. He joined the IP two years after your father.'

Bill would have been ninety next year if he'd survived. That's forty-five years he was cheated out of, half a life.

'We're trying to get hold of his address. Assuming he's alive and has all his faculties, he'll know a lot more about your father and the Parallel Government than you'll find in the archives.' He scowls. 'Still no answer from this Bhosle to your emails?'

I shake my head.

'If the worst comes to the worst, Modak's widow may still be around. She should remember something of those times. She was a fair bit younger, I recall.'

'I don't know how to thank you, Rajeev.'

'Most happy to help. But first we've got to run down where he lives – or used to live.'

I nod.

'So what are your plans now?'

I shrug.

'I'll try and find out when Poel gets back. What about getting away yourself for a few days? You could do worse than start with Nasik. That's where your father seems to have spent most time, if he didn't go to Sindh. The training school's well worth a visit. Ask for Mrs Goel, the director.' He laughs enigmatically. 'But don't say I sent you.'

I wonder if there's anyone Rajeev doesn't know. But why the disclaimer? 'Perhaps I should head straight for Pune?'

My host considers a moment, before shaking his head. 'Better to wait until we're sure about Modak. From Nasik, you're only a few hours north of Pune by bus and while you're looking round there, we can carry on hunting for Modak.'

'It might save time to go straight to Kolhapur and try to find Shinde and Bhosle?'

Rajeev shakes his head. 'University vacation time by now. They could be away. Keep them for later; if we don't find Modak then you can try down there.'

'You think they'd be co-operative?'

My host shrugs. 'Jealous types, these provincial historians. You've read Nirad Chaudhuri. Just don't give the impression you want to write about the Patri Sarkar. They probably think they own the subject.'

Later, in my hotel room, I pore over Kamte's *From Them to Us*, published in 1982. Disappointingly, there's no mention of Bill. But the author describes how he himself was supposed to have been sent to Satara in May 1944, just as Bill left. This was in order to help suppress 'the "Patri Sarkar" agitation, which was notorious for its treatment of informers, real or imagined'. While diverted at the last moment to Dharwar, some distance from the disturbances, Kamte nonetheless dismisses the 'baseless reports' of police brutality in Satara. This seems telling, given his occasional criticism of white colleagues, from whom he apparently suffered some degree of prejudice. On the other hand, Kamte's a policeman himself, so he would probably protect his own, wouldn't he? Indeed, his disclaimer about police brutality is somewhat undermined when Kamte describes a crowd of demonstrators he was confronted by early on in his appointment to Dharwar: 'I asked them to disperse, failing which they would get a beating.' Was this typical police strategy at the time? If so, what light might it shed on Bill's alleged behaviour at Chafal?

All in all, this feels like a breakthrough. Here's the first documentary counter-evidence to Shinde's accusations. If only Rajeev can run down Modak. I wonder what he's like. I can't afford to think of him in the past tense. If he and Bill worked side by side against the Parallel Government, presumably he'll be pleased to see me and talk? His evidence may prove crucial. Suddenly, remembering Rajeev's earlier comment, I'm arrested by a strange feeling. Perhaps I *am* becoming a detective, like Bill. Yet he's the chief suspect in this case. However, I'm also acting for the defence. Are the roles compatible? Bill's words echo across the decades from the Ugalla River.

'*You have to collect the evidence. Then it's for other people to decide.*'

CHAPTER 5

My Father's Friend?

As I'm packing up my hotel room to leave for Nasik, Rajeev rings. He can't keep the excitement out of his voice. 'We've found Modak.'

'What?' My heart pounds.

He dictates an address in Pune. 'You should go straight away. It seems his son has come over from the US for Christmas. They may go away somewhere or whatnot.'

'Do you have a number?'

'I'm sorry, no.'

I consider rapidly. Nasik will have to wait. In view of Shinde's accusations, meeting Modak's the priority.

'I was just on my way to the train station.'

'Good. My dear friend, please to keep me advised of your movements. I will always aid you with every helpfulness. Now, a little word.'

'Yes?'

'Modak has the reputation of being cranky. His fellow-officers rather avoided him.'

'Why?'

'He's a bit ... he always felt hard done by.'

'Was he?'

'Well, he was always something of an outsider. For one thing, he's Christian. His father converted. He was a district magistrate under the British. A big fish. But they sacked him during the war.'

'Why?'

'I don't know. Anyway, try to humour him. He could be a gold mine.'

'I can't thank you enough, Rajeev.'

'Modak had a difficult career,' he adds, almost absent-mindedly.

'How so?'

'It must have been very hard for him after Independence. Do you know, he actually shot his own future boss during the Patri Sarkar agitation? When Nana Patil tried to escape from Sangli jail – in 1943, I think. Shot him in the back as he was running away.' His voice tails off meditatively. 'Yes, then your intended victim becomes chief minister of Maharashtra and you're still in the force. To Nana's credit, he never held it against Modak. He could have finished his career at a stroke.'

Rajeev's warning tone doesn't detract from my elation. If Modak's cranky, it won't be on my account.

Victoria Terminus is heaving, except for an area cordoned off with plastic tape, which, apart from a guard or two, is ominously empty. It's hard to believe that so many people were gunned down here barely three weeks ago. I get a train easily enough and we're soon on our way. It's a relief to escape the intensity of Mumbai. Tiredness and heartache are slowly soothed by the laboured rhythm of the train chugging inland towards the Sahyadri mountains, known to the British as the Western Ghats. We climb ponderously through run-down Raj-era stations, each a shade cooler than the last, where I sense the ghosts of Kipling's lovers and clubmen hovering on the platforms. The landscape ripples into ever deeper gorges beneath forested crests, the occasional village in a clearing dwarfed by huge blue skies.

As we reach the Deccan plateau on which Pune is situated, my apprehension mounts. I'm investing hugely in finding Modak. If anyone can vindicate Bill, it'll surely be his comrade-in-arms of eighteen months during the Parallel Government agitation. But will Modak be willing to talk? What if he's drawn a line across those troubled times, given what was evidently an awkward transition between service in the imperial Indian Police and its post-Independence successor? Yet he obviously did well enough, reaching the rank of commissioner. Now I think about it, I don't remember any mention of him in Shinde's account. Why not, if he was in Satara at the same time as Bill, and especially if he shot one of the leaders of the insurgency?

Central Pune is an unpleasant contrast to the still-gracious Fort area of Mumbai where I based myself; unsurprisingly, perhaps, since the city's population has doubled to more than five million in just fifteen years, with no perceptible investment in infrastructure. At the station, long queues of Christmas travellers snake round the concourse, right into the road, each person clinging to the one in front like disaster victims.

'Is for ticket offices. They do like that to stop queue-busters,' my taxi-driver explains.

Getting around is one continuous dodgem-car snarl of close shaves, klaxons and frustrated drivers. For the first time, I see the kind of poverty I expected in Mumbai: disabled boys tapping at our windows, old men in rags, bewildered families squatting amongst their possessions on the teeming pavements, perhaps regretting their decision to migrate to the city. The driver weaves in and out of the bedlam, hand glued to his horn, overtaking any which way he can, mounting the pavement when all else fails.

Happily, the hotel I've booked turns out to be a delicious oasis of smoked glass and cool marble, with friendly and efficient staff. The receptionist shows me on the map where the Modaks live and recommends the German Bakery, on the same road, for a late lunch.

'Everything's prepared with sterilised water, only,' she affirms.

I shower, change and catch an auto-rickshaw back through the mayhem round the station towards Koregaon Park. I feel as vulnerable as an egg in my open-sided carriage, staring aghast at the throbbing buses which bully beside us, inches away.

The pollution's palpable as fog and I have to clamp a hankie over my nose against the fumes. Eventually we turn into the relative calm and green of 'The Cantonment', the old British garrison area and now HQ of the Indian Army's Southern Command. Nothing's visible behind the endless walls, with sentries at every corner, saluting the pennanted 4×4s which bustle past. Koregaon Park's leafier still, though the greenery's already gathering a rime of post-monsoon dust.

There are suddenly a fair number of Westerners, most clad in long maroon shifts. This area's home to the Osho commune, where Bhagwan Rajneesh returned after being expelled from Oregon – with or without his collection of Rolls-Royces, I can't remember. Along the pavements, shiny-faced acolytes greet each other with long hugs. Soon the tuk-tuk arrives at the German Bakery. But being this close to Modak, I'm suddenly too on edge for lunch. Instead I settle on cappuccino and a coconut macaroon.

As soon as I've finished, I head down Koregaon Park Road, searching for no. 22. Vendors' stalls clog the pavement, evidently catering to Oshoites, displaying regulation maroon robes, sunglasses, curios and cases of Red Bull. To my surprise my destination turns out to be a scaffolded house with workers slapping render on the front. It's a while before they can find someone who speaks English. His face and stick-like arms are caked with cement dust.

'House empty. Before Mr Sinha. New owners now.'

There's no answer when I phone Rajeev's mobile out on the street. When I call Inquiries for his landline, he's listed as ex-directory. Nor do they have any E.S. Modak. I feel crushed. My quest seems to have come to a dead end again. I wonder if I should return to Mumbai.

Since I've paid for my room, however, I decide to take a look around Pune while I work out a plan. The Osho commune is supposed to be interesting, so I head there first. It's down one of the streets leading at right angles off Koregaon Park Road.

Strolling down Lane Two, as it's called I realise I've stumbled on an architectural jewel. It's all Art Deco buildings, in much better condition than those in Mumbai. Perhaps the monsoon's not so damaging inland, or the owners more particular. I photograph a few houses, before finding myself outside a spectacular double-storeyed specimen with a curved frontage, painted fresh sage-green. The garden's gorgeous, huge trees edging a smoothly shaved lawn. More vibrant colours, but the borders are clearly modelled on the English cottage garden. Seeing a man on the drive, I think it polite to ask permission for a photo. He doesn't understand, but signals me to wait.

He soon returns, accompanied by a bent, white-haired woman with a deeply lined face, wearing a white sari with tinselly gold-embroidered hems. I explain my interest in architecture.

'Of course you may take picture,' she smiles.

'Was this the British area during the Raj?'

'No. We Parsis built here in the 1930s. What are you doing in Pune?' She pronounces it the old way, Poona.

'My father was in India in the 1940s, and I was told one of his colleagues lives in Koregaon Park.'

'What did your father do?'

'Indian Police.'

She nods with unmistakable approval. 'Who are you looking for?'

'E.S. Modak.'

She straightens up a little, beaming. 'Emmanuel? He lives in Lane Four. I don't remember the house number, but it's next to an office block with plate-glass windows.'

'22?'

'Yes, that's it, 22/4 Koregaon Park Road. Just after a sandy track on the left.'

It's another huge stroke of luck. I can barely restrain myself from hugging her. Either Rajeev or his contact omitted the lane number. It might have proved catastrophic.

I race back to the main road, as though Modak may only

have minutes to live. I'm soon at the sandy lane and see the name plate, engraved in italics, on a low gate: 'E.S. Modak, I.P. (ret'd.)'. I hesitate. What exactly am I going to ask? Will it be too much of a shock for him? I approach down a short drive lined with alternating pots of orange and mauve bougainvillea. Screening the house are lacy-leafed papayas and spiky shrubs with forsythia-yellow blooms. A dusty Christmas wreath hangs on the front door. It seems ominously quiet. A few moments after I ring the bell, however, the door's opened by a plump young woman with glossy hair and tired eyes.

'Hello,' she says grumpily, 'we were expecting you before lunch.'

I'm completely thrown. 'Expecting me?'

'Aren't you here about buying the washing machine?'

I set her straight with a nervous laugh. 'Is Mr Modak in?'

'They're having their nap. Can I help? I'm their daughter,' she adds snappishly, sensing my reluctance.

Is there some mistake? She can't be more than twenty-five. Perhaps Modak remarried. But I've had so many surprises in India that I simply nod and offer my visiting card.

'My father and he were colleagues.'

Her expression softens. 'Enter, enter, please.'

'I can come back later?'

Her head wobbles deprecatingly as she shows me into a rectangular living room with ceiling fans and comfortable, old-fashioned furniture, before disappearing down a corridor. The Christmas cards are outnumbered by silver-framed photos of children and grandchildren. Above the mantelpiece hangs a scabbarded dress sword, identical to the one my younger brother inherited. The ornately chased hand-guard gleams against the faded white walls. It's all very Western. Even the floral rugs could be from Peter Jones.

Eventually, nerves on fire, I hear shuffling. Out of the gloom of the corridor emerges a very old man in loose cream pyjamas. I recognise him at once, although age has whetted the beaky nose and tautened the skin across his cheekbones. His ears are more pronounced than in the photo in Rajeev's book, and his lips are string-thin now. In one trembling hand he holds my card.

'Moore-Gilbert,' he mutters after a moment, glancing from me to the card and back again, 'Moore-Gilbert. Well I never.' He signals me to sit, before lowering himself stiffly into an armchair.

The girl, who's been hovering attentively, like a nurse, seems satisfied and disappears. Modak examines the card again before nodding uncertainly.

'Do you realise, I last saw your father more than sixty-three years ago.'

The awful passage of time stuns both of us.

'I understand he died in Africa in the 1960s. How did it happen?'

As I explain, Modak examines me forensically, as if verifying my connections to Bill.

'Now tell me about yourself and why you're here.'

He's rather hard of hearing and I have to go slowly and repeat myself at times. His expression makes me wonder whether he's in pain or perhaps displeased to have been tracked down. Once he's grasped the outlines, my host starts to lever himself up. I'm about to offer help when his sharp look forestalls me.

'I must tell my wife. This will cheer her up. She's a bit low because our son left to catch his flight this morning.' He shuffles back the way he came. When he reaches the corridor, he calls out in a matter-of-fact tone: 'Kiron, dear, Moore-Gilbert's come.'

'Who? Who?' The voice is tired, faint.

'Moore-Gilbert,' Modak shouts feebly.

A frail figure soon appears, clad in a one-piece scarlet sleeping-suit, like an infant's. The fine features are still beautiful, grey-white hair thin but smartly cut and the same beaky nose as her husband. Huge luminous grey eyes blink out of almost translucent skin. When her husband shows my card, she slowly breaks into a smile. She seems as moved as I am.

'Bill's son? I can't believe it.' She shakes her head wonderingly. 'But let's have tea first. Perhaps you'd like cake, too?' She calls through to the daughter.

While we wait, Mrs Modak tells me about the church service they're going to later. She complains that fewer and fewer attend these days. I'm impatient to get onto Bill, but don't want to be too pushy, so I begin by asking if her family is Christian.

She nods. 'My father converted. He was one of the Bengal terrorists.'

What?

'He threw a home-made bomb which wounded a policeman. In 1917.' The pride in her voice is unmistakable.

'But he was underage and was made a ward of Cornelia Sorabji, that brilliant lady.' The first Indian woman barrister, if I remember right.

'They let him off on condition he left the country. Miss Sorabji sent him to Durham to study, where he lodged with a Reverend William Trotter. That's how it happened.'

I explain that I did my own undergraduate studies there. 'What did he read?'

Mrs Modak chuckles disarmingly. 'You see, with his, er, interest in chemistry, that was the logical thing. When he returned after the Great War, he gave up politics and became one of India's leading industrial chemists.'

I'm struck by the apparent incongruity of Modak, IP, marrying the daughter of a 'terrorist'.

'You know, you look like your father.'

I'm startled. All my life I've been told I resemble my mother more. Nonetheless, I'm glad she's brought the subject round.

'But he was bigger than you.'

Again, I'm surprised. I know for a fact I'm an inch taller. Is

Bill in sugar-cane fields

her memory playing tricks? Perhaps she means more heavily built, which would be right.

'A very handsome man. We often had him to dinner when we were in Satara. Being a bachelor, he appreciated home cooking. Charming company.'

I breathe easier. I try to imagine what Kiron looked like when Bill knew her.

'Yes,' Modak chips in, 'he'd drive round from the Inspection bungalow in his station wagon. Sometimes we went to the club for tennis or badminton after work, though neither of us drank. Quite unusual for policemen in those days.'

'When did you first meet him?'

Modak coughs croakily. 'Well, I first heard about your father at training school in Nasik. I arrived the year he left. I was told two things. First, he used to cut up nationalist newspapers to use in the toilet. No one was sure whether it was an economy measure to support the war effort, or a political statement.' Thin lips rubber-band into something like a smile. 'Also, he was a duffer with Marathi. He failed the exam thrice.

He really had to cram for the final attempt, or he'd have been out on his ear.'

I can't be sure whether Modak's scoring a point.

'Rather than relying on the pandits, he apparently found a local lady friend to help. If so, it worked. When the viva voce began, they asked him to state his name and so forth. He's said to have replied in perfect Marathi: "Good Lord, gentlemen, this is the fourth time I've appeared before you and you still don't know my name?"' Modak chuckles scratchily.

Once more, I can't quite decipher his tone. What does he mean by 'lady friend'? Yet I'm intensely grateful for these anecdotes which bring the Indian Bill alive.

'Then, one day during the Patri Sarkar disturbances, the district superintendent told me your father would be joining us. He was supposed to be on his way to Belgaum, if I remember right, to deal with some incident of sabotage and came to us at the last moment. Hobson was the DSP's name,' Modak adds with a flicker of distaste. 'He took me out on the veranda of Satara police station, pointed to Shivaji's old fort on the clifftop opposite and said: "This Moore-Gilbert's so fit, he'll be able to run up to the gate of Ajinkya Tara and back in fifteen minutes. He'll soon sort out the terrorists round here." I remember being startled. It took that long in a car.'

'And did he?'

Modak smiles ambiguously. 'He was certainly very athletic.'

'Can you tell me more about the Parallel Government?'

My host brings his fingertips together in an uneasy gesture of prayer.

'Well, we live in a different world today, of course. But from our point of view then, they were terrorists, pure and simple. We treated them as criminals rather than politicos.'

This sounds like Rajeev. 'Why?'

'We didn't want them to accrue prestige. In any case, they often behaved like common dacoits, running about the rural districts, robbing and beating people.'

'The Government of the Bastinado,' Kiron adds with a pained expression. 'You know, like Mussolini's thugs.'

I nod sagely. But I'm still trying to process what lies behind the unspoken distinction between her father and the Parallel Government. I infer from Modak's use of the derisive nickname, Patri Sarkar, that time hasn't modified his views of the movement. He grimaces, as if in confirmation of my hunch.

'When they caught someone who was – according to them – a collaborator, they'd say: "You've made yourself a donkey of the British, so we'll treat you like one." Then they'd nail horseshoes into the soles of the victim's feet.'

I'm shocked. Shinde never mentioned anything like this. But also encouraged. There *is* another story, after all.

'Once I was called to investigate a train hold-up. I arrived to find they'd killed the driver and guard, so there'd be no one to testify against them. Completely unnecessary. Threatening reprisals against people's families was their usual way. Very effective. They created such a climate of fear that our job was made almost impossible. There was anarchy in much of Satara. Apart from one district in Bihar, nowhere took up arms against the British to such an extent. Between them and the pressure from above to solve the problem, our lives weren't easy.'

'That's why my father was sent there?'

Modak nods, but a shadow passes over his face. Sensing I'm on delicate ground, for reasons I can't fathom, I deflect the conversation onto the weekly confidential reports which I hope will express Bill's point of view.

'Yes, I had to write them, too, once I became DSP.'

'Would a special additional DSP like my father have done so?'

Modak reflects a moment. 'I think so.'

'I was told they were destroyed after thirty years?'

'Not sensitive material. Not in my time, at least.'

'Do you know anything about a secret Memorandum

my father's supposed to have written about the Parallel Government?'

An aggrieved expression sours Modak's face before he shrugs. 'First I've heard of it. Have you tried Mumbai?'

As I explain my travails, I wonder whether Bhosle has got this wrong, too.

'Well, these things could be in Satara, you know. I don't imagine that storage is a problem in the rural divisions.'

'Is it worth trying here in Pune?'

Modak shakes his head, and confirms that in those days Satara reported to Belgaum.

'Are you planning to visit Satara?'

'I'm not sure yet.'

'It would give you a better idea of what we were about, your father and I.'

Before I can explore the possibility, Mrs Modak gets up.

'My dear, the driver's coming in twenty minutes, we should get ready.'

Her husband nods. 'Of course. I'm so sorry, Moore-Gilbert, but we'll have to stop for now. Can you come tomorrow for high tea? I'll try to find photographs. I'd ask you for elevenses, but I have to see the doctor and then we're out for luncheon.'

As I gather my hat and sunglasses, I hear Mrs Modak's low voice.

'Why don't you give him the books, Emmanuel? Perhaps he can help with Ashoka?' She turns to me. 'My husband's written a memoir and two novels.'

I'm stunned. This could be my gold mine. But I'm arrested by the uncertain look on Modak's face. His wife gazes at him insistently.

'Very well,' the ex-policeman concedes.

I wait uncertainly while he pads down the corridor after Kiron. I wonder who Ashoka is, and what help I can possibly give. The daughter returns to gather the tea things. I'm puzzled by her, too. Mrs Modak would have to have had her in her sixties. Besides, she behaves more like a servant.

My host soon returns with three books which he hands me, one by one. This is incredible. The memoir's entitled *Sentinel of the Sahyadris: Memories and Reflections*, and was published in 2001. The front cover is a painting of a deserted fort overlooking a verdant ravine. I wonder if this is the one in Satara which Modak mentioned.

'You'll find a lot in it about our problems with the Patri Sarkar. The other two are detective novels. I always liked Erle Stanley Gardner and Agatha Christie. I've tried to give them an Indian slant.'

One's called *The Guru and the Policeman*, and, according to a quick scan of the blurb, involves a fraudulent holy man whose Western devotees come to grief while searching for enlightenment. Is this Modak's commentary on the Osho commune? The other, *No Place for Crime*, boasts a black-and-white photograph of a man lying in a pool of blood, revolver, banknotes and jewels scattered beside him. 'Set in India of the 1940s and later,' the sleeve announces, 'this police novel focuses on the experiences of a young police officer whose career starts with the British and continues long after they have folded their tents and gone.' With trembling fingers, I turn to the contents page. There are four chapters: 'Nasik, Satara, Nasik Again, Bombay.' This surely draws on Modak's experiences in the 1940s?

My host signs each book laboriously, 'with warmest regards'. I'm shaking with excitement as I thank him. By tonight I expect to have a substantial counter-narrative to Shinde. I ask if Modak knows his book. He shakes his head.

'Every Tom and Dick has had his say about the Patri Sarkar. And Hari,' he adds with his rubber-band smirk. 'Only those who were there really know what happened. Shall we say five-thirty tomorrow afternoon?' Modak adds, handing me his card. 'We don't want you getting lost again,' he chuckles creakily.

~

Back at the hotel, the evening's turned surprisingly cold, a reminder that we're high on a plateau and its December, after all. I settle under my covers and thirstily examine Modak's books. I wonder whether to begin with *No Place for Crime*, since it was the first to be published, some twenty years before the memoir. But since it's facts I'm after, I decide to start with the latter. *Sentinel* is a 300-page hardback, only the first quarter of which looks relevant, the rest being devoted to Modak's career after 1947. In the index, I find several entries for Bill. Oh no, not again. The first page I cross-reference sets the tone: 'Have I given the impression that ... all British police officers were like Hobson and Moore-Gilbert? There were plenty of good capable officers ... I was unlucky to have to deal with two of the worst.'

A couple more such passages, and I'm winded. Coming from someone I'd assumed was friendly with Bill, as well as a comrade-in-arms, the impact's worse even than reading Shinde. However, this time I react quite differently, at least to begin with. I'm furious. Modak has children himself. How would he feel if someone gave them such things to read? Even if Kiron caught him off guard, he could surely have found some excuse not to offer the book. And why was Kiron so keen for me to see this stuff, after such warm words about her old acquaintance?

With an enormous effort, I remind myself that after reading Shinde, I made the decision to find out the truth, however painful or inconvenient it might be. Heart aching, I start again at the beginning. I learn that Modak was in fact born in Satara, where his father was deputy collector, the administrative number two in the Raj system. He entered the PTS shortly after Bill had graduated, leaving a lingering reputation as an overbearing presence in mess life. Their first meeting is represented with distinct ambivalence. Greeting Modak with 'a friendly handshake' on arriving in Satara, 'the handsome blonde giant' boasts that he'll mop up the saboteurs '"within a month"'. Modak comments acidly: 'SM Moore-Gilbert stayed on in Satara for a year and a half, and caught nobody, not even one single dacoit or saboteur.' Here's an unpleasant incident involving Modak's former head constable, Gaikwad, whom Bill had apparently sneakily appropriated: poor Gaikwad's obliged to carry his new boss across a swollen stream, because Bill couldn't be bothered to remove his boots. Hard not to see this as an allegory of the ordinary Indian policeman, or even Indian, burdened by the lazy, autocratic British.

This is small beer, however, compared with Modak's testimony about Bill's brutality against supporters of the Parallel Government, which he claims to have witnessed on two occasions. Annoyingly, he doesn't mention dates or places, commenting simply that:

> He [Bill] could hardly use the Bastinado, but he could do something faintly akin to it. He would go to an important village, collect their friends [supporters of the PG], take them to the *chavadi* [village office], where the police patil and his watchmen had gathered all the male villagers present in the village. Then he would begin to thrash the suspects, one by one, Gaikwad assisting him all the way.

Modak's not simply morally disgusted. He argues with Bill that such measures will be politically counterproductive, alienating the villagers and making elimination of the insurgency more difficult. *Sentinel* then asserts that Bill reported Modak's objections to DSP Hobson, who subsequently turned against his Indian subordinate, making it impossible for him to work effectively.

There are some crumbs of consolation, however. Like Kamte's memoir, Modak rejects talk of 'atrocities' in the nationalist press. He claims 'only' twenty-five people were killed by the police during the entire three-and-a-half years of disturbances in Satara, most of them in the course of firing on rioters who'd been warned to disperse. None of these deaths are ascribed to Bill, thank God. Nor does he repeat Shinde's allegations of ill-treatment of women and old people. I'm also relieved there's no hint of racism in Bill's troubled relations with his colleague. Indeed, given Modak's accusations, it's heartening, if bizarre, to read that: 'To me, at any rate, all during his entire stay in Satara, [Bill] was polite and pleasant.' But there's no getting away from it. Independent eyewitness testimony – from a colleague, moreover – clearly confirms Bill's brutality against civilians.

Yet if he seems unambiguously condemned by this new evidence for the prosecution, I'm more conscious than ever that he has no one to speak up for him now. While I can't possibly condone what he's accused of doing, I'm soon aware of problems with Modak's account. These begin with his reaction to news of Bill's secondment. Talking to Kiron that night, the aggrieved ASP complains: 'I have come to one definite conclusion: the British are not fit to rule India or any other place.' Why does he react so badly? Professional pique? The appointment of an outsider like Bill might have reflected badly on those, including Modak, already dealing with the Parallel Government.

More importantly, there appear to be serious contradictions over the issue that most concerns me. Indeed, Bill and Modak fall out over the question of police brutality in quite unexpected ways. One occasion involves a sub-inspector called Walawalkar, who'd been recommended by his deputy superintendent for the Indian Police Medal after arresting a notorious bandit. Bill somehow discovered that the dacoit's wounds were not inflicted while resisting arrest – as the citation claimed – but when the man was in custody. Modak was instructed to investigate further, leading to Walawalkar's dismissal and the deputy superintendent's transfer from Satara.

Modak comments darkly that his unwilling role in all this caused a steep decline in his popularity within the force. Given his condemnation of Bill's illicit violence, why was he so reluctant to help get rid of a bad apple?

The second incident's even more telling. Here comes Bill one day to Modak's camp in a place called Tasgaon. With him is a woman claiming to have been tortured following a police raid on a Parallel Government safe house in Patan, fifty miles away. Describing the case several decades on, Modak's still scandalised, ostensibly because – in the absence on leave of the authorised medical officer in Patan – Bill himself examined her (albeit in the presence of her uncle). Her private parts had indeed been badly burned with cigarettes. Bill now asks his colleague to take the woman to the medical officer in Tasgaon, for independent corroboration of her injuries. But Modak refuses, because the brutality occurred in Patan, outside his area of responsibility (although we've been told earlier, quite specifically, that technically he had jurisdiction over the whole of Satara District). It seems that he doesn't want to get involved only because Bill's broken the rules of the Police Manual by performing the physical examination himself. My father explains that the local women he approached refused to act as witnesses, for fear of reprisals. But Modak continues to demur. So Bill leaves in a huff, taking the woman with him and complaining of Modak's unco-operativeness.

Not simply because I'm his son – or is it? – I think Bill comes out of this part of the narrative, at least, rather better than his accuser. Modak's refusal to help sits uneasily with his repeated cricism of DSP Hobson's wooden adherence to the Police Manual. More to the point, isn't Modak far too ready to wash his hands of a female torture victim? Very odd, too, that he expresses no disquiet at the methods used to get information from the woman. Indeed, he comments matter-of-factly of his replacement head constable that Pisal 'had a way with witnesses'. And if Modak already knew Walawalkar's 'methods were questionable', why hadn't he intervened before?

I also can't help feeling Modak protests too much that he took no part in the kind of behaviour he accuses Bill of. For example, there's an almost hysterical rebuttal of an accusation in one journal, edited by Gandhi's grandson no less, that Modak tortured a nationalist leader after arresting him. Above all, if he so strongly objected to the methods Bill allegedly employed, it's difficult to comprehend why he didn't report it sooner. Especially since he implies that his belated complaints to the inspector-general hastened the transfer of both Bill and Hobson from the district. Why wait so long? After all, Walawalkar was summarily dismissed and his immediate superior seconded, although their misdemeanours were mild by comparison.

Perhaps most important, from my point of view, even, according to what's obviously hostile testimony, Bill was evidently prepared on at least some occasions to come down heavily on police violence, even when it involved a fellow IP officer like Walawalkar's Deputy Superintendent. Moreover, the woman torture victim whom he went so far out of his way to help was a suspected supporter of the dissidents. Surely that counts for something?

Equally, Modak's assertion about Bill's ineffectiveness in Satara is contradicted by the author's admission that he learned a great deal about strategic thinking, and the importance of determination and attention to detail from his incubus. *Sentinel* acknowledges that Bill was decorated for his good work: 'Very soon after their transfer, the announcement came that both Hobson and Moore Gilbert [sic] were awarded the Indian Police Medal for their meritorious services. I got nothing.' While I'm grateful to Modak for filling in this lacuna in Bill's official service record, the whiff of sour grapes is unmistakable.

And what was that Rajeev told me? Why is there no mention

of the shooting of Nana Patil in Modak's memoir? What else has been omitted? The inaccuracies, too, are troubling. Modak claims Bill was simply an assistant superintendent of police like himself, implying that he tried to pull rank during incidents like that involving the female torture victim. Yet the *History of Services* is clear Bill was a special Additional District Superintendent, as Modak himself acknowledged this afternoon, and thus unquestionably his senior. Even so, Bill didn't order his subordinate to take the woman to the medical officer; he simply tried to persuade him to do so. Hardly evidence of overbearing behaviour.

Enough of the problems with *Sentinel*. I'm going to have to investigate further. Although I've satisfied myself Modak isn't a wholly reliable witness, it's not enough to allay my sorrow and anger with Bill. For the first time, I wonder whether he didn't have a stupid side. Even if he believed passionately in the Raj – and I can remember nothing from my childhood suggesting any great ideological investment in 'the white man's burden' – he must have realised that the behaviour Modak describes would fatally undermine its last vestiges of moral authority, especially since the war was framed as a struggle against fascism. I feel ashamed and somehow incriminated once again, as if my own political ethics have been tainted by association with Bill's role in such events. I can't imagine what his victims felt, dragged from their charpoys in the middle of the night, stripped and thrashed in public to extract information they might not have had. What did Modak go through, watching a foreigner abuse fellow-Indians, even if he was unambiguously part of the Raj himself? Is there anything in my childhood which suggests Bill might have acted so unjustly?

The Australian missionaries who run the bush hospital an hour from Manyoni are coming to tea. The boy dreads these visits. Mrs Rowlandson's forever talking about God in her brassy, cheerful voice. Her husband's jolliness is more laboured, as if he's perpetually missing sensible, civilised New South Wales and can't wait to get back. The boy's father grimaces when the visit's announced. Normally he looks forward to company. But he's been in a bad mood these last few days, and his children have been treading carefully. So the boy's relieved to learn at the last minute that Mr Norton, the district officer from Singida, will also be there, bringing his smart car. Ever since helping the boy's father hunt down the man-eater in his district, the two men have been firm friends.

In the early afternoon they all have to brush their hair properly, scraped into partings on the left, and put on clean clothes. 'No bare feet and scrub your nails,' their mother reminds them briskly. The boy's aggrieved. They've had to come back early from exploring the tumbling basalt rocks on the hill overlooking the village. A bit longer and they might have made contact with the troupe of baboons which has recently arrived.

Now they sit, trying not to fidget, at the table on the veranda where the good china's being given an outing and napkins lie furled in Sunday rings. The cook's made scones, but the mouth-watering floury smell can't entirely compensate for Mrs Rowlandson's loud, jokey complaints about the the wet-season roads. The boy glances at his father. His jaw's set and he lets his wife do the talking, perking up only when the priest mentions the forthcoming Ashes series, alerting his host to reports from home about a young leg-spinner called Richie Benaud. Mr Norton responds by chaffing him about Frank Tyson and Alec Bedser. Just as his father's spirits seem to be lifting, Mrs Rowlandson asks the boy whether he's looking forward to going away to school. He wilts under her beaming goodwill, trying to keep one ear tuned to the cricket conversation. If only she'd pipe down a notch or two.

Kimwaga, dressed in a starched khaki jacket for the occasion, brings in the tray. He's not yet accustomed to wait at table and frowns with concentration as he sets down teapot, butter, milk and sugar, before laying out fish-knives for the scones.

'Mpumbafu,' the boy mutters, swatting a fly from the butter dish, 'you fool, you've forgotten the doilies.'

He thinks he's only murmured as Kimwaga goes past, but the disapproving hush quickly disabuses him. Mr Norton coughs and his father glares. Kimwaga's expression remains impassive as he turns quickly back towards the kitchen. He hasn't seen Dempsey come in behind and trips over the dog. The remaining cutlery clatters from his tray onto the Rev. Rowlandson.

'Now see what you've done,' his mother scolds the boy.

He gazes fiercely at the needle-work in the tablecloth, hot-faced, afraid to look at his father, thoroughly grateful now when Mrs Rowlandson brightly resumes her praise of boarding school.

Later, they wave off the visitors. First to go are the Rowlandsons, in their clumsy van. Mr Norton, pipe wedged beneath his RAF moustache, revs his mud-spattered DKW, with its Olympic rings on boot and grille. The rear wheels spin as he taxis down the drive before shooting off on his next mission.

'Can we get a car like that?' the boy asks his father with his most ingratiating smile. Recently DKWs have begun winning the East African Safari, a source of local pride as the toughest and longest road rally in the world.

His father takes him roughly by the arm. 'I want a word with you. In my bedroom.'

Terror seizes the boy. This has happened three times before. Once when he stole some money from the trouser-pocket of a family friend. Once when he twisted Darwin's tail and the monkey's screeches brought his parents running. The last time when he snaffled and ate an entire packet of ginger biscuits, later denying all knowledge of its whereabouts. He's dragged along beside his father now, feet barely touching the ground.

As soon as they're indoors, the boy begins to cry. But there's no deflecting the fury.

'How dare you talk to Kimwaga like that in front of guests? At any time? Didn't you see how embarrassed he was? After everything he does for you. Why do you behave like a guttersnipe?'

'I was only joking, daddy. I'll say sorry.'

But he knows that when his father's made up his mind about something, he won't be deflected. Now he resembles the ogre in Jack and the Beanstalk, his expression murderous. This time he reaches not for the purple slipper but for his long-handled hairbrush. Knowing this giant's wife won't rescue him, the boy prostrates himself on the bed, as if appeasing an angry god. But he threshes wildly when his father takes hold of him. It's no use. In seconds, he's exhausted. His father flips him over easily, holds him down and starts to beat him. The pain's excruciating, as if boiling water is being splashed on his backside. The six strokes over, the boy can't move. He feels as if he's melted into the bed.

Later, when he's calmed himself and visited Kimwaga in his quarters, and his mother's patted him on the head, the boy gingerly enters the living room, where his father's listening to the radio. Will the grey eyes be soft like dawn, or the battleship colour of thunderclouds?

'I went and said sorry, daddy,' he mutters.

'Good boy. Come here,' his father smiles, almost shyly. 'Want some mango?'

Despite the smarting pain, the boy settles gratefully on his father's knee.

In turmoil, I get up to close the window. The temperature's dropped dramatically. In these early hours, the street is jaundiced-looking under yellow sodium lights haloed with frantic insects. The front wheels of empty auto-rickshaws are turned inwards, like the heads of birds at rest. A ragged old man's sleeping on the pavement opposite. He seems so peaceful, stretched out like that, despite the chill, eyes closed, head on one crooked arm, the other hand tucked inside his tattered shirt. I envy him momentarily. There's still Modak's novel to read. I turn back to my rumpled bedclothes in dread.

CHAPTER 6

Bill or 'Bill'

Opening *No Place for Crime*, I'm mindful of the blurb on the dust jacket of *Sentinel*:

> He [Modak] believes that if the writing of prose (in any genre) is to be meaningful, it must be true to life and reflect life. He believes that a writer who has had to face drama in his daily life, does not need to scour the recesses of his imagination to get lively and living detail; it is there waiting for his pen.

It's soon clear the novel reflects this conviction. Many of the characters have identical names and functions to people in the memoir, including Bashir, Modak's driver, and his trusted head constable, Pisal. Others are thinly disguised. The underground leader Vasantdada (Nana) Patil morphs into Anna Bala Jadhav, District Magistrate Chambers returns as DM Burke, and Inspector-General O'Gorman as IG O'Flynn. Some characters in *No Place* are composites, however, notably the wooden and hen-pecked DSP Tomkins, an amalgam of Hobson and his ineffectual predecessor, CMS Yates.

By contrast, the protagonist Arvind Kumar seems at first to bear little relation to the Modak of the memoir. He's much more likeable, partly because he has a sense of humour – even, occasionally, at his own expense. You have to admire his stubborn pursuit of the murderers of the 'untouchable' woman Vasanti, who has no one to stand up for her. Like her, Kumar has fallen foul of outmoded social attitudes: his girlfriend's family consider him beneath her. The protagonist shows both determination and ardour to overcome the obstacles they erect. But he's altogether more vulnerable than the strident

Modak of *Sentinel*, on one occasion confessing to his fiancée that he sometimes suffers from an 'inferiority complex'.

Yet Kumar is obviously autobiographical. Like Modak, he spends part of his childhood in Satara, where his father was an important official. He, too, is a Christian who marries a Bengali woman. Kumar is likewise highly anglicised and employs a similar stilted diction to his creator, peppering his speech with words like 'thrice' and 'elevenses'. After probation at the PTS in Nasik, furthermore, Kumar's posted to Satara, where the Parallel Government is beginning to cause problems. Not only does Modak's memoir rehearse many of the major incidents from *No Place*, but whole conversations are repeated verbatim. These include not only fractious debates over strategy with his superiors, but even intimate conversations between Kumar and his wife.

The representation of his principal colleague therefore interests me compulsively. It's soon obvious that Bill Pryce-Jones is a close approximation to the Bill Moore-Gilbert of Modak's memoir. The novelistic 'Bill' differs in minor ways; he drinks and smokes and has an irritating verbal tic, exclaiming 'Kiss me gently!' whenever something surprises him. Can't imagine my father being so precious. He's also still at the PTS when Kumar arrives. Yet the similarities far outweigh these trivial divergences. The physical description of 'Bill' in *No Place* anticipates almost word for word the one given twenty years later in *Sentinel*. Many of the incidents involving him are already familiar, and some of his exchanges with Kumar have been cut-and-pasted. Here once more are the stories Modak told me, about the newspapers cut up for lavatory paper and his colleague's problems with Marathi.

What's strikingly different, however, is the tone in which *No Place* portrays 'Bill': far more positive, affectionate at times. We're introduced to him as the author of an elaborate practical joke which he co-ordinates in his capacity as mess president. En route at night from Nasik station to the PTS, the new recruit's car gets flagged down by 'bandits'. Kumar's Indian escort leaps out of the car and opens fire, forcing the 'assailants' to scatter. At dinner, a still-shaken Kumar is solemnly informed that he must swear on the Police Manual to sleep with his sword. Only as he's about to head off to bed, weapon to hand, is Kumar told the whole evening's been an initiation rite. Thereafter 'Bill' is thoroughly obliging and helpful to his new colleague, explaining everything from the peculiarities of particular instructors to where to shop in Nasik. Contrary to what one might expect of such an institution ('Bill' even warns Kumar against 'sucking up' to the teachers), the mess president insists from the outset on the use of first names.

'Bill' is represented well in other ways. For example, he's strikingly polite to the mess staff, bookending the most trivial request with 'please' and 'thank you'. He's also an outstanding probationer. On one practice operation, he's given the role of dacoit leader and hunted by colleagues through the hills round Nasik. Despite the logistical advantages the 'police' enjoy, 'Bill' eludes capture, turning himself in only long after the rest of his gang has been captured and his pursuers have returned to base. True, 'Bill' spoils his success by 'smirking', but Kumar's nonetheless impressed, as he is once again when his fellow-cadet completes an assault course – under live fire, for God's sake – in record time. After graduation, 'Bill' carries many of these qualities into his police work. He even runs up to the fort overlooking Satara in five minutes, not the fifteen of Modak's memoir. And contradicting *Sentinel*'s account of Bill's lazy exploitation of Gaikwad to carry him over the stream, *No Place* records how 'Bill' once walked cross-country for two miles in his stockings, in order to surprise some saboteurs. Time and again, furthermore, the novel emphasises his personal courage during the pursuit of the Parallel Government.

Indeed, Kumar's relationship with 'Bill' in Satara is initially far less conflictual than the corresponding one in *Sentinel*. It's 'Bill' who supplies the tip which enables his subordinate to arrest a notorious dacoit, providing the newly qualified ASP with his first major professional success. While several raids which they mount together end disappointingly, in this narrative the failures are clearly joint ones. Also starkly contrasting with Modak's memoir, there's acknowledgement that his colleague achieved considerable success against the Parallel Government (thereby justifying the award of real-life Bill's Indian Police Medal). Look here: immediately before 'Bill's' transfer from Satara, Kumar ruefully acknowledges that 'the other Sub-Divisions are free of sabotage activity while all the gangsters have come over to mine.'

Very dishearteningly, however, this success is accounted for by his comrade's brutal methods. *No Place* refers to one incident, not recorded in *Sentinel*, in a place called Kumtha. Capturing someone suspected of sheltering dissidents, 'Bill' begins to 'beat him on the buttocks with a *bharmappa* [a stiffened piece of leather with a handle attached] in front of all the villagers. Priya howled and yelled, but did not disclose anything. Pryce-Jones then made him lie down flat on the floor and began to beat him with the edge of the *bharmappa*. He had a theory that it hurt more.' The beating only stops when Kumar protests that enough is enough. After quarrelling with 'Bill' over his cruelty, the still-protesting subordinate storms back alone to Satara. I get up and check my map. Yes, Kumtha's a real village in the southern part of the district.

The narrative of 'Bill's' violence is shocking. Nonetheless it feels less damaging than the allegations in *Sentinel*, for three reasons. First, 'only' a single individual is beaten by the character in the novel. Second, the violence employed by the Parallel Government both precedes 'Bill's' and is much more extreme, echoing Modak's remarks yesterday afternoon. The novel also repeats his claims about the gratuitous killing of the train crew, and follows it with a graphic description of the thrashing of a suspected informer. After several warm-up blows, the unfortunate victim is 'roughly upended' and his feet tied together. A 'gangster' begins

> to beat him on the soles with a stick slowly and rhythmically. After a few strokes, Thakur began to howl and yell but the gangsters continued the beating. Thakur defecated. The gangsters poured a bucket of water over him, but continued the beating. The villagers watched all round without uttering a word, until one of them said, 'He seems to have fainted.' But still the *dhup-dhup* of the beating went on.

The assailants only desist when even a woman whom Thakur has supposedly victimised protests that any more and they'll 'murder' the now unconscious man.

Above all, 'Bill's' behaviour seems slightly less reprehensible here because his Indian colleague is himself clearly complicit in police violence. Whereas *Sentinel* denies any such involvement on Modak's part, early in the novel Kumar witnesses a constable using the *bharmappa* on a prisoner: 'Shiva was held by two policemen in the posture of a public school boy getting six of the best.' This beating, however, continues for fully fifteen minutes. Although he throws up later, the ASP doesn't intervene at the time, despite knowing such methods are strictly prohibited by the Police Manual. Indeed, Kumar's subordinates are later allowed to justify their brutality as follows: '"What other kind of interrogation could have helped in getting Shiva to admit the offence? ... What choice have we? If we can't detect cases, we're branded as inefficient."' Further, it's notable that while arresting the nationalist leader, the pinnacle of his career in Satara, Kumar himself administers several blows to an obstructive henchman.

So the novel makes it clear that the culture of police violence which Kumar belatedly complains about long preceded 'Bill's' arrival in the district. Significantly, when he first witnesses the use of the *bharmappa* on a suspect, Kumar steels himself because he 'remembered how another ASP had cried when he had seen a similar interrogation, and how he was ever afterwards branded as a weak and soft officer.' Here's something else. *No Place* harps on the pressure exerted by successive inspector-generals to end disturbances which were beginning to pose a serious threat to British rule. But if a green light had been given to use extreme measures against the dissidents, why did Bill intervene against the rogue Sub-Inspector Walawalkar and on behalf of the tortured woman in Tasgaon?

Something else also unsettles me Modak's half-admiring, half-deprecating insistence on his colleague's womanising. I picked up on my host's ambiguous tone when he referred to Bill's 'lady friend' during our meeting. Now I see that *Sentinel* comments: 'As for the ladies, they were all charmed with his "shy" smile and his boyish behaviour.' He's also represented as having an eye for Indian village beauties.

Beryl Grey, one of Bill's 'girl-friends in India'

In the novel such hints are developed. 'Bill's' 'shy, naïve smile' particularly charms the DSP's wife, who becomes tongue-tied when talking about him. His relations with Indian women are more troubling, however. While at the PTS, 'Bill' has an affair with the servant of a colleague – much to Kumar's horror. It's not clear whether the protagonist's disgusted by 'Bill' sleeping with a low-caste woman, or the crossing of racial barriers, or – by contrast – whether he objects to the unequal power relations involved. Later, 'Bill' plans to sleep with another Indian woman while spending the night at a colleague's. The woman mistakenly goes to the wrong end of the veranda and gets into bed with his fellow-officer, an orthodox Brahmin, whose scandalised protests abort the tryst. Neither Kumar nor his creator appear to appreciate what strikes me as the obviously farcical nature of the scene. In another incident with similar comic potential, 'Bill' offers the recently married Kumar some man-to-man advice about how to keep his wife happy, leaving the young Indian ASP boggling haughtily at his colleague's worldliness.

I spend hours trying to square Modak's two accounts of Bill. Given the strongly documentary feel of *No Place*, I can't help inferring that the older author edited his memoir to Bill's disadvantage, for reasons which I can't fathom. What is the relative truth status of each text, one apparently fictional, the other non-fiction. It's a problem much debated in autobiography criticism? Didn't Richard Steele famously claim that 'the word *Memoir* is French for a novel'? And Paul de Man once commented that 'the distinction between fiction and autobiography is not an either/or polarity but one that it is undecidable.' Yet I have no reason to distrust the thrust of Modak's descriptions of Bill's behaviour towards suspected supporters of the Parallel Government, whether in real life or fictional guise. It's dawn before my heartache soothes enough to let me fall asleep.

~

It feels as if I've only just dropped off when my mobile rings. It's Rajeev, bright and enthusiastic.

'Well, did you find him? Are you alright?' he adds as I struggle to collect myself. To my surprise, I'm chilled to the bone.

'It's been a bit depressing, to be honest, Rajeev. He gave me his memoir. Very negative about my father.' I relate the gist.

It's his turn to hesitate. 'But as I said, Modak's a bitter man.'

'Doesn't make it any easier.'

'My friend, how are the other British represented?'

The penny drops. Bill, Hobson, Mountain, Smith, Yates are variously lazy, incompetent, bullying, sticklers for pointless rules or a combination of these qualities.

'There you are, then. He never forgave the Raj for dismissing his father.'

I recall Modak's line in *Sentinel* just before the Satara episode ends: 'I have no love lost to the British because they were unfair to me and unfair to my father.'

'Why didn't Modak resign, if he felt so strongly? They were very tough times, my friend, and required firm measures. I told you what the Patri Sarkar got up to. Some of those saboteurs were fifth columnists, they tried to make contact with the Japanese … Remember Gandhi himself condemned them.'

It's little consolation, and I tell him so.

'So what are you going to do now?' Rajeev asks uncertainly.

'I'm supposed to have dinner with the Modaks this evening. But I'm not sure I'll go.'

'Do so, my friend, I beg you, you may find out other things. Don't be put off by his crankiness.' Discomfited by my silence, Rajeev tries another tack. 'You know why he wrote that memoir? Get hold of J.F. Rebeiro's *Bullet for Bullet*. See what his colleagues thought about Modak. Rebeiro claimed he was a coward, and riot-prone. *Sentinel*'s his apologia.'

'What?'

'Everywhere Modak went, especially when he was in charge

of policing Kashmir, controversy and commissions of inquiry followed. Does he write about that?'

'I've only read the stuff about Satara. But he can't have been that bad if he finished up as top cop in Maharashtra.'

'My friend, if you stick around long enough, you get there eventually. Isn't it the same in your profession?'

I make a mental note to read on in *Sentinel* when I've got the energy.

'Make sure you keep me informed about your movements. Anything I can do, just let me know. Oh, and when you see him, ask Modak to identify the other cadets in that photo I gave you. That would be a big help to me.'

'Will do. If I go ... By the way, any news of Poel?'

'He isn't back yet. I'll keep trying.'

'Thanks, Rajeev,' I respond wearily.

'No dark thoughts, now,' he encourages gently. 'Ask yourself why your father won the Indian Police Medal if everything Modak says is true.'

I need time to think. Unsure whether I'll be able to face the Modaks later, I eventually phone, complaining of a stomach bug. Kiron answers, warm and sympathetic.

'You must be careful about the water, even in the good hotels. There's a good pharmacist near you. Do you want me to ring them and have something sent over? Try to rest and if you feel better, give me a ring this afternoon. I'd love to get your advice on something.'

Putting the phone down, I'm suddenly sick of my whole trip. If I could get back to England today, it wouldn't be too soon. I've been away rather less than a fortnight, yet it feels as if my life's been turned upside down. My room shrinks like a cell. I've got to get out. On the spur of the moment, I decide to bring forward my visit to nearby Yeravda, where Gandhi was imprisoned after his 'Quit India' speech – the event which precipitated the Satara uprising.

Before going down to breakfast, I wander over to the

window and look onto the street. An auto-rickshaw's revving up, exhaust clouding the chilly morning air. Across the street a knot of onlookers has gathered on the pavement, breath steaming. It's a violent shock to see them bending over the old man from the night before, his body now shrouded head to toe in a blanket. A policeman makes notes languidly. It's no doubt my own sense of vulnerability which generates the raging sense of guilt which suddenly overtakes me. Did the poor fellow die of cold while I lay on the bed, sweating over my petty concerns?

~

It's a surprise to discover that Gandhi's 'prison' was actually a palace belonging to the legendarily wealthy Aga Khan, leader of the Ismaili sect. It's an enormous three-storeyed wedding cake, icing-sugar-white, with Moorish lancet arches, its extensive grounds an oasis after the turbulent inner city. Surrounding it are cooling stands of flame tree and jacaranda, leaves filamented like fish skeletons, clumps of graceful oleander and blushing hibiscus. On the ground floor, Gandhi's rooms are closed off by glass screens. So it was from here that he denounced the Parallel Government. I wonder what Bill thought about his intervention? In his bedroom are a wafer-thin mattress, spinning wheel, writing materials, bookcase, red carpet, overlooked by a portrait of the Mahatma cradling his ill, white-haired wife, Kasturba. Next door, the austere white-tiled bathroom looks like it hasn't been touched since his release. A simple pair of sandals lies in one dusty corner. Hard to tell whether husband's or wife's.

There's an extremely peaceful, meditative atmosphere, enhanced by the absence of other visitors. In the hush, I try to internalise the meaning of Gandhi's attachment to non-violence, an attachment so intense that he was prepared to condemn an insurgency as passionately committed as himself to India's freedom. I know from his autobiography how hard Gandhi tried to comprehend and empathise with his opponents, while pursuing his conceptions of truth and justice with inflexible determination. It's deeply moving to connect such values to the sacrifices he made for them right here. In his portrait, the eyes remain warm, mischievous and lively despite his evident grief for Kasturba, who was soon to die, still a prisoner. The British attempt to isolate him suddenly strikes me as not only unjust, but ludicrous. Gandhi's spirit was the source of his power and it must have percolated, an untameable will-o'-the-wisp, through the keyhole of the padlock on his door.

Behind the palace, two huge urns contain the couple's ashes. As I contemplate them, the world suddenly clicks back in gear. I'm not to blame for my father's alleged behaviour, nor am I responsible for the death of the old man on the pavement. Perhaps being here also prompts my reconsideration of Modak as the morning wears on, the attempt to see things from his point of view. I can only sympathise with his disgust at police brutality, however tardy his protests might have been. Most of all, I'm struck increasingly by the ambivalence beneath his memoir's hyper-confident narratives of the brilliant policeman, the ardent and persuasive lover, the moral scourge of the British. His position was probably untenably awkward. As an Indian, Modak could never be fully part of the Raj, however much he might once have wanted to be. The nameplate on his gate, inscribed 'IP' rather than the post-Independence 'IPS' (Indian Police Service) suggests a lingering identification with the Raj, as does the interior of his home and Christian faith. But although he disclaims any direct experience of racism on the part of his British fellow-officers, and even though power had been nominally devolved to a Congress government in Bombay before war broke out, the system remained structurally racist. Otherwise Bill's colleague Kamte would have had no need to be on guard against slights in the way described in *From Them to Us*.

According to *Sentinel*, an Englishman could join the IP with O-levels, while Indian candidates had to have degrees. The viceroy could still declare war on Germany and Japan over the heads of the elected legislatures, and heap insult on injury with the totalitarian Defence of India Rules. Most of the 100,000 people detained alongside Gandhi were held without trial. And even if the British men Modak met ostensibly treated him as an equal, their female counterparts sometimes didn't, as both his texts complain. How much was Kumar's 'inferiority complex' an individual personality trait, how much a product of contact with the British? To this degree, he reminds me of his namesake, Hari Kumar in Paul Scott's *Raj Quartet*, although Scott's character is far more tragic – and far less autobiographical – than Modak's.

At the same time, as Rajeev also intimated, Modak would inevitably have been regarded as something of an outsider to Indian society. It was doubtless bad enough to be from a family that had disavowed its Brahmin roots; as a policeman, he'd have been strongly identified with the ever more unpopular Raj. He must have felt increasingly vulnerable from 1942, as the Parallel Government stepped up its attacks on perceived collaborators. If, as seemed likely then, Britain was to lose the war and India fell to the Japanese, a sorry fate almost certainly awaited functionaries of the *ancien régime*. At the end of the war, his prospects couldn't have seemed bright, what with Independence on the horizon. His real political beliefs in the 1940s remain unclear. In both books, the Parallel Government is occasionally represented almost as a liberation movement, social as well as political, directing its attacks as much against landowners and moneylenders as the Raj. As an Indian, he must surely have felt at least some identification with their aims? In the novel, Kumar's sister is questioned by the police on suspicion of aiding the underground. It's hard to know if this is fact, or a fiction which nonetheless expresses Modak's own feelings at the time. Or does it express a convenient retrospective change of heart by someone who had to make his way in post-Raj India?

I wonder too why Modak's father, the District Magistrate, was dismissed, and when. Perhaps that was decisive in recalibrating his son's vision of the Raj. The sour way Modak sometimes represents Bill (and other British colleagues) might be consistent with that, even if professional rivalry wasn't involved. Perhaps, justifiably, Modak also felt he'd been unfairly marginalised following his complaints about tactics, as indicated by his ignorance about the secret Memorandum Bill supposedly wrote. Maybe the memoir simply reflects the bitterness of old age, with Modak's reputation under attack from former colleagues like Rebeiro. I sense it'll be impossible to get to the bottom of it. My academic training reminds me that there's no such thing as definitive truth in memories, only interpretations of events. As Salman Rushdie observes: 'Memory ... selects, eliminates, alters, exaggerates, minimizes, glorifies, and vilifies also, but in the end it creates its own reality.'

For all the pain they've caused me, then, I'm still intensely grateful for the insights Modak's texts provide into the Bill of the 1940s. I couldn't have hoped to get much of this information any other way. I feel more at peace by the time I get back to the hotel, but I'm physically exhausted. Where the old man's body lay this morning, a makeshift stall has already been set up, selling single cigarettes and fluorescent sweets, overseen by a tinsel-golden god mounted on the frame. There's no one to remember him now, nothing to record his having been. For some obscure reason, his abrupt erasure makes me feel I have to see the Modaks again after all. Perhaps Rajeev's right, other things will come out, material excised from the memoir, which will help me better understand the young Bill and preserve his memory. After lunch I phone Kiron, who's delighted to hear I'm better. The goodwill in her voice makes me feel ashamed of my earlier stratagem.

Lying down to rest in the afternoon, I examine the photo that Rajeev gave me. When it was taken, my father was rather less than half the age I am now. What must it have felt like, at twenty-five years old, to be given such responsibility, taking on well-organised, armed insurgents, in a district the size of Wales, and equally mountainous in parts? I try to imagine one of my PhD students being entrusted with such a task. It seems inconceivable. And me? If the demands of the time had placed that burden on my shoulders, how would I have responded? To what and to whom would I have understood my loyalties to lie? I feel less and less in a position to judge Bill. I eventually fall asleep with the photo cradled on my breast.

When I wake, there's only an hour before the appointment. I place the picture amongst the others photocopied by my aunt Pat. I look again at the page of his 'girl-friends in India'. I must ask Modak if he knew Beryl Grey or Maria. Perhaps they were also in Satara at the time. I wonder again about Modak's insistence on Bill's womanising. How much is fiction, how much true?

Eric Balson's proving impossible to prise out. However fast the boy tears down the concrete drive towards the garage door on which the stumps are chalked, however quickly he whips his arm over, as his father's taught him, Mr Balson picks out the tennis ball unerringly and flogs it beyond the nettles into the vegetable patch. His own sons seem reluctant to run for it, as if they don't want to diminish their father's glory, so the boy and his brothers have worked themselves into a lather retrieving the ball. The boy takes the opportunity to give the Brussels sprouts a cuff. He's always secretly glad when his mother mournfully reports another nocturnal raid by an elephant. They can take the lot as far as the boy's concerned. If they didn't grow sprouts, perhaps the elephants wouldn't come, he's helpfully suggested.

There's a welcome break when his younger brother finds a chameleon in a shrub and they all gather round, hoping it'll change colour before their eyes or flick out its tongue like a sticky rubber band at the ant it's shadowing. The creature moves jerkily up the twig, swivelling each eye independently of the other beneath miniature horns, one eye on them, the other fixed on its prey. Close up, it's something out of a prehistoric horror film: scaly skin, long tail and horns. What a size its forebears must have been in the age of dinosaurs. With a shudder, the boy imagines himself in the place of the ant which the chameleon is steadying itself to strike. The insect disappears in a blur of plum tongue swifter than a slingshot. The excitement over, they trudge back to resume the game.

Mr Balson's the Public Works Department officer at the Ngorongoro Crater, where the boy's family moved after their posting in Manyoni. A boyish, sandy man, he seems in awe of the game ranger. His wife's an impossibly pretty, slim, blonde woman who seems much too young to have three sons. The oldest, Alan, is closest to him in age and the boy often visits their house a mile or so away down the red murram road. It's worth the risk of running into game, because of Viva's wonderful puddings, gluey mousses and moist crumbles that the boy's mother never makes. She always offers second helpings, spooning out the dessert with laughing blue eyes, as if anxious he doesn't get enough to eat at home.

The boy has decided he's in love with her, but he's not sure what it means exactly. Certainly not what was shown in Samson and Delilah, *the most recent flick his father's taken him to see. They drove all the way to Arusha, ninety miles distant, he's such a fan of Hedy Lamarr. 'History's Most Beautiful and Treacherous Woman', the poster indelibly proclaimed. But the boy hated Delilah. So mean to Samson, she couldn't have loved him, for all her breathy protestations. It's something about her eyes, hard and depthless like the chameleon's. Utterly unlike Viva's. Sometimes the boy's jealous of Alan, his mother so dotes upon him.*

Perhaps it's because his father's disappeared that Mr Balson's now so expansive, laughing and joking while a succession of bowlers tries to dismiss him. Usually he's reserved, though always pleasant. Sometimes he brings his family round in the evening to watch the game gathering on the salt lick the boy's father constructed on the ridge opposite their house. However, he will often say nothing, listening respectfully as his host talks about the population patterns of different species or poaching problems in the Conservation Area, while the wives discuss schools or long leave. The boy's father has told him that Eric's asked about a transfer to the Game Department.

The boy wants his turn to bat. There's only one way to get the visitor out, and that's to get his father back on bowling. Even fresh from the office in his clicking brogues, he's too good for all of them. But where is he? He slipped off, saying he needed a drink. That was twenty minutes ago. Now Eric's racing towards a double century. Surely his father won't want his record beaten? He'd better warn him of the danger.

He's not in the kitchen or living room. Strange, because there in the corridor are his shoes. Kimwaga shakes his head when the boy asks if he's seen him. The child sets off into the garden. Round the rough-grassed lawn, his mother has planted borders edged with red-hot pokers which nod stiffly in the changeable breeze. She's sitting at the far end, in a deck-chair, reading a book in the shade, as if keeping watch over her creation. One night, a few weeks before, some buffalo broke down the fence and congregated gruffly on the lawn. Calling his son, the boy's father led him out onto the front steps and threw a thunder-flash, laughing as the tossing shadows stampeded back the way they came, trembling the ground. The following day, his mother wept over the destruction. Now she looks too absorbed to disturb, so the boy crosses the garden to return to the cricket match, on the other side of the wing where the bedrooms are. He hears another triumphant shout from Mr Balson and feet haring towards the vegetable patch.

He crouches behind a shrub under his parents' bedroom window, in case he's called to wade through nettles again. For *a while he watches a dung beetle laboriously rolling its freight across the flowerbed. When someone shouts that it's his turn to bowl, the boy begins to straighten up. As he does so, he glances in through the metal-framed window. He freezes in his half-squat. A few inches away a man's back fills the square of glass. He recognises the short-sleeved Fair Isle sweater immediately. But that's not what arrests him. A delicate white hand is moving tremulously up his father's shoulder until it finds the neck; it pauses there, before fingers search again, twisting like tendrils in the short hair of the nape. Beyond his father's bent head, the boy can see curling blonde hair. He's paralysed. If he moves, he may give himself away. Yet he doesn't want to see. Something deadly dangerous is happening. Like the fight with the cook.*

Suddenly the tableau shifts sideways, the bodies pressed closer together. Surely they'll see him now? But the boy stifles his panic. His father's always telling him to keep still if he senses danger in the bush. It's the first lesson of the wilds. To his huge relief, their eyes are closed. The mouths slide softly on each other, as if lips are slipping in their search for traction. Viva's hand moves again, caressing his father above the collar, fingers opening and closing like tender scissors. The boy's close enough to see goosebumps on her downy forearm. There's an expression on his father's face the boy's never seen before, a gorged, flushed relaxation which makes him even more confused. Viva simply looks like she's dreaming.

Holding his breath, the boy crouches again. Slow as he can, he backs towards the garden. Should he tell his mother straight away? If he doesn't, he'll be doing something just as wrong as what he's seen. What about Mr Balson? He dismisses the thought immediately. He knows there'll be an almighty row if he says anything, with the Balson children here. Then he won't be able to go round any more to play with Alan, and there'll be no more chocolate mousse or Viva's loving looks. Oh no! What if his mother has to swap with Viva? Or worse, the game ranger with his would-be apprentice? Suddenly, the boy's furious with his father for putting them at risk. Trying to compose himself, he runs round the back of the house and rejoins the game. Just as he arrives, there's yelling enough to wake the dead. Ames has caught Mr Balson. He stayed out by the vegetable patch and clung onto a skyer.

'Come on, Bill, your turn,' Mr Balson shouts, when the congratulations die down.

Viva comes out first. She's smiling, composed. After stooping to give her middle son a hug, she approaches the boy and ruffles his hair. With the same hand which a few minutes ago was running through his father's. Despite himself, the boy feels transfigured, included in a magic triangle. As Viva pours everyone lemonade, the boy's father appears. His shoelaces are undone and he's whistling the theme from Never on a Sunday, *a fixture on the gramophone these days when it's not the awful Russ Conway.*

'Sorry to have been so long on the choo. *Must have been the curry last night.'*

Mr Balson laughs politely.

'Isn't this bliss?' Viva laughs, sipping from her glass.

At first the boy's ecstatic that everything's back to normal. But soon the doubts return, and the fury. He approaches his older brother Ames.

'I've got something really important to tell you. Get Barney as well.'

Their half-brother, ten years older, has recently finished at Winchester. They've never lived all together, the children, and the boy's unsure of this serious, remote young man with frizzy hazel hair quite unlike theirs, and such easy lines of communication to their mother. Ames looks bemused and goes unwillingly. But as the pair return, something in Barney's set expression puts the boy off. He remembers schoolmates whose parents have divorced. Only one or two, but everyone behaves as if they've been in a road accident or have a rare disease. Besides, there's that serenity on his father's face and Viva's dreaminess. Can anything which makes people so happy really be wrong? The boy has a sudden vision of Samson in the entrance to the temple, the columns quivering as he strains his sinews. In the time it takes for his siblings to arrive, he's changed his mind.

'It's nothing, sorry,' he says.

'What's wrong with you?' Ames demands. Barney simply stares, as if the boy's once more proving himself an idiot.

What does bliss mean, the boy wonders, as his father cheerily seizes the bat. Kiss he knows. Is bliss what you get from the sort of kiss Viva gave his father, or Delilah gave Samson, not the peck on the cheek his parents exchange or which his mother gives the boy? Or is it something softer, shimmery, liquid, which lights you up golden from within, making your face shine the way his father's and Viva's do when they steal a glance at one another? Whatever, perhaps it isn't the same as love.

CHAPTER 7

The Pendulum Shifts

On my way to the Modaks for high tea, the auto-rickshaw driver's exuberant.

'They're showing these terrorist bastards, *yaar*?' he says with a vengeful laugh.

'What do you mean?' For an awful moment I think India's retaliated against Pakistan for the Mumbai attacks.

His puny frame seems to swell with pride. 'Gaza. The *Yehudi* are showing them what for.'

It's no surprise that some Indians should be favourably disposed towards Israel, a few of whose citizens were amongst the targets in the recent outrages. I presume the man means there's been an artillery bombardment or rocket strike against the Hamas leadership. I shrug. The attrition's been endless since Ariel Sharon unilaterally pulled out of the Gaza enclave, leaving its population imprisoned within a ring of iron. Despite my distaste at his glee, I've more pressing things to think about, notably how I'm going to manage this next meeting with the Modaks. I just hope I get there before the fog of exhaust in which we're stuck suffocates me.

When I arrive at 22/4, Modak's not yet back. Kiron looks frailer today, dark rings under her eyes. She's wearing an ivory ankle-length dress and a pair of tennis shoes.

'Must be the wretched traffic delaying him. Make yourself at home,' she smiles sweetly, ushering me through the dining room to a small courtyard with a bench and blue-tiled circular table. The walls are lined with potted plants and there's an enticing smell of citrus and jasmine. Once her daughter's brought an extra chair and cushions for the bench, the young woman retires again to fetch drinks.

'Did you read Emmanuel's books?' Kiron asks eagerly, once I've again insisted I'm fully recovered from my 'digestive problems'.

'Started *No Place for Crime* but I haven't got that far. Spent a lot of the day sleeping. Thought I'd read them in the order they were published.' I've decided on this ruse so as not to embarrass Modak. Although part of me badly wants to challenge him, I don't want to put him on the defensive in case he has further information.

Kiron flutters, almost girlish. 'What I wanted to ask, you being a literature professor, do you have contacts with publishers?'

'Only academic ones, I'm afraid. Why?'

'Well, Emmanuel's written this new novel about King Ashoka, who ruled India two thousand years ago and converted to Buddhism. I think it's terribly good, but no one's interested here. We're forgetting our heritage in this mad rush to be American. I can't tell you how delightful Pune used to be in your father's time. The Oxford of the East. Pensioners' Paradise. Not any more,' she adds ruefully.

I smile sympathetically.

'What do you think of *No Place* so far?'

Even though I've prepared myself for the question, I find it hard to answer. 'It's very interesting on events in Satara,' I mumble. 'And I learned a lot about police procedure at the time.'

Kiron smiles, as if I've paid her a compliment.

'Bill Pryce-Jones is based on my father?'

'Well, my dear, he was rather a writer's gift, rushing around the district with his machine gun, chasing those people. He certainly had glamour.'

At this point the young woman returns with a tray. She's wearing jeans with a white long-sleeved shirt. Puppy fat shows above the collar. She pours me fizzing gin and tonic and juice for her mother.

'I'll be off, then, mummy. My shift starts at six. See you later.' Her hand rests for a moment on Kiron's arm before she turns to me. 'Goodbye, Mr Moore-Gilbert. Enjoy your meal.'

'So you can't help with Ashoka?' Mrs Modak asks despondently when the door slams.

'I'll ask around when I get back to the UK,' I offer. 'I'll write and let you know.'

'My sons tell me the market for historical novels is bad at the moment.'

I nod. 'Where do they live?'

'One's in South Africa and the other just went back to the United States.' Anticipating my query, she adds: 'You see, it would have been hard for them here as non-Hindus.'

'Your daughter's the only one with you?'

Kiron leans forward confidentially. 'She's our adopted daughter.'

She tells me the story. The girl's biological mother came from rural Bihar and was sold into prostitution, passed from gang to gang until she ended up in the Falkland Road cages in Mumbai. Modak discovered her during a drugs raid. The woman said she preferred to stay in her brothel rather than be sent home. She feared reprisals from the people who first peddled her and abuse from her family, which had been content to have one less superfluous female mouth to feed. Modak took pity and invited her to join his household. The couple adopted her infant child in due course. The mother worked her way up to cook and it's she who's preparing high tea. The daughter's recently graduated from university and now works in the personnel department of an IT company. As the story unfolds, I remember Vasanthi, the 'untouchable' character in *No Place*, whose brutal killers Kumar pursues so determinedly. I'm impressed. Clearly Modak shares his protagonist's admirable desire for social justice. I now also better understand the girl's self-effacing demeanour in her parents' presence.

Just as Kiron finishes, the front door bangs to again and soon her husband comes shuffling out to the courtyard. He's wearing a loose red-and-black check shirt and grey slacks, his skin almost colourless in the fading light. I can't interpret his expression. Is he pleased to see me or not?

'Sorry I'm late.'

'Moore-Gilbert's started *No Place*, Emmanuel dear,' Kiron announces, patting the cushion beside her on the bench, 'he thinks it's awfully good.' She has to repeat herself as her husband cups his ear.

'Yes, I haven't had time for *Sentinel* yet.'

Is that a flicker of relief on my host's face? He, too, seems very frail today.

'Sorry you've been unwell,' he mutters.

'I'm fine now, thank you.'

'I wasn't sure you'd be coming. I got out some photographs, anyway.'

'Thanks so much. I have some for you as well.'

Modak shuffles back indoors, returning a few minutes later with two large black albums. But his archive's a disappointment. There are dozens of black-and-white photos, fixed at the corners with stamp hinges, pages separated by crinkly semi-transparent sheets. The first one which Modak shakily removes shows him with Mountbatten, inspecting a guard of honour. His evident pride seems another example of his Raj-identification. Other photos feature various politicians met as his career progressed. I wonder again how my host felt after Independence, as the servant of the people he'd pursued in the 1940s. It's fascinating to see the leaders of the Parallel Government, Nana Patil and Y.B. Chavan. But these pictures date from the 1960s. The commentary stumbles along as Modak tries diligently to remember. However, he's behaving as if I've come to research his life rather than Bill's. I try to be patient. Anyway, what am I hoping for? He can't be expected to suddenly retract his accusations. Besides, I'm not supposed to have read *Sentinel* and I can't think how to probe without revealing that I have.

By the time Kiron calls us for food, I'm frustrated and rather bored. It's a relief to come inside to the delicious aromas. We sit at the dining table as a middle-aged woman with hennaed hair in a centre-parting brings out the dishes. Looking at her, solid, comfortable and smiling, it's hard to imagine what would have become of her but for Modak's kindness.

'Beef curry, dal and paratha,' Kiron explains, waving round the dishes like a conductor, 'rice and *methi maloo*.' This last looks like spinach fried with plenty of garlic. 'And one of your father's favourites,' she adds fondly, pointing to lamb cutlets and coarsely mashed potato flecked with skin. 'We often had it in Satara.'

The English food looks insipid. But to humour Kiron for going to the trouble, I help myself. Like Bill before me, I imagine, I mitigate the blandness of public-school chow with a dollop of acid mango pickle. Modak looks at me keenly.

'Fully recovered, I see.'

Is there a hint of knowing irony?

Over the meal, I show him my Aunt Pat's photos. He immediately identifies the ones of the PTS. None appear to have been taken in Satara, though he doesn't recognise all the locations. I deduce that those are from Bill's later postings.

'I remember his "Woodie" well,' Modak remarks, pointing to a picture of Bill sitting in a Ford station wagon with timber framing. 'We had to buy our own cars in those days, though we got an allowance. That's Sergeant Staines, the drill instructor,' he comments, pointing to a figure in long shorts to whom Bill is listening with a half-smile. 'Ex-Guards. He always used to say, "Mr Modak, walk straight now, don't waddle like a duck." We were called "Mr", like at Sandhurst,' he adds proudly.

Police-Probationer Bill listening to N.A.P. Smith, Inspector-General of Police (in homburg) and Charles de Vere Moss (in pith helmet), Principal of Nasik PTS c. 1940

'And these two?'

Bill looks on respectfully as two older men confer, like a schoolboy privy to a discussion between masters.

'On the left's Smith, the inspector-general, and the other's de Vere Moss, the principal.'

'"Pembroke" in your novel.'

Modak smiles appreciatively. I show him Rajeev's photo.

'This is the intake before mine. That's Ted Dodwell and Michael Mountain, can't remember the chap between them.'

I make a note for Rajeev. Mountain features in *Sentinel* as a colleague who escapes Satara for a cushy post in Air Raid Precautions at the local hill station, thereby doubling Modak's workload. My host tells one or two anecdotes about each figure, recaps aspects of the probationer's life described in *No Place for Crime* and explains the syllabus he and Bill followed. There were four main elements. First, instruction in the Indian Penal and Criminal Procedure Codes and the Bombay Police Evidence Acts, with lower and higher exams in successive years. Subsidiary courses covered Hindu law. Second, study of two Indian languages. Hindi was compulsory, with the choice of another lingua franca of the province, Marathi, Gujarati or Kannarese. Then, Physical Training. This included drill, weapons, riding and team sports. Finally, the Police Manual and Investigative Procedures. When I look up, Kiron's eyes are shut, as if she's exhausted, or has heard it all many times before.

She perks up again when the cook appears to clear the plates. After a portion of kulfi and what resembles spotted dick, which I dutifully swallow, she excuses herself to make some phone calls. Modak and I retire to the courtyard again for coffee. An oil lamp's been lit, attracting a large grey moth. I ask my host to look at the photos of Bill's 'girl-friends in India'. He doesn't recognise either. Maria's uniform, he suggests, indicates that she might have been based at Deolali army camp, outside Nasik.

'Your novel suggests Bill Pryce-Jones had an Indian girl-friend at the PTS. Did my father?'

It takes Modak a while to understand what I'm asking.

'Out of the question,' he says firmly. 'Such things were not allowed.'

'But in your novel ...'

'My dear Moore-Gilbert, you're a literature person, you've heard of novelistic licence. Some of the British certainly did such things. There *was* a man in Nasik, Gumbleton-something. But not an IP officer. Good Lord, no.'

Modak sounds very like the orthodox Brahmin officer whom 'Bill' scandalises in *No Place*.

'But you talked about a lady friend the last time I came?'

'Yes, yes,' Modak responds testily, 'but that's quite another thing. I had a great English lady friend, the wife of the executive engineer in Satara. It doesn't mean ...'

He gazes impassively, as if the subject is closed. I wonder why 'Bill' is turned into such a womaniser. Perhaps it's simply to give his character colour after all. I take a deep breath and ask about the novel's treatment of police brutality.

'How much of that was "novelistic licence"?'

My host looks uncomfortable, but he confirms the documentary nature of this aspect of his narrative, without mentioning Bill explicitly.

'Regrettably, some officers thought it the most expedient way to get results. They were wrong. As I said yesterday, it simply fanned the insurgency. On the other hand, it wasn't to be compared with what the Patri Sarkar were doing.'

Startled, I explain that I read Kamte's memoir in Mumbai. 'Was it common practice to beat demonstrators?'

'My dear Moore-Gilbert, you have to understand what it's like to be faced with a violent stone-throwing mob which won't disperse and reckon the probable loss of life and property if they have their way. Sometimes we had to use live rounds.'

I'm struck by that 'we'. But his look tells me that this subject, too, is closed. Damn it. I'm never going to find out exactly what was fact and what fiction in *No Place* – or in *Sentinel*.

Kiron returns, looking very tired. Although it's only seven-thirty, I sense it's time to leave.

'There's a lady who'd like to meet you, if you're free now. She knew your father.'

After all the talk of 'lady friends,' I'm startled. 'Who might that be?'

'Her name's Dhun Nanavatty. A Parsi. Widow of K.J. Nanavatty, who joined the IP a few years before your father and Emmanuel. They worked together, he and Bill. If you're free, she'd like you to go round.'

'Now?'

'In an hour. It's not too late for you?'

Kiron explains where Mrs Nanavatty lives, fifteen minutes in an auto-rickshaw.

'I said I'd phone back if it's not convenient.'

What luck. Thank God I didn't cancel my meeting with the Modaks. This could certainly make up for the lack of new information here.

'More than happy. Do you know when and where they were together?'

Kiron frowns with concentration, pulling at her lower lip.

'In fact, do you know where my father went after Satara? His Service Record's incomplete. The last entry says Ahmedabad, in early 1946.'

'That's where he must have been with Nanavatty,' Modak chips in. 'Keki was up there for quite a while, running the Home Guards.'

'Didn't Moore-Gilbert go somewhere on the coast?' Kiron counters.

'I don't think so, my dear,' Modak responds moodily, 'I'm sure your father stayed in Ahmedabad until Independence.'

Kiron shrugs deferentially. 'Perhaps Dhun can tell you.'

'Now, I've made some telephone calls, too,' Modak intervenes rather abruptly. 'In case you want to go to Satara.'

Startled, I explain that I'm waiting for a call from Rajeev about Poel and the SIB archives.

'Well, I phoned the DSP anyway. They'd be delighted to show you round. It might give you a better sense of what we were about. And you can see the fort your father used to run up to.'

I'm doubly glad I didn't cancel. 'Thank you, Mr Modak, that's very kind.'

'Not at all. Who knows, they might be able to dig up those confidential weekly reports. And if they don't, ask to see the Part IVs.'

'Part IVs?'

He nods. 'The station's annual records. They provide an abstract of the main developments, communalism, crime, traffic and so on. They don't throw those away.'

The thought suddenly occurs to me. 'Do you know anything about my father's involvement in putting down the Hoors? I've been told that's why he got the job in Satara.'

'The Hurs of Sindh? I don't remember him talking about them.'

Surely, if Professor Bhosle's right, Bill would have discussed that earlier rebellion with his colleague in the course of preparing a strategy for dealing with the Parallel Government? If he didn't, either he was never in Sindh, or this is further evidence of the distance or mistrust between the two men. Maybe Modak's simply forgotten, as with some of the names in the photographs. How much can anyone be expected to remember after sixty-odd years?

When I get up, Modak gives me another of his visiting cards. On the front, above his details, he's written 'Sent By' in a trembling script: on the back, the name and phone number of the DSP in Satara.

'I hope you enjoy meeting Dhun,' Kiron says, shaking my hand warmly. 'Do try to get to Satara, it's only a few hours and the drive's beautiful. Ah, Satara,' she adds wistfully, 'we had some happy times there. It was just after we married.'

Modak's face, however, suggests otherwise. 'If you come back this way, be sure to drop by,' he mutters.

I leave with mixed feelings. Kiron's a darling, without a bad bone in her body. As for Modak, he's too complex to grasp in two sittings.

~

There's time to kill before my appointment with Mrs Nanavatty. I consider going back to the Samrat, but can't face being poisoned again just yet in an auto-rickshaw. Instead I head for the German Bakery to consider my options. As I walk down Koregaon Park Road, I doubt the wisdom of going to Satara. While heading south into the territory of the Parallel Government would be another adventure, the likelihood of finding Bill's weekly reports seems remote. The Part IVs would no doubt be interesting, but I've already got a grasp of the main events which concern me. And since Bill wasn't the resident DSP, I doubt he'd have had much input into those. I'm also getting a little anxious about time; it's more than half-way into my trip. Probably better to head back to Mumbai, and be in a position to ask Poel to chase down the missing files as soon as he returns.

When I arrive at the café, it's overflowing with blissed-out maroon-robed Oshoites and I head instead to another one across the road. That's packed, too, with what look like young professionals and students, chatting animatedly on sofas, sipping peppermint-flavoured tobacco through their shishas. I take a table near the plasma screen. It's showing some English-language news channel and the banner reads 'Breaking News: Assault on Gaza'. It's far more serious than I realised from the auto-rickshaw driver. Wave after wave of air bombardments are underway. Modern Empire deals with 'terrorism' rather differently than in Bill's time and it's reported rather differently, too. Foreign correspondents are corralled on a hilltop some kilometres from the conflict; behind them massive columns of smoke mushroom over Gaza City, rising in poetic slow motion. At least at Guernica and Coventry, the population had a few minutes' warning of the bombers. Now death comes silently out of cloudless skies, long before the jets' noise can be heard. A horse-faced Israeli army major insists her country's prepared to do everything necessary, for as long as it takes, to 'degrade the assets' of the 'terrorist entity'. Nothing about what's going on at the receiving end.

'This chair free?' a man asks, in a northern European accent.

I'm relieved to be distracted. He's slim and tanned, dressed in loose orange cheesecloth trousers and a pale-blue waistcoat with bulging pockets. Despite a crease-less complexion, his thick copper-gold hair's streaked with grey. I motion him to put down his crash helmet and bag, a flimsy cotton foldover worn like a bandolier. He goes to the counter and returns with a plate of stale-looking macaroni cheese.

'Starving,' he explains, 'just got in from Goa.'

'You came by bike?' I'm astounded.

He gestures outside. 'Moped. Before that I crossed over to Madras and back.'

I take to him immediately. Travelling India on a moped sounds pleasingly crazy. He assures me it's not so bad. The Honda's extremely manoeuvrable, though he checks the brakes religiously every few days.

'And I always use earplugs. The truck klaxons, man, they blow you out of your seat otherwise.'

Anders is sixty-two, Swedish, and has fallen into the habit of wintering in Goa. He goes home in spring, spending the warmer months on his boat, moored in one of Stockholm's harbours. Mostly he eats fish which he catches himself, and saves his pension for winter breaks. He got bored this time and decided to do some travelling. Despite India's apparently enthusiastic embrace of globalisation, foreigners still can't buy any sort of vehicle in India, so a local friend did it for him.

'You certainly travel light.'

He dangles his bandolier from one finger. 'That's it. Change of clothes, my documents, toothbrush and a book. What's that you have there?'

I hold up Gandhi's *Autobiography*. Anders looks sceptical. 'Got anything lighter you've finished with?'

'Perhaps back at my hotel.'

On my recommending the Samrat, Anders decides to check it out. 'I've been in some real dumps this trip, man. Like to treat myself every so often to a hot shower.'

He asks what I'm doing in Pune, and I give him an abbreviated version.

'Sounds amazing,' he responds. 'Never really talked to my old man after my parents divorced. Regret it now. Not that he had an interesting life in the colonies or anything, he was an accountant in suburban Stockholm. But what he felt, how he looked at things, what was important, I never thought of asking before he died. You gotta grab a chance like this, squeeze it for all it's worth.'

I explain my dilemma over Satara.

'Satara, you gotta go, no question,' he declares. 'You're meeting people here who knew your father. Maybe the same will happen down there. Perhaps there's some old constable who worked with him?'

What an idiot I've been not to think of that before. Modak may be the only survivor from the officer cadre of the IP, but that was minuscule compared to the other ranks.

'You're on a roll, man, go with the flow.' He smiles at my doubtful expression. 'Mind you, personally I'd prefer to spend time in Pune.'

I explain I haven't seen much apart from Yeravda, not even the local attraction, the Osho commune.

'I dropped by just before I came here. Thought I might spend New Year there. I hear the parties are wild. Get most of my chicks on the internet at home. Shame that's not so well developed yet in India.' He grins wolfishly. 'Goa's full of hotties. But with AIDS it's too much of a lottery. Should have started coming thirty years ago. Want to come for a drink?'

I decline, citing my appointment with Dhun.

'OK, maybe see you later at the Samrat.'

As I leave the café, I make the decision to head for Satara. Anders is right. Who knows what I might turn up there? Besides it's entirely possible that Poel may be away until the New Year. In any case, Satara's only a few hours away, so I won't lose much time if Rajeev calls me back from there. Go with the flow; I repeat the mantra as I step into the road to hail an auto-rickshaw.

~

Mrs Nanavatty's is even more modest than the Modaks', a two-bedroom flat in a small development one block in from the reeking river which drags its viscous carcase through the north-east of the city. I'm met at the door by a striking woman with short dark hair who tells me she's Mrs Nanavatty's daughter, Erna. It's difficult to judge her age, and I'm wary after my experience with the Modaks. Mrs Nanavatty, however, is clearly very old. She's tiny and stooped, face deeply lined behind pebble glasses which make her toffee eyes look huge. She has piled-up thick grey hair and wears a wrap over one shoulder like a toga, half concealing a blue silk top. A faint scent of cardamom hangs in the air.

'Come in, my dear, so pleased to meet you. I couldn't believe it when Kiron phoned me to tell me you'd come. Do call me Dhun. Now I'm ninety-four, so you'll have to speak up.'

Her eyes are much younger, almost playful as she motions me to a white leather armchair in the cramped living room. I feel much more at ease than at the Modaks'.

'A peg?'

It takes me a moment to remember she's using the Raj-era term for a shot of liquor. I ask for fresh lime-soda instead. Erna bustles out to the kitchen. No servants here. I slowly realise why the room feels claustrophobic. It's crammed with game trophies, of the kind familiar from childhood, antlers on the walls, a leopard skin hanging. In one corner is a pair of elephant tusks, thick ends capped with engraved brass. Jammed between the glass coffee table and the sofa is a display cabinet. The familiar IP sword sits next to another I don't recognise.

'My son's,' Dhun explains, 'just retired from the army. Lieutenant-General.'

Husband and son stare down from portrait photos on the wall. Mr Nanavatty's resembles the official one of Modak in Rajeev's book. His black-and-white face is strong and bony, the expression frank, a touch of irony in the half-smile. The son's picture is full colour, and shows him receiving further medal to add to the impressive collection adorning his resplendent dress uniform.

'It was taken when R.K. relinquished Northern Command. He was in charge of Kashmir and Jammu.'

Clearly being non-Hindu has done her son no harm.

Once Erna returns with the drinks, Dhun asks about me and my trip. She expresses concern about the Modaks. In poor health, with their sons overseas, to her they seem very vulnerable now.

'So how did you know my father?' I ask when the preliminaries are over.

'I first met him right here in Poona, one Police Week. It must have been soon after the war started.'

'Police Week?'

She nods. 'A lovely event. Part formal inspection, part *bandobast* – that's dress parades – part public relations, to show off what we were about. But very social, too. There were balls and drinks and sports events. Everyone came up from the districts and the training school. It was the highlight of the year. I met your father at the governor's ball. He was a striking man, very charming. Keki and Bill got on from the start, despite Keki being a fair bit senior. They shared an interest in *shikari*.'

'Hunting?'

'Yes. There was a rule in those days at the PTS that every probationer had to go into the hills alone and bag a kill before they graduated. It didn't have to be big game, though there were plenty of tigers and leopard round Nasik in those days. Keki gave your father advice on where to look. They hunted together later, once or twice.'

'That's funny, because he became a game ranger in Africa.' Looking at all the trophies, I wonder if I've made a faux pas.

But Dhun smiles. 'Yes, he and my husband used to write to each other long after your father moved to Tanganyika. Bill said that if Keki wanted to come out and hunt, he just had to find his fare and everything else would be taken care of. Keki so wanted to go, but he hummed and ha'd and put it off and put if off and then the dreadful news came about the air-crash.' She looks at me with melting eyes.

'Your father was so young. Keki was terribly upset. He always said Bill was one of the finest men he'd known, and kept kicking himself for not having taken the opportunity to visit before. We were all devastated. I used to correspond with your mother after that. We never met, of course, but after Bill was killed I wrote to say how sorry I was and she wrote back and after that it was mainly at Christmas. Once she went to New Zealand, however, we lost touch. What happened to her?'

As I explain how she died a few years ago in Australia, I have a sudden vision of my mother in Gorleston-on-Sea, poring over the pale-blue aerogramme smothered with exotic stamps, explaining it came from a former colleague of Bill's who'd been posted to western India.

'That would have been us. We were in Assam in the late 60s and early 70s. During the Naxalite trouble. Keki was transferred to try and squash it.' She smiles ruefully. 'There's always some terrorist trouble in India.'

'Where did Bill and he work together?'

'In Ahmedabad. They were helping to set up the Home Guards.'

'Wasn't the war over by then?'

'Yes, but the new provincial government wanted more police auxiliaries. Everyone could see law and order was going to collapse. There was already trouble between Jinnah and Gandhi and Nehru. It was clear the Muslims would break away. There was lots of communalism, it had only been suppressed by the war.'

'It was a training post?'

Dhun nods. 'But there were so many riots, your father and Keki were often called out. It got very vicious: home-made bombs and acid and some of the rioters had arms.'

'Do you recall my father being wounded?'

She reflects a moment, before shaking her head. 'You know, everyone was getting injured. The police were completely out-numbered, caught in the middle of mobs who wanted to get at each other. Sometimes they had to call the army in. But the police took the brunt. Without them, it would have been much worse than it was.'

'Imagine what it's like to be attacked by an angry mob,' Erna interjects.

I recall Modak's comments earlier. 'Terrifying.'

'Keki always said your father was one of the bravest offic-ers he knew,' Dhun continues, as if she hasn't heard.

This is more like it. I feel my spirits lifting. 'Was Bill still in Ahmedabad during Partition?'

Dhun ponders. 'Do you know, I'm not sure, I've a feeling he might have been transferred before Independence. But the last time I saw him, I remember him saying it was a terri-ble mistake, Partition, that it'd just give the green light to the extremists. And he was right, look what happened. All those death trains and the rapes and killing of children. And we're still at each other's throats sixty years later. With nuclear weapons now.'

'Kiron thought he might have been posted somewhere on the coast.'

'I can't be sure, my dear. Have you checked his Service Record?'

I explain the dead end in that respect.

We talk for another hour or so, but Dhun can add little to what she's already said. A lot of the time that Bill and Keki were in Ahmedabad, she remained in Pune for the children's schooling. She glances fondly at her daughter. I can hardly believe Erna's in her seventies. With her dark hair and unlined cheeks, she doesn't look any older than Anders. It's conceiv-able Bill could have played with her as a child, hoisting her onto his shoulders as he later did me. Before I can ask, Erna explains how, after school, she worked long years in a clothes export company in Mumbai before retiring to Pune to look after Dhun. I infer that she never married, and wonder why not. When I tell them I'm planning to go to Satara, Erna jumps up.

'Then you absolutely must look up an old friend of ours, Farrokh Cooper. He runs a big engineering works down there. His father was the first Indian prime minister of Bombay, before the war. He'd be delighted to help you. I'll ring him right now and let him know you're coming.'

Any remaining doubts about the next stage of my trip dissolve. It's as if it's all been planned. Above all, I'm immensely reassured by Dhun's account of Keki's relations with Bill. This is what I'd hoped to hear from Modak. It's the first unambiguously positive account of Bill this whole trip. Maybe the pendulum's beginning to shift, after all the allegations in Shinde and *Sentinel*. Still, nagging doubts remain. Keki worked with Bill well after Satara, and in completely different circumstances. Pursuing the Parallel Government and preventing communal massacres are chalk and cheese.

Erna returns from the adjoining room a few minutes later. 'I phoned Farrokh and he's going to book you into the Regency. He says it's the only decent place in Satara. How are you getting there?'

'Bus, I guess.'

Erna looks concerned. 'Have you travelled on Indian buses?'

I smile complacently. 'It'll be an adventure.'

She seems dubious. 'Have you reserved?'

'Thought I'd wander over in the morning.'

'No time like the present. They can fill up. I'll take you down to Swargate and drop you afterwards. I insist.'

Before I leave, I show them my collection of photocopies. Dhun looks fondly at Bill, but she doesn't recognise Beryl or Maria.

'Do you know if he had an Indian girlfriend?'

Dhun ponders. 'I seem to remember something about the

sister of the Gaekwad of Baroda. But I don't know if it was romantic.'

Nothing's too much trouble for Erna. She ferries me in her tiny car to the bus station and supervises my purchase of a ticket on the next day's 'Volvo', as inter-city buses are apparently known here – she point-blank refuses to let me catch anything else. Then she drives to an ATM before leaving me at the Samrat.

'You really must stop for longer on your way back,' she says. 'Give my mother time to try and remember more. It's all so long ago now. We'd love to have you for dinner and really talk.'

I watch Erna's tail lights disappear with a feeling of regret. How generous people are here. Even Modak, whom I can't really make out, has gone to trouble to smooth my way. Why, if he was so hostile to Bill?

I've barely shut the door to my room when there's a knock. It's Anders, in a damp t-shirt, the lower half of his body wrapped in a towel.

'Can you help me out, man? Soon as I got in from the bar, I washed all my clothes in the sink. This American chick I met just rang. Wants me to come over to her hotel. But my only trousers are wet and I can't go out to buy some more.'

We're roughly the same build. Laughing, I show him what I have. 'Make sure you don't stay out the night,' I add mock-solemnly. 'I'm leaving at six-thirty tomorrow morning.'

CHAPTER 8

The Ghosts of Satara

From Swargate, the 'Volvo' grinds its way through ugly, gridlocked suburbs until eventually we reach the new dual carriageway running south to Bangaluru. There's no hard shoulder, however, and the inner lane's choked with pedestrians, bicycles, auto-rickshaws, motorbikes and herds of animals. Rural India, vast as it is, seems to be disappearing apace, Pune's tentacles spreading far along the motorway, small hotels in bare plots, half-finished filling stations, stalls with shining produce which women risk their lives to lean out into the hurtling traffic and wave imploringly. The bus barrels along in the overtaking lane, darting inside when it's hogged by labouring trucks, some piled high as double-deckers with precarious arrangements of sacks and crates. The countryside becomes increasingly parched and dun as we approach a series of ridges. We climb steepling passes, one after another, where the road shrinks to a single lane of lurching hairpin bends and ill-tempered klaxons.

Four hours later, as we descend the last incline towards Satara, the landscape changes markedly again. The plain in which the city's situated is a lush patchwork of emerald sugar cane and jade orchards, extending as far as the eye can see. The temperature's warmer and the air seems softer, too, more like the tropics than Pune. I'm dropped at a busy intersection and hop into an auto-rickshaw, where I'm suddenly overcome by nerves. At last I've reached the main theatre of action, the seeming pinnacle – or nadir – of Bill's Indian career.

First impressions of Satara are positive. Seen from the broad, tree-lined approach road it's much less ugly and polluted than

Pune, and has more the character of a country town. There are even bullocks grazing in the middle of the final roundabout out of which, of all things, a fifteen-foot replica Eiffel Tower soars. Looming over everything, a mile or so beyond, is a fort on a cliff-encircled height. It's the one on the cover of Modak's memoir, but now with spindly telecommunications masts jutting out of it. What did Bill feel when he first entered Satara, charged with his onerous brief? Perhaps the same mixture of excitement and apprehension as grips me now.

At last I'm somewhere Bill spent significant time. My sense of connection with him intensifies when I get to my room, at the top of the eight-storey hotel. It's not as nice as the one in Pune, but has the great advantage of a balcony. I step outside with the bellhop and he points out the police headquarters, way down to the left, half hidden by a dense canopy of trees. Beyond is a collection of miniature yellow buildings, like children's blocks from this distance, which he tells me is the Rajah's 'new' palace, built in the eighteenth century. North and west, the eroded flanks and flat-topped bluffs of the Sahyadris rise through the dancing haze like buttes in a western. I wonder which of those hills Bill scoured, which ribbon roads below he raced along in his 'Woodie'.

After lunch I take another auto-rickshaw to the police station, about a mile away. We pull up at an imposing, double-storeyed building made of dark laterite blocks. The veranda which Hobson took Modak out onto in *Sentinel*, immediately before Bill's arrival, runs the length of the first floor to massive turrets at each end. 'Satara Police 1913' is painted in blue and white, next to a long run of Marathi letters in golden plastic above the main entrance. A khaki-clad constable shows me into a ground-floor room where his superior examines Modak's card, before sending him off with it again. Phones ring and intercoms crackle. I wait, inhaling the aroma of bodies and masala tea, under the curious eyes of half a dozen policemen and some anxious-looking civilians. Was this the duty room in Bill's day, too? There's a large map of Satara District on one wall, subdivided in different colours. Everything's in Marathi, so I can't read it; but I try to guess which are the villages which Shinde and Modak mention.

A pretty woman constable enters, and motions me to accompany her. How many times did Bill stride up these very stairs? On the first floor, she knocks at a door and opens it to reveal a sleek-skinned, smiley man of about forty, with film-star teeth. He's holding Modak's card.

'Deputy Superintendent Kulkarni,' my escort announces, saluting him crisply.

He stands up to shake hands, before motioning me to a chrome chair at his imposing desk. I look at the name boards. They're in English, and list every DSP since the station opened. Some of the names are familiar: de Vere Moss, principal of the PTS when Bill was there, had charge earlier in the 1930s, following Freddie O'Gorman, Modak's favourite inspector-general. Later come C.M. Yates, about whom *Sentinel*'s so rude, and Modak's bête noire, James Hobson. After 1945, all the names are Indian; they include Dhun's husband, K.J. Nanavatty. But here's a surprise: there was an Indian in charge as early as 1929. Perhaps the IP was more progressive than Modak's given it credit for.

'DSP Mutilal's out of station just now. But he's given instructions about your visit. So your father worked here?'

I point to the board. 'Special additional superintendent under Hobson.'

Kulkarni reaches across the desk and shakes my hand again. 'Privileged to meet you.' He nods emphatically. 'Tea?' My host shouts for an attendant and settles back in his seat, asking about Bill's career. When I mention the Parallel Government, he laughs, as if it's a great joke. There's a knock at the door and another officer enters, swagger stick under one arm. Kulkarni rises and salutes.

'Mr Sanjay Shinde. He's the ASP these days.'

Shinde's a slimmer and smarter version of Kulkarni, with an equally luxuriant moustache. He beckons me to a sofa beneath the name boards, where he examines my visiting card while I wonder anxiously whether he's related to Bill's chief accuser.

'So you are professor of English at the London University?'

I nod.

'I studied literature, too. You like *Crime and Punishment*? My favourite work of all time.'

We discuss books. Shinde's very well read, and his English is excellent; this he attributes to a lengthy spell in Kosovo as part of the UN peacekeeping force.

'First time I understood the position of Muslims in Europe,' he comments. 'Made me see their situation here in a new light.'

Before I can ask him to explain further, he inquires about my trip.

'This would have been your father's office,' Shinde declares, when I've repeated my story. 'Unless he was given Mr Modak's when he arrived?'

If so, I'm sure Bill's colleague would have mentioned this additional irritant. I look round hungrily, trying to work out what's survived from the 1940s. The noisy ceiling fan, perhaps, spinning lopsidedly? And was this teak desk where Bill mapped his operations? I ask what problems today's police face.

'Quieter than your father's time,' Kulkarni laughs, flashing his teeth.

'When you have democracy, it's never quiet,' Shinde adds. 'When you don't have democracy, it's never quiet. Same as your father's time, there are always agitators waiting in the wings. We're worried about reprisals for the attacks in Mumbai.'

'Are there many Muslims here?'

'Not as many as before,' Shinde says. 'Too many politicians make political capital out of them. And out of incitement against Hindus from other parts of India. They make a mockery of the Constitution.'

'Money's short, as well,' Kulkarni complains. 'We don't have the resources to do our job properly.'

Shinde nods. 'Especially vehicles. Spares always a problem. Would you like to look around?' he suddenly asks, as if this is why he's come by.

I'm taken back downstairs and through an arch to the rear of the building. We pass a cabinet of tarnished sports cups and another filled with ancient weapons, muskets and crude-looking pistols.

'Home-made, seized from *goondas* over the years,' Shinde explains.

Did the Parallel Government rely on such crude equipment? Out back are perhaps two acres of crushed murram. A squadron of women recruits in white tops and khaki trousers wheels about to an instructor's bark. Beyond, rows of tiny cottages slope away, like the game scouts' lines I remember from Tanganyika.

'Other ranks' housing,' Kulkarni confirms.

I take the cue. 'Are there any old constables around still from my father's time?'

Shinde ponders a moment. 'We don't have lists. The pension people in Mumbai will know.' Catching my look of disappointment, he smiles. 'I'll ask. How long are you staying?'

'It depends. I'm waiting to hear from a friend.'

He nods.

'Two names I have from that time are Gaikwad and Pisal. I'd be particularly interested to track them down.'

Kulkarni jots the names in his notebook. Next I ask about the confidential weekly reports. Both men again look doubtful but promise to inquire.

'Mr Modak also said that every main police station keeps Part IV records. Could I possibly see the ones from that time?'

Shinde's eyes light up. 'You mean our annual reports?

Summaries of trends? You'll have to ask when Mr Mutilal gets back tomorrow.'

I comment on the military feel of the station. Kulkarni explains that the old Bombay Police was modelled on the nineteenth-century Irish constabulary, and the modern force has retained its khaki uniform. It seems an ominous precedent.

We're now outside a long hangar-like building to one side of the parade ground, with a shallow-pitched roof of corrugated iron. The sky above's a flawless blue. Shrieking harlequin parakeets tumble through the flame trees behind, scattering orange blossom on the ground. An enormous grey lizard watches warily from its rock while a mongoose scuttles past. Rikki-Tikki-Tavi. I remember arriving in Durham for undergraduate studies, how alien it seemed after the southern England I'd slowly grown used to. What must Bill have felt, a wide-eyed nineteen-year-old, coming to such a wildly different place?

Army liason, 1945 – Bill front row, fifth from left

'Will you say something to the men?' Shinde suddenly asks. I'm startled. 'Which men?'

'We have a cadre of constables passing out this week. A few words, please, Professor, before their class?'

I have no idea what to say. Still, it seems impolite to decline. Inside, there are perhaps 150 male recruits, seated at desks like exam candidates. They rise as one as we take our places, and Shinde addresses them in Marathi. He taps his swagger stick in one palm, turning occasionally to gesture towards me, while I try to imagine Bill here, giving his troops a pep talk before a raid. When the introduction finishes, the audience breaks into enthusiastic clapping, seemingly delighted at this unexpected diversion. I briefly explain my family connection with the Satara force and wish them luck in their future careers. I receive more thunderous applause, and the probationers all rise again as we exit. I'm bemused and flattered in equal measure.

Once we've inspected the armoury, where Shinde explains the different training programmes of the ordinary and armed constabulary, which Bill had charge of, we return to Kulkarni's office. Two men in civilian clothes are waiting outside, one fiddling with his camera.

'We hope you don't mind,' Shinde smiles, 'this is a reporter from *Young India*.'

Wasn't that Gandhi's newspaper? I tell my story once again while the correspondent makes notes. His teeth protrude slightly, making his mouth look swollen. Then I sit between Shinde and Kulkarni for photos. That accomplished, the reporter gives me his card and invites me to get in touch if he can be of help. I explain I'm after a constable of the time and he nods genially, promising to ask his contacts. My hosts offer more tea, which I decline. I've taken enough of their time. Besides, I'm dog-tired from all the emotion of Pune.

'It's been a long day. But I'd like to come again tomorrow and take some photos myself.'

Shinde smiles. 'Of course. Your transport awaits.'

Once again, I'm thrown. 'Transport?'

Kulkarni laughs. 'Mr Mutilal's orders. You are our VIP guest.'

This is unbelievable. 'But aren't you short of vehicles?'

Shinde shrugs. 'It's yours as long as you're in Satara.'

Sure enough, here's a police 4×4 outside the main entrance, with uniformed driver. It's painted black and white, strips of yellow and red lights across the roof and the gold Maharashtra Police logo on the front doors.

'And a constable will be posted outside the door of your hotel room.'

Kulkarni must be joking. 'That's too much,' I protest, when I see he isn't.

'Same for every VIP.'

Thoroughly embarrassed, I try to joke my way out of it. 'But everyone at the hotel will think I'm a criminal.'

Shinde laughs, before turning to Kulkarni. They each take out a visiting card. 'Ring either of us whenever you need the car. Someone will be available as your guide.'

'I can't thank you enough. It's so wonderful to be here.'

Head spinning, I get in the vehicle and am driven back to the hotel. I'm relieved that it's just the driver and me. Perhaps they've forgotten about the room guard. Modak's certainly pulled out all the stops; despite my reservations about him, I'm intensely grateful. What kind of reception would an Indian receive, if he came to a police station in England and said his father had worked there during the war and could he look at the files? Probably be banged up. However, there's no chance to make sense of my astonishing welcome. A squat man in jacket and tie is waiting in reception, thinning hair, very fair skin and pouchy, grey-blue eyes.

'Farrokh Cooper,' he announces, hand outstretched. 'Room alright?'

'Really kind of you to organise it.'

'Erna's a very old friend. She told me about your father. My parents must have known him. Now I thought we might go to the Club for a drink.' There's no 'might' in his tone. 'All the British belonged before Independence.'

There's icy air-con in Farrokh's luxury saloon, and *Turandot* blares from the speakers.

'What school did you go to?' he suddenly asks as we swing past the Eiffel Tower. 'I was at Bryanston.'

'Enjoy it?'

'Very much. Often drop in when I'm in the UK on business. We have designers in Shoreham-on-Sea. We're one of the biggest industries in Maharashtra. Automotive products mainly. Sell all over the world.'

Soon we're curving down a long drive shaded by gigantic jacarandas and Farrokh pulls up in front of a long, low building with lancet windows which reminds me of a church. According to Kipling, such places were the social cement which held the Raj together. The foundation stone proclaims the Club was opened by a Mrs Piers, wife of the collector, in 1895. My heart's racing as we sign in at the desk. Bill must have spent a lot of his leisure time here, when he wasn't at the Modaks' or the homes of other officials.

'It was closed for forty years, but we're slowly redoing it. There's a swimming pool now. Otherwise it's pretty much as always.'

The first room Farrokh shows me has a beautiful wooden floor, with faded lines painted on the parquet.

'This is the badminton room, which doubled up as the ballroom in the old days.'

So here's where Modak and Bill thrashed a shuttlecock across the net after frustrating days chasing the Parallel Government. It looks gloomy in the gathering dusk, bare bulbs strung along the apex of the roof.

'What's that?' I ask, pointing to a large-scale model of a fort in a glass case.

'Pratapgad,' Farrokh responds, 'one of Shivaji's most important strongholds. He built them all over the district. It's where he killed the Mughal general Afzal Khan. Disembowelled him with a clasp in the form of a tiger's claw,' he adds with relish.

'Look here,' he beckons, leading me into a billiard room with a full-size table; he whips the cover back to reveal immaculate forest-green baize. On the walls hang evocative cartoons from British times. 'Snookered!' one proclaims, showing a Bertie Wooster type in Rupert Bear trousers leaning ruefully on his cue as a fat old man ushers a pretty girl out of the room before him. A water-stained poster in a battered frame explains the rules of 'Russian Pool'. Through an arch is the card room, darkly varnished chairs grouped in fours round felt-topped tables. I can almost hear clipped voices calling for someone to make up a hand of whist or rummy.

'Today's members are more interested in the gym.'

'How many are you?'

'Thirty or so. Not enough of the right kind of people nowadays.'

The bar's been redone with formica. To one side's a shelf of dimpled tankards, opaque with age. I wonder if Bill brought his with him to Tanganyika. To my surprise, no bottles are displayed.

'One of the conditions of our alcohol permit, strangely enough,' Farrokh explains.

We sit outside in the flagstoned courtyard while the waiter prepares our drinks. A smell of boiling lentils wafts from the kitchen. As Farrokh barks into his mobile, I examine a shallow trough jewelled with water lilies, over which a dragonfly hovers on wings of azure gauze. The temperature's perfect now the sun is setting.

'Ah, here they are,' Farrokh announces as two men, well into their sixties, come through the bar. 'Gujur, my press secretary and Mr–, head of personnel.' I don't catch the name.

Farrokh waves me impatiently to stay seated and they take their places deferentially where he points.

'Now we're all assembled,' Farrokh says, once he's ordered them soft drinks, 'tell us about yourself and why you're here.'

For the third time today, I tell my story. My host looks absent-minded and the personnel man struggles to keep up. But Gujur's clearly interested. The problem is that I can barely understand his English. I think he's talking about the Parallel Government.

'Villains,' Farrokh interrupts him acidly. 'The amount of trouble they caused us.'

'What do you mean?' I ask.

'Always agitating our workers to go on strike, sabotage the war effort. What did they expect them to eat if they downed tools? There was endless intimidation. The police were always coming out. Probably your father did, too. After the war, we learned they had a cell in the workforce.'

Gujur says nothing during the tirade, but the personnel man seconds his employer with nods and grunts.

'I also work for G-TV,' I understand Gujur to be saying.

'He'd like you to do an interview tomorrow morning.' Farrokh makes it sound like a fait accompli. 'Don't worry, he'll bring along someone to interpret,' he adds ungraciously.

I hope Gujur doesn't register the rudeness. The personnel man then tells some halting stories about the Parallel Government, repeating the one Modak told about its adherents shoeing their victims like donkeys.

'When Nana Patil had his leg amputated later in life,' Farrokh butts in again, 'it was poetic justice. The police were too soft, that's why they didn't crack them. They should have used the same methods as the Patri Sarkar.'

Farrokh's manner and his peremptory assertions jar. But I resist the temptation to suggest that, as Modak asserts in his books, the police did do things which weren't entirely dissimilar. 'Is Cooper a Parsi name?' I inquire instead.

He chuckles. 'No. We Parsis often took the names of our trades. Paymaster, Engineer and so forth. My great-grandfather made barrels in Bombay.'

As Farrokh drives me back to the hotel, I ask how he feels about the Raj now. I guess he might just be old enough to remember it. He turns down *Turandot* for a moment.

'You know the biggest mistake the British made? Not allowing us to develop a motor industry. My father suggested it, but they didn't fancy the competition. You see? They had a habit of alienating even those who were most pro them. And now we're buying up what's left of your car firms, Jaguar and Land Rover,' he smirks, exhaling whisky over me. 'Not allowing us to industrialise was a serious error of judgement, though no doubt people like Gandhi would have disagreed.'

But what about Nehru's five-year plans and the great leaps forward, I want to ask; surely India didn't awake only when globalisation and deregulation arrived?

It's still only eight o'clock when he drops me, and after dinner I wonder what to do for the evening. Back in my room I turn on the television to check out G-TV. I can't find it, but the bombing of Gaza is apparently continuing relentlessly, to silence from Western governments, according to the reporter. There's a problem with my reception and I get only spectral black and white. Perhaps that's why the footage reminds me of the assault on the Warsaw Ghetto. A youth stalks a broken-up pavement, armed with a slingshot, scanning the skies. Gaunt, cowled women crouch in the ruins of buildings, small children huddling in their skirts like chicks, choked in the drifting smoke of intermittent fires. A howling man accompanies an ambulance crew wheeling a girl burnt by white phosphorus, which has apparently bored through to the bone. Who are the terrorists, who the terrorised, here?

I switch off the TV in disgust and pick up *Sentinel*. The account of Modak's career after Satara offers little relief, however. I look first for references to Rebeiro. The first comes while Modak was police chief in Pune in the 1950s, when a communalist riot erupted. Judging by the author's tediously detailed justification of his actions, particularly his apparent sudden disappearance during the trouble, as well as acid comments about Rebeiro's own role in events, I guess this was the occasion for the latter's charges against his superior. There are several further bitter passages about his subordinate, in which the accusations of cowardice and incompetence are repaid with interest. The rancorous point-scoring casts tantalising new light on *Sentinel*'s caustic representations of Bill.

More interesting still, especially in relation to the Mumbai attacks and what I've just seen on TV, is Modak's account of his role as police chief in Kashmir in the 1960s. Once again, much of this is a knotted narrative of accusation and rebuttal. In particular the author's at pains to deny that he contributed in any way to the vortex of civil disobedience and repression into which Kashmir descended during his time in charge. Instead, Modak shifts the blame onto politicians, whose interference prevents him doing his job effectively. Shades of his denunciations of Hobson during the PG disturbances. He re-emerges from this part of the text as an injured idealist, the unwitting dupe of dark forces in Delhi determined to impose India's will on Kashmir's Muslim majority. Summary executions, rape, ethnic cleansing to make way for the transfer of Hindu settlers, looting, detention without trial – all appear to have been staple behaviour among the Indian police and army units brought in to deal with the unrest. It makes the British repression in Satara seem like the proverbial picnic. Rajeev's denials notwithstanding, I wonder again how far this wretched history of occupation created a thirst for revenge among the Mumbai attackers, or at least their handlers. But it doesn't take me a great deal further in understanding Modak's take on Bill.

Putting the book down, I consider my options. Much depends on when Rajeev gets back to me about Poel and whether my new friends at the police station here can turn up the documents and people I'm after. But then the thought occurs to me in a blinding flash. Since DSP Mutilal's put the car at my disposal ... My heart starts pounding. Getting out my file, I pore over the notes from Shinde which I managed to salvage before fleeing the SIB archives. I cross-reference them with Modak's texts. Amongst the villages where Shinde alleges outrages involving Bill allegedly took place, Kumtha's the only one mentioned by Modak. At first I think it's the best place to ask to be taken. But according to *No Place for Crime*, 'only' a single individual was abused there and the chances that he'll still be alive are probably remote. At Chafal, I remember, scores of people claimed to have been victimised. Here it is on the map. A bit far from Satara, perhaps seventy kilometres. Would the police let me have the 4×4 for a whole afternoon? The enigmatic Modak's words echo through my mind: 'Only those who were there really know what happened.' Is this the place to test Shinde's account?

But I'm soon overtaken by uncertainty. How will I react if the villagers confirm Shinde's evidence? I can't even be sure they'll want to meet the son of their former persecutor, if that's what Bill was. Yet having come this far, I can't let nerves get in the way of my investigations. Too much rides on them. As I thrash over the possibilities, the phone jangles. I assume it's Rajeev. Perhaps he's going to summon me back to Mumbai.

'Glad I caught you,' a thin voice says, 'it's Srinivas Dongare. I'm downstairs.'

It takes me a moment to recollect that he's the journalist from *Young India*. Has he found me an old constable?

'There's someone who wants to meet you. He's been in Satara for the week-end, but he's heading back to work in Mumbai first thing tomorrow. I bumped into his son this afternoon.'

'Who's that?'

'His name's D.Y. Patil. A lawyer. He knows a lot about the 1940s. We should go at once if you're free. He needs to make an early start.'

As with Kiron and Dhun Nanavatty, one thing's leading to another here.

'My wife and children,' he explains, when I reach the lobby, turning to a pale-skinned, delicate-featured woman and two young daughters who look like they're in Sunday best. 'They wanted to meet you.'

Despite this assurance, all three quickly retreat a step or two behind the paterfamilias. Srinivas leads the way to a battered Maruti saloon. His womenfolk somehow cram into the back beside a couple of large aluminium camera cases. It's cramped in front, too, and the shock absorbers feel worn out. But it's not far to D.Y.'s and I'm too intrigued to care. Go with the flow, I remember Anders saying. Last night already seems to belong to another life. Time has taken on such strange properties since I arrived in India. My mind and body feel overloaded, stretched to breaking point.

D.Y. lives further along the same road as the Satara Club. When we pull up in front of a two-storey villa, a young man's on the veranda. Introducing himself as D.Y.'s son, he shows us into an elegant drawing room. It's much more Indian than Dhun's or the Modaks', with what look like Rajput paintings on the wall, a lovely inlaid gateleg table and chocolate raw silk curtains. One wall's lined with bookcases containing uniform runs of forbidding legal-looking tomes in dark leather bindings.

'Glad you could come,' D.Y. smiles as he extends a hand. 'So you're the son of the famous Gilbert? That period's long been my hobby.'

He's a big, strong-looking man in his fifties with dark patches under his eyes and a piercingly intelligent expression. His son looks strikingly similar, the same ready smile and powerful frame.

Over soft drinks, D.Y. and I talk while everyone else listens respectfully, as if this is a masterclass. My host states that he's a Marxist and proud of the Parallel Government. Like Shinde, he asserts they were nationalists, not thugs, and turned to violence only as a last resort. When I repeat the stories I heard at the Club about the shoeing of suspected collaborators and the trouble at the Cooper works, his face clouds.

'The Coopers were loyalists. Farrokh's grandfather was knighted by the British. But they were pragmatists, too. They must have known about the Prati Sarkar cell.' He uses the respectful name. 'But the Coopers didn't denounce them. They knew the workers would have walked out. It suited both sides. The Coopers carried on making profits, and the nationalists carried on smuggling out parts to make weapons. They couldn't have done so if there'd been a general strike.'

My mind boggles. Right under his nose, the biggest factory in Satara was supplying Bill's opponents. D.Y. then tells me about the movement's founders. After their arrest, the initiative apparently passed to a second, more radical cadre of dissidents.

'At least two of that group are still alive who would have known your father. G.D. Lad, the field marshal. And Naganath Nayakwadi, who carried out some of the most daring operations. One bank robbery made him famous throughout India. They both had narrow escapes from Gilbert.'

I can hardly believe my ears. 'Do you think they'd meet me?' I stutter hopefully.

D.Y. looks discomfited. 'To be honest, I don't know.' He stands up and goes to a bookshelf, returning with a book in Devanagari script. Flicking through it, he finds the page. 'Gilbert was a *dushtoman* officer.'

What?

'Villainous,' D.Y.'s son interjects, seeing his father struggle for the right word. 'Also cunning.'

I feel uncomfortable, but this isn't the time or place to launch into a defence of Bill.

'Where do they live?'

D.Y. shrugs. 'Kolhapur way. There are some historians down there who've worked on the movement. They'll know.'

'Abasaheb Shinde and Arun Bhosle?'

He looks surprised. 'You know them?'

'Not personally. But I've been thinking of going down to Kolhapur to introduce myself.' It's suddenly much more tempting. 'Perhaps they could set up a meeting?'

'Well, it may be worth a try. But if you do go see Lad and Naganath, don't turn up in a police car,' he smiles.

'I told him about your escort,' Srinivas explains.

'Naganath says we just replaced the white sahibs with brown ones. And the police still do the same dirty work they always did.'

'Do they?'

D.Y. nods sorrowfully. Still, the police have been so generous to me, especially here in Satara, that it seems churlish not to acknowledge it.

'Of course,' my host says with a short laugh when I've finished praising Kulkarni and Shinde, 'you're a foreigner and a professor. And there's still an aura about the old IP.'

'Would you be able to give me the details of that book you quoted from?'

'It's in Marathi. I have three others which also talk about Gilbert.'

That's seven books I've discovered, in less than three weeks, which feature Bill. I wonder what he'd have made of his posthumous celebrity.

'When we get a moment, I'll get my son to translate the relevant passages. Can you leave your email?'

I nod gratefully, giving him my visiting card.

Mindful of D.Y.'s early start, I'm about to get up when the lawyer leans across the arm of his chair. 'You know, the British behaved very strangely at times. Almost as if their heart wasn't in the battle.'

'What do you mean?'

'Let me show you.' He says something to his son who goes to the bookshelves, returning with an old atlas and a map. D.Y. lays the two side by side.

'You see modern Maharashtra? Now look how Bombay Province was in the 1940s.'

The boundaries are quite different. Along the south-eastern edge of the old British territory are a number of enclaves: Aundh, Miraj and Sangli.

'Princely states. Technically independent, albeit under the eye of a British Resident. See how close they are to Satara? Well, a fugitive just had to get to one of these territories and he could cock a snook at the British.'

'What?'

'Yes. Unless it was in hot pursuit, and strict rules governed such chases, your father and his colleagues would have to get the permission of the princely administration. Of course, it was rarely refused, but by the time all the paperwork had been completed, the suspect would have slipped into the next state. And so it went on, round and round from one place to the next.'

'That's ludicrous. Why?'

'The British wanted to use the Rajahs as a counterweight to Congress. So the government wouldn't allow anything to compromise their prestige.' He shakes his head, chuckling. 'Yet they still expected their police to crack the Prati Sarkar!'

I now remember *Sentinel* complaining about the obstructiveness of certain princely states. What did Bill make of all this?

'Aundh in particular actively sympathised with the rebels. The prince was educated at Oxford before the war, where he became a communist. If you want to understand why the British had limited success against the underground, you need to understand factors like that.'

I nod. But I'm busy calculating the chances of meeting a couple of Bill's former antagonists. 'Do they speak English, those two leaders of the Parallel Government?'

'Lad, some. He was at the Ayurvedic medicine college in Pune when the war began. Naganath very little. You'd need an interpreter.'

I presume it won't be too hard to find one. 'You know, my father spent eighteen months hunting them without success and it looks like I might catch up with them in a day or two.'

My host explodes into laughter. 'Tell that to Naganath if you get to see him. He'll like that.'

Despite my exhaustion, it's going to be hard to sleep. What wouldn't I give to meet the very men that Bill pursued? I'm beginning to hope Rajeev doesn't ring.

CHAPTER 9

Against the Tide

At breakfast, the waiter hands me *Young India*. Bizarre to see myself on the front page, looking earnest, sandwiched between Shinde and Kulkarni. I'd expected perhaps an inch buried deep inside. Soon I notice Gujur in reception, accompanied by Srinivas.

'Mr Cooper said eight o'clock,' the latter informs me, offering his hand with a smile.

I don't remember the arrangement being so precise. Farrokh's even booked the conference room.

'It'll go out this evening,' Srinivas explains as I'm fitted up with a mike. 'I'll also ask if any old policemen who see it can get in touch.'

'Thanks, Srinivas. And also for fixing up last night. I'm really grateful.'

After a couple of trial takes, the interview begins. Gujur and I find it hard to understand each other, and I'm glad to have Srinivas on hand. I realise I'm beginning to get bored with telling my story. After an hour, the cameraman declares himself satisfied and leaves. Gujur and Srinivas, however, linger.

'How many people are likely to watch?'

'Could be a million,' Srinivas laughs.

He says he's a media graduate, and designs websites in addition to the freelance journalism which provides the bulk of his income.

'Mr Gujur wants me to tell you a bit about Satara. Give you some context for your researches.'

Farrokh's colleague grins expansively as he palms back lank, greasy hair, evidently more comfortable out of his employer's shadow.

'Satara means "Seven Hills" in Marathi. After Shivaji conquered the city in 1663, it became the centre of his empire. From here he drove the Mughals north.'

'And freed the land?'

'For a while. After his death, the Mughals returned, until they were finally forced out again in 1706. When the British encroached, there were several wars, the third of which they won decisively. They ruled through Shivaji's descendants until 1839 when they deposed Rajah Pratapsinh because he was alleged to be plotting against them. They installed his brother Shahaji in his place. When Shahaji died in 1848, he had no male heir, so the British simply annexed the territory.'

Gujur looks aggrieved. Little wonder. The doctrine of 'lapse', whereby the British refused to recognise adopted male heirs in princely states, was perhaps the most cynical device used to extend British dominion in India, and a principal cause of the 'Mutiny'. I ask if it spread to Satara in 1857–8.

'No. Pratapsinh was organising an uprising, but it was discovered a week before due time. They exiled him and his immediate family to Karachi.'

'Did the Parallel Government look back to this tradition of resistance?'

Gujur smiles. 'Of course. Shivaji invented the idea of *Hindavi swaraja*, Indian self-rule, three hundred years before Gandhi. He was also a pioneer of guerrilla warfare and knew how to tie down much larger conventional forces. However, the PG were modernisers. They didn't want the feudal princes to get back their old powers.'

'Isn't there still a Rajah here?'

'The family occupies the palaces, but they lost their privileges in the 1970s and don't have real influence.'

The intercom buzzes as my history lesson winds down. It's

Kulkarni, to say that DSP Mutilal's expected shortly and I should come in to ask about the reports.

I leave at once for the police station. Kulkarni's in his office. To my surprise, he's in a pink shirt, jeans and sandals, and reeks of cologne.

'May I offer you one?'

He thrusts a tray of luminous, soapy-looking sweets towards me with his dazzling smile. They look like they might dissolve even his tooth enamel.

'To celebrate,' he explains. 'I'm being promoted to ASP with immediate effect. Transfer to Pune in the New Year.'

I congratulate him and take a candy. It's sickly sweet, but spiced as well.

'DSP will be here in one minute only.'

I've got used to the elasticity of Indian minutes, and pass the time taking photos of the station. Kulkarni doesn't seem to mind where I poke my nose. I end up on the roof, amongst a thicket of antennae, facing Shivaji's fort. It's like a stage set in the crystal light. On the other side of the road, I suddenly realise, is a prison. Inmates have gathered at a barred window, chaffing a detail of convicts repairing the wall below. It's grim and forbidding, despite the prisoners' apparent good humour. I wonder uneasily how many people Bill sent there. As I watch, a white saloon with flashing roof lights approaches from the direction of town.

By the time I get downstairs, constables are snapping salutes one after the other along the first-floor veranda. DSP Mutilal looks roughly the same age as me, but he's rather short, with cowlicks over his bald patches, a wart beside one eye and a paunch which strains the buttons on his uniform. He expresses delight I've come and shows me into his office. It's much like Kulkarni's, but with several different-coloured phones and intercoms arranged across an even more imposing desk. Incense perfumes the room, thin smoke curling from a brass container on his desk towards a small, plastic-garlanded figurine of Ganesh occupying one corner. Once I've rehearsed my story yet again, I ask about the station archives. Mutilal buzzes an intercom. Soon an attendant appears, clinking a tray of tea glasses, followed by an elderly man in civilian clothes.

'My steno, Mr Walawalkar. Tell him what you need.'

Not a relative of the miscreant sub-inspector whom Bill got sacked? Or the horrid man in SIB? The archivist listens earnestly and mutters something to Mutilal before disappearing.

'He says we should be able to find the Part IVs fairly quickly. The weekly confidentials may take time. Could you come again tomorrow?'

We chat some more before Mutilal's mobile rings. He sits up straighter. 'Yes, sir,' he concludes the brief conversation, before standing up.

'That was the commissioner. We're preparing for an inspection. If you'll excuse me, there's so much to organise.'

I get up, too. 'I'm extremely grateful. Especially for the vehicle.'

'The least we could do, dear Professor.'

I take a deep breath. 'Would you mind if I took it as far as Chafal? I was thinking of going tomorrow.'

Mutilal's eyes light up. 'Ah, you want to visit the famous Mahadeo temple?'

I nod, relieved his prompt has made it so easy. The DSP beams approvingly.

'One of the most important *mandirs* in all of Maharashtra.'

Back in Kulkarni's office, Shinde's arrived, looking extra smart today, silver braiding twisted through the epaulettes of his field-grey shirt.

'Have to supervise the welcome for the commissioner,' he explains, 'there's a practice parade at twelve. Now I have some good news for you. We managed to contact a veteran constable called Dhoni. He's not very well, so he can't come in person. He lives a couple of hours north.'

Brilliant. The morning's getting better by the minute. 'Could I drop by in the car, maybe?'

Shinde shakes his head with a wry grin. 'His wife says he's got diarrhoea, so it might be awkward. They're expecting us to phone his son's shop. You ask the questions and I'll relay them.'

It takes time to get through various intermediaries before Dhoni gets to the receiver.

'He says he's happy to speak to the son of Gilbert. He would have liked to come to see you.'

I'm in a lather of expectancy. 'In what capacity did he know my father?'

The answers emerge haltingly. Dhoni was promoted to the armed constabulary in 1944, the year Bill arrived. As a junior policeman, he never spoke with him at any length. But he remembers accompanying Bill on one raid. Usually, big anti-insurgency operations involved calling backup troops from something called the Special Reserve Police Battalion. But there wasn't time on this occasion. Bill and his squad were already in the field when they received a tip-off. Dhoni can't remember the name of the village for sure. It might have been Mangsoli. They all piled into the 'Woodie' for the occasion, some of them standing on the running boards, because their bus had broken down.

'So nothing's changed,' Shinde comments wryly.

On the outskirts of the village, they were confronted by a sizeable crowd which had just burned down the *chavadi* and its store of village records. Thoroughly worked up, the mob could have overwhelmed them with a concerted rush. For some reason Bill was without his Sten gun, and the six constables and two head constables had only breech-action .410 muskets, painfully slow to load.

I'm surprised at the feeble firepower. As children in Africa, we used .410s to shoot birds.

'What happened?' I ask.

Bill and his team apparently faced down the demonstrators and made them disperse. In the confusion, however, the ring-leaders vanished.

'Were there any reprisals?' I steel myself to ask.

Shinde looks uncomfortable, and for a moment Kulkarni's sparkling teeth retire.

'He says they left as soon as they'd had the fire put out and questioned witnesses.'

'What were his impressions of my father?'

Shinde starts laughing as he listens to the answer.

'What did he say?'

'Your father was very strict. Everyone knew what they had to do. He didn't tolerate slackness. You see?' he grins. 'Exactly as a senior officer should be.'

I next ask if the constable can remember any personal stories about Bill. He repeats that the gap in rank meant they had very little personal interaction.

'He used to eat the same food as the men when they were in the field. He loved chapattis made with *jowar*. No pickles were too hot for him.'

I smile.

'He's complaining about his bowels,' Shinde chuckles, one hand over the receiver, 'perhaps it's talking about pickles. Better let him go.'

I convey my thanks. I'm so relieved that Bill apparently didn't abuse villagers as a matter of course. But would the constable really have told me if he did?

'No word on Gaikwad or Pisal?'

They shake their heads. As we chat about preparations for the forthcoming *bandobast*, the attendant knocks.

'Mr Walawalkar has found something for you,' Kulkarni translates. 'The car will come after lunch to give you a tour.'

The steno's office, which doubles as the records room, is further along the veranda and offers a now-familiar mix of mouldy mailbags, broken-down chairs and ancient typewriters.

On the desk, however, are some promising-looking ledgers with marbled covers, tied with faded ribbon. Walawalkar motions me to sit beside him.

'I think this is what you're after.'

The Part IVs, covering the station's work from 1938 to 1947, are brisk and to the point. First I examine 'Subversive and Revolutionary Movements'. For the years 1938–41, successive DSPs record 'nil'. However, in April 1943, CMS Yates declares: 'I could write a book about what has gone on here since August 1942 [the month of Gandhi's arrest].' Was it that bad? He then corroborates what D.Y. Patil told me: 'Suffice to say that the movement would have been comparatively negligible in this district were it not for the activities of Congress persons in Aundh State, helped, behind the scenes, by the APPA Sahib, the Raja's son ... He is a menace. The Politicals at Kolhapur are carried away by his charm and think he can do no wrong.' What a ludicrous position the British put themselves in.

I'm also struck that neither Gandhi's release nor the war's end effected much improvement in the security of the District. In July 1945, just after Bill's departure from Satara, James Hobson complains: 'Saboteur activities still continue and at the moment it has taken the form of bastinadoing government servants and private individuals who have helped government ... everyone is too frightened to give information.' Modak's bête noire seconds Yates's complaints about the continuing malign influence of Aundh, but conjectures that the Rajah is increasingly frightened by the number of 'gangsters' lodged in his territory. The DSP's frustration is expressed forthrightly:

The trouble is particularly difficult to deal with and the police have had little or no success in dealing with it generally. Officers with the very highest reputation, when posted here, seem to get an attack of palsy, for none of them seem to assert themselves to effect arrests, though all will talk for hours about some indefinite action in the future. It is a disheartening business.

I'm jolted by these last remarks. Given that Hobson was his immediate superior, it's impossible to escape the inference that Bill was one such ineffectual 'officer with the very highest reputation'. This lends support to Modak's more jaundiced observations about his colleague. Perhaps I need to rethink my initial responses to *Sentinel*. Interestingly, Hobson also seconds aspects of his subordinate's ambivalence towards the Parallel Government: 'So far everyone … who has been dealt with [by the movement], in addition to being government servants, are privately all bad characters who have extorted money or goods from the public for their private use under colour of their office.' However, a later entry by Bill's old friend Keki Nanavatty provides a rather different perspective. In July 1947, weeks before Independence, he decries the amnesty offered to Parallel Government activists in April 1946: 'It was a mistake to have pardoned such heinous crimes as cutting off a man's limbs or murdering him because he helped the Govt.'

I then browse other entries, to investigate the effect of the political unrest on law and order more widely. From 1938 to 1941, Satara seems to have been as quiet as today. According to 'Labour Movements and Strikes', however, 1942 was clearly a turning point. Trouble flared at Cooper Engineering and other industrial works in the region during attempts to form a trade union. 'Ordinary' crime also increased exponentially. In April 1943, Yates comments that a Mang gang in Patan *taluka* (subdivision) has 'committed over seventy dacoities [armed robberies] in a few months … They thought, and rightly, that the Police were busy with the [unreadable] movement and that their vigilance was reduced.' Isn't Patan where Bill picked up the woman torture victim? The following year

Hobson observes that 'the ordinary criminals cash in on political crime to further their object.' Taken together, the records paint a picture of a district almost out of control at the time Bill arrived and continuing very restive after he left.

'Are you finding everything needful?' Walawalkar asks, when I gather up my notes.

'Very helpful.' I show him a couple of entries which refer to the confidential diaries kept by DSPs.

'We're still looking, sir Professor.'

I lunch in my hotel room, trying to make sense of what I've read. Why did Bill get the IP medal if, as Hobson seems to suggest, his work in Satara was ineffective? And why, indeed, did Hobson? Perhaps Modak was right to be bitter about the awards. Am I ever going to get to the bottom of things? My baffled speculations are interrupted by the receptionist, who calls up to say the vehicle's arrived. When I go downstairs, instead of Kulkarni, who I'd assumed would be my guide, a tall, languid man gets out. He's dressed in a blinding white shirt, black slacks and impenetrable sunglasses, which he doesn't remove before saluting.

'Sub-Inspector Phule, sir. To escort your outing.'

The road to Shivaji's fort overlooking Satara is steep and winding, flanked by thick bush. Unless some now hidden path existed, there's no way anyone could run up to it in half an hour, let alone five, or even fifteen, minutes. It takes us a good quarter of an hour in the groaning 4×4, the driver lurching against Phule as he negotiates the hairpin bends. Another myth about Bill is being debunked, somewhat to my chagrin. We labour to a stop at a massive gatehouse, its narrow aperture easily defended from the bulging towers either side. From here a precipitous footpath leads to the crest of the hill, where thick walls girdle the cliff-edge. They enclose several acres of coarse, parched grass, where there's nothing except for some ancient stone rainwater tanks, telecommunications masts and a windswept guardian's cottage, its tiny garden bursting with sweet-bright flowers. To the south, the drop's even more sheer, the distant dual carriageway I came on a frail thread through the landscape.

Phule keeps half a pace behind, swinging his binoculars, more like a bodyguard than a guide. I eventually tease out that he's from Pune, where his wife and two children live. He's been in the force for eight years and loves it, he insists lugubriously. In his wrap-around shades, he looks like an actor and I half hope he'll break into a Bollywood routine when we climb the ramparts. But he's more concerned about snakes than the panorama. It's eerie here, wind howling with the sorrows of the hosts who died attacking and defending the fort. I wonder how often Bill came up here. Would it have been safe to walk on his own, or did Gaikwad accompany him as Phule does me?

On the ramparts, he hands me the field glasses. Following his pointing finger, I can just make out another fort, Sajjanghad, on a distant peak. The same style and period as Ajinkya Tara, it's a place of pilgrimage now, Phule explains, containing a seventeenth-century temple and the mausoleum of Shivaji's guru, Samarth Ramdas. He describes the hold Ramdas had over Shivaji, and how the saint's commitment to the independence struggle of his time began one dark night when he bumped his head against something while walking a path through local woods.

'When he looked more closely, he realised it was the dangling feet of a villager hanged for refusing Mughal tax demands,' Phule concludes gloomily.

I wonder if Bill heard these stories, and understood how deep-rooted resistance to foreign rule was in this area's traditions. What did he know about the indigenous religions?

'Did Ramdas have family?' I ask. I can't remember whether Hindu priests are allowed to marry.

Phule nods. 'Yes, his descendants are still an important clan with extensive land holdings round Chafal.'

I almost squeal with surprise. The cue's irresistible. But my heart's beating so violently it takes me a while to broach the subject. Phule looks surprised.

'Why not a hill station like Mahabeleshwar? Especially now, in the strawberry season. Or Aundh museum? Many curiosities, from all over the world.'

'I'm told the temple of Mahadeo's very beautiful.'

Phule frowns. Perhaps he's been anticipating more exotic outings. But the die is cast. We agree to head for Chafal tomorrow afternoon.

~

Farrokh seems in a bad mood when he swings by the hotel soon after Phule drops me. He complains his wife and daughter have stayed on another day in Pune, to do some extra shopping for the little party they're having. Will I still be around next week-end?

'I may be going to Kolhapur.' I almost certainly will if I don't hear from Rajeev soon.

He looks surprised. 'Well, come and have a drink now.'

Farrokh's tone doesn't brook any hesitation. This time he takes me to his home. It's near D.Y.'s, with a watchman at the gate and a posse of guard dogs chained to stakes, which erupt aggressively as we approach. The house is large, hard to tell what period. The interior's modern Western, with an enormous open-plan kitchen boasting a humming chrome fridge and shiny worktops. Farrokh takes me upstairs into an equally spacious drawing room, cool and cream with plump armchairs and sofas. He puts on a CD, so loud I can barely hear him as he stoops over the drinks cabinet.

'Recognise this?'

I nod. Beethoven's *Pastoral*. Farrokh holds up two bottles, Ballantyne's and Courvoisier. I point to the whisky. We sip our drinks in silence for a while. But Farrokh's fidgety and soon gets up to change the music.

'How was Gujur's interview?'

'Fine. What time's it on? Couldn't find the channel in my room.'

Farrokh shrugs dismissively. 'Recognise this?' he asks again. This has the feel of an exam. '*Elvira Madigan.*'

'Please!' he retorts. 'Mozart's piano concerto number 21.'

Unsure of how to soothe him, I ask after his business. Farrokh immediately relaxes and is soon talking volubly about how well it's going, the new export markets he's negotiating.

'Not bad for a company that began in beer barrels, eh?' he concludes. 'Guess how much I'm worth?' Farrokh calculates rapidly on a pad, before waving it triumphantly. 'At today's exchange rate, 250 million sterling.'

I can't think what to say. Fortunately, my embarrassment's relieved by a volley of barks. Farrokh gets up and goes to the window.

'Come down and meet them.'

His wife and daughter are soon in the kitchen, stacking booty on a worktop as a servant struggles behind with the larger bags. Mrs Cooper's a fine-looking woman who greets me cursorily before excusing herself to go and shower. The daughter lingers a moment. She's in designer jeans and embroidered shirt, a cream silk scarf loose round her neck. I wonder if Farrokh's grooming his daughter to take over the business. She answers his questions about drinks for the party before disappearing down the same corridor as her mother. I get the feeling the house is zoned, women here, men upstairs. It sits oddly with Farrokh's aggressive modernity.

I'm keen to get off and see if I can catch Gujur's interview, but Farrokh seems reluctant to relinquish me.

'What did you do today?'

When I've explained, he leans forward. 'All this VIP nonsense,' he scowls. 'Why don't they concentrate resources on proper police work?' Perhaps sensing he's been abrasive, Farrokh suddenly smiles sharkily. 'Would you like to meet our Rajah? No doubt you'll be wanting to write a travelogue about the mysterious East when you get home?'

I'm beginning to dislike my host, but it's too good an offer to refuse. Aside from anything else, it might give me more insight into the fragile political alliances of Bill's time. 'Thanks, Farrokh. But not tomorrow afternoon, please.'

'Why not?'

I shrug. 'I'm going to meet some people.'

'I'll call in the morning to confirm.'

'Not before ten, please,' I say with a yawn. 'I need a lie-in. Haven't been sleeping well.'

'Tired? But you're on holiday.'

'Sort of,' I concede.

'I don't take holidays. Work ten hours a day, even now.'

Why, when he's already so rich? Surely there are other things in life. As if reading my thoughts, Farrokh grimaces.

'And I'll carry on till I drop.'

While he refreshes our drinks, I ask about Modak. 'Do you know why his father was sacked?'

Farrokh looks at me keenly. 'Why do you ask?'

'Just wondered, since he was a colleague of my father's.'

'No, I don't.'

Instinct tells me he's concealing something.

It's a relief to escape at last. Farrokh seems irritated again when I decline his offer of a lift. Am I letting the side down by walking? But he's downed a fair quantity of spirits and I find driving in India scary at the best of times. He accompanies me past his ravening hounds to the junction, which is bathed in patchy moonlight. I'm thankful for it, because the street lights are few and far between. I vaguely recognise some constellations. We can't be far off the latitude of Tanzania here. But I can't name them. Bill never got to finish teaching me the tropical stars. Despite the deep, rustling shadows of the trees, I feel perfectly safe. Indeed, so far on my trip I haven't experienced the slightest sense of personal danger. The Mumbai attacks seem a world away. Hard to imagine the atmosphere of fear there must have been while Bill was here. Reaching the main road, I pass an imposing colonial building, lights ablaze at the end of a long drive. The sentry salutes crisply, before confirming it's the district commissioner's, the setting in *No Place for Crime* for a glittering dinner which Kumar and 'Bill' attend in honour of the governor of Bombay. I imagine the 'Woodie' pulling up in real life and Bill checking his wing collar in the mirror as he's saluted through.

Ajinkya Tara fort's a brooding black mass in the moonlight. Built long before the British arrived, it continues to endure imperturbably. Difficult to understand how a handful of foreigners could have hoped to bind to them the civilisation this monument represents, especially once the people turned against them. Force, though no doubt the simpler option, was inevitably insufficient in the end. At best Bill would only have been sticking his finger in the dyke. Did he know that, or did blind obedience or an iron sense of duty drive him on regardless? Perhaps it was the confidence of youth. Or wilful obstinacy.

On the way back to camp, the boy's father is teaching him natural history. The rock hyrax, he says, with that wondering look which always makes his son's heart melt, is the closest zoological relative of the elephant. The boy laughs. Yes, the hyrax has a long snout, but how can such a tiny rat-like darting thing be connected to the majestic tembo? *His father asks why he's laughing, when it's scientific fact. Later he explains the difference between the social life of termites and of* siafu, *the fearsome soldier ants. At school, the pupils egg each other on when they arrive in their marching columns, innumerable miniature legionaries. It takes nerve to grab them behind their bulging heads. Soldier ants are agile and quick, and their pincers dig deep and painfully into flesh. Even when the bodies are pulled off, they don't release their jaws. The trick's to offer the hem of your shorts to bite on so you end up with a chain of totem heads clamped to the cloth. He with the most trophies wins; and the bleeding when the ants catch you makes being top head-hunter all the sweeter.*

But the boy finds the description of the termite colonies too far-fetched, and says so. How can a whole scaled-down sky-scraper, with millions of inhabitants, revolve around a single queen? His father's smile tightens.

'You'll see for yourself,' he says quietly.

When they've had afternoon tea, he calls some of the men. They're mystified when he tells them to fetch picks and strip off their shirts.

'Choose one,' he commands the boy.

Stretching across the plain, every hundred yards or so, are rock-hard, red steeples, many ten or twelve feet tall, scattered amongst occasional baobabs. The boy loves those colos-sal trees, their branches, disproportionately flimsy, more like crazy roots; the fruit's equally bizarre, leathery, distended gourds, like rugby balls swaying in the breeze. Kimwaga has told him that after Creation, the baobabs became too proud of the beautiful foliage they'd been given. In retribution, God pulled them all up and stuck them back upside down. The termite towers are equally intriguing. Every grain of sand's been ingested by its inhabitants, coated to fuse it to the next one with a mortar durable as concrete.

The boy feels ashamed at the trouble he's causing when he sees the game scouts take up position. They've had a long day, and have been looking forward to their boiled maize and stew. His father's taking it too far. But the boy's fascinated, too. He compromises by pointing to a smaller column, perhaps seven feet high, only ten or twelve round the base. The scouts look at one another disbelievingly. But they set to, singing rhyth-mically to encourage each other as they take turns with the picks. The iron spikes rise and fall, sometimes skidding off the surface, painfully chipping a way through the obstinate defences. The ground begins to swarm with indignant pale blobs. But they're no problem. Unlike siafu, termite soldiers are blind and sluggish. The boy's mesmerised by the muscular effort of the scouts, the bass grunts which accompany the singing, the clang of the downward strikes, the obdurate resistance of the earthworks. A little way in, the colour's darker red because the ants' cooling system keeps things a little moister. The interior's honeycombed, endless passages broken up by wider galleries, some filled with supplies – desiccated wings, a patch of fur, even a tiny bone, so white it's like a ghost's vertebra.

It takes more than an hour to demolish most of one side of the pillar. The shadows of the baobabs are creeping rapidly towards them and the first stars emerge, sparks struck off the blinding afternoon sun. As the scouts tire, the boy's father strips his own shirt off. He's hairier than his men and more heavily built. Soon the sweat's running down his back, too. The scouts now rest on their pick handles to watch. The earthwork turns chocolate as his father approaches the centre of the hive. Unlike the men, he neither sings nor grunts. Even when it's getting too dark to see properly, and the fruitbats have begun to zigzag overhead, he continues, breathing heavily, great shoulders labouring to heave the pick skywards. Finally a couple of scouts resume their work. If they don't join in, everyone's labour will be wasted. Bwana ndogo, little bwana must find his queen, one mutters, before it gets pitch black.

As the Milky Way forms in the satin night sky, delicate as dandelion fluff, seemingly close enough to touch, his father sends the men for a hurricane lamp. He says that anyone who wants to eat now can do so. Only Hamisi returns, with the light and filtered water. On safari, it's carried in crate after crate of old Gordon's Gin bottles with orange and cream labels. His father drinks off half of one, before hanging the lamp on a stick which he jams in the wrecked battlements of the termite colony. The head game scout stays to offer advice on where to dig next. The mosquitoes, about which the boy's father's usually so punctilious, have become persistent. Only when the boy complains softly that his ankles are being bitten, does the digging stop.

'Can't have you catching malaria,' he mutters. But he seems grateful for the interruption, his great chest pumping, shoulders slumped as he picks up his shirt and flicks it free of the writhing pus-balls.

'Damn queen,' he says. 'Probably took one wriggle further back every time the pick landed. I imagine she's skedaddled over the other half of the anthill. We should have started from both sides at once. But I wanted you to see it in cross-section.'

On the way back to the tents, the sky blazes with stars. There are so many, the heavens so deep and at the same time depthless, the boy feels vertigo. And a sudden aching sense of sadness. It's as if the contents of the tower have been tipped into the vast black bowl, the millions of tiny beings still pulsating with life but now separated forever.

They revisit the excavations the following morning. The colony's empty. Not a single ant remains amongst the rubble. The ruined interior has already dried to the same rusty colour as the outside. Wind whistles softly through the abandoned passages and galleries.

'Sorry, old chap,' the boy's father murmurs. 'We'll try another time.'

The boy, awestruck by the absent millions, can think of no adequate response.

CHAPTER 10

A History Play

When the phone jangles at seven a.m., I awake bewildered. Another disturbed night. I've been dreaming about Bill, but disorientation drives the details from my mind.

'Farrokh here. Rajah Udein's away, but his uncle's happy to show you round the old palace. Eleven-thirty?'

As usual, there's no negotiation. I'm put out. Farrokh could have left a message at reception. I told him I wanted to lie in, in order to gather my strength for the afternoon. But there's no question of going back to sleep. Today may prove the most significant of my whole trip. I wonder anxiously what Chafal will be like, whether we'll be able to find eyewitnesses. How will Sub-Inspector Phule respond when I tell him my true reasons for wanting to go there?

Breakfast over, I head to the police station in an auto-rickshaw. Lorries and vans are parked outside, disgorging constables, and Kulkarni's in full dress uniform, smile dulled, as if he's eaten too many sweets since yesterday.

'Preparations for the *bandobast* going well?'

'Very good. Just a few adjustments before the first parade,' Kulkarni says, beaming again as he takes me to the window Bill must have stared out of so often. A lone bugler's practising on the saluting podium, now covered with bunting.

'The DSP's up at the sports field,' Kulkarni explains. 'The intra-districts start today.'

'Aren't you taking part?'

He chuckles. 'Once upon a time.' He swerves his hips comically. 'By the way, congratulations on your TV appearance. My wife and I enjoyed it.'

'I never got to see it. Do you think it'll flush out any more veterans?'

Kulkarni shrugs. 'We were lucky to find even one after all this time.'

'Well, thanks for your efforts. I'd better pop down to Mr Walawalkar. Hope everything goes off well.'

The steno, however, has had no luck. 'We are finding weekly confidentials from the 1950s, but nothing from British times,' he apologises.

I mention Shinde's history of the Parallel Government. 'He definitely consulted them.'

'Yes, sir Professor. But did he see them in Satara?'

'I don't know.'

'Only other possibility here is district commissioner. I called. But he's out of station.'

'Until when?'

Walawalkar waggles his head ambiguously.

'Do you know where the Inspection bungalow is, where my father stayed?'

Again the deprecating head-waggle.

I'm deflated. This has been my best chance of tracking down Bill's reports outside of Mumbai. I've heard the voices of so many of those concerned during his posting here. Chafal villagers are quoted in the deposition to the Congress activist that Shinde based his accusations on, and I hope to speak with some of them again this afternoon. Former colleagues – Modak, Hobson and the old constable – have had their say. Now there's even a lead to two of the surviving underground leaders. Everyone has made themselves heard, it seems, except Bill himself – other than in tiny snippets in the SIB files. I'll simply have to go to Kolhapur. Bhosle and Shinde are my route not only to the nationalist leaders, but to the correct archives in Mumbai. It's my last hope if I want to hear Bill's voice. If I set aside two or three days for Kolhapur, there should still be opportunity to get back to Mumbai and search in the right places before heading back to England.

There's time to kill before my appointment at the old palace. Returning to Kulkarni to ask if Phule can pick me up after lunch, I decide to walk round Satara and check out some of the other places Bill might have frequented. Better than hanging around the hotel getting agitated about this afternoon. Along the road back into town, there's a colonial-era stone post office, doubly grand against the messy concrete buildings which have encroached on either side. Would Bill have come here to pick up his mail? Not far away are the original British garrison quarters from the 1850s, rows of neat, low barracks built of brick and tile. Some boys are playing cricket against the end wall of one block. They offer the ball and laugh when I shake my head.

Further on I stumble on the old British graveyard. Once inside, the stench is overpowering. It's evidently an open-air jakes now. Headstones poke through unkempt scrub like worn-down molars. A couple of raised tombs remain, plinths cracked, inscriptions too worn to read on the patches of marble no one's managed to chip away. From one corner comes the thin whine of puppies. The scene is as pathetic as it's depressing. The best efforts of the conquerors to preserve their memory, effaced by wind and sun and monsoon rains, and those who piss and shit on their monuments.

I catch an auto-rickshaw to the airy, green former British cantonment area. No one can identify the old Inspection bungalow. However, there's an intriguing church. St Thomas's is in bad repair. It's locked, but my driver rustles up a caretaker from the gaggle of huts which have mushroomed in the grounds. The interior's austere, despite the tinsel Christmas streamers rustling above the hardwood pews. The guardian says the congregation's healthy, though the Anglican Church of India faces increasing competition from evangelical Protestant sects funded from America. Hindu revivalism isn't an issue in Satara, he says. Brahminism has always been viewed with suspicion amongst Mahrattis, who don't accept their lowly position within orthodox Hinduism. Indeed, the Brahmins of Satara were slaughtered to avenge Gandhi's assassination by caste fundamentalists. Then the guardian tells me his daughter's studying public health in Wolverhampton.

'The Black Country,' he grins proudly. 'Do you know, she's doing missionary work in her spare time, amongst the British themselves.' I can't help enjoying the irony.

A brass wall-plaque catches my eye, the engraving just legible:

In Remembrance of Francis Charteris Davidson who joined the service in November 1914 from which time he served as Assistant Collector and Magistrate at Satara. In July 1916 he entered the Indian Reserve of Officers and in March 1917 was appointed to the South Waziristan Militia in which Corps he was serving as Captain and Adjutant when he was killed in action at Sarwakai in Waziristan on the 10th of May 1917 in the 27th year of his age. This tablet was erected by his brother officers of the Indian Civil Service.

South Waziristan. Part of the North-West Frontier Province where Aunt Pat claims Bill also served, an area now pock-marked by US drone strikes. Ninety years on, and the territory is once more an epicentre of rebelliousness. The impotence of Empire, then and now, in the face of a few thousand (hundred?) lightly armed but highly motivated opponents, strikes me forcibly.

Later, the auto-rickshaw drops me at the old palace. It's a substantial half-timbered building, set on a slope rising to the abrupt bluffs beneath Ajinkya Tara. Like St Thomas's, the fabric's in poor condition and it fronts onto a busy square, occupied by a market. The palace was doubtless once some distance from Satara but the town's grown voraciously up to it. An old man opens the door to my knock, and I'm unsure whether it's the Rajah's uncle or a retainer. He dons Gandhi spectacles to examine my visiting card before ushering me into a dark hall. The klaxon of a passing truck makes me jump. I think of Anders on his scooter. Soon the old man returns with someone in a loose white cheesecloth shirt and what look like pyjama bottoms, matching his bone-white hair and moustache. He's plump and has the rolling walk of someone with a bad hip. Rajah Udein's uncle introduces himself in a muffled voice that prevents me catching his name. He ushers me down the corridor into the most extraordinary room.

First glance reminds me of the Hall of Mirrors at Versailles: rows of beautiful, badly tarnished mirrors, diminishing in size as they rise twenty feet up on three sides of the cavernous space. At an angle between the ceiling and walls hang portraits, many of European officers and ladies whose costumes and hairstyles come straight from Jane Austen. Indian nobles in traditional dress are interspersed among them. At the far end, twice the size of its companion pieces, is the unmistakable likeness of Shivaji. The ceiling, painted gold, brown and blue in faded geometrical patterns, sprouts enormous, ornate chandeliers. They're barely visible through grimy plastic sheets, taped top and bottom, wrapping them like surreal mechanical fruit. In the smoky mirrors, they multiply uncannily. Neon tubes pulsate erratically, accompanying the wobbly fans. Judging by an ancient dais on a tattered pink carpet, I assume this was the durbar hall, where guests and petitioners to the Rajah would have waited. There's an odd, faint, marzipan smell.

The far half of the hall boasts several divans upholstered in tired purple velvet. Chinese vases with rampant dragons fill the alcoves beneath the windows facing the market, shutters closed, perhaps for privacy or to abate the constant noise of traffic. Faded gold brocade bolsters lie scattered on the floor. My host seems strangely nervous, smiling uncertainly at every compliment I pay as we wait for the inevitable tea to come. It's accompanied by a selection of sweets like those Kulkarni offered me yesterday. These taste like they're made from condensed milk. I ask about the history of the old palace. To my surprise, Rajah Udein's uncle is unsure when it was built. The words rumble from somewhere deep inside him.

'It was requisitioned by the British when they annexed Satara,' is about as much as he can muster. 'My family had to decamp to the new palace until they built the Residency. The district commissioner's, today.'

'What were relations like between your family and the British?'

My host shrugs. 'Good and bad, it changed.'

'What about in the last war?'

'We raised troops, of course. Some fought in North Africa.'

I tell him a little about Bill's time in Satara.

'A difficult period,' he mutters non-committally. 'Probably my father knew him.' He seems so uncomfortable, pinpricks of perspiration gathering on his brow, that I don't have the heart to press him.

'Have things changed very much for your family?'

'Oh yes.' He strokes his white moustache mournfully, easing one foot over his opposite thigh into a half-lotus posture. 'There's just me and my wife now. We only have ten retainers. In the old days ...' He sighs, before resuming. 'My grandfather used to tell me about the *dasara* processions every September, with squadrons of mounted cavalry and seventy elephants. There was a nine-day festival with readings of the sacred texts and actors and dancing girls and the British Resident gave twenty-five-gun salutes.'

I feel I'm tumbling into some Kipling fantasy. He was obsessed by the hereditary princely Indian rulers; in his fiction and non-fiction alike, they're a byword for conspicuous consumption, which he half deplores and is half dazzled by. They also epitomise the conflicts between tradition and modernity which continue to work themselves out in India today. Here, it feels as though tradition is making a feeble last stand.

I wonder if Bill came by and, if so, what he made of it all. Then I notice a series of what look like enamelised tableaux.

'May I?

Close up, they prove to depict different stages in Napoleon's coronation as Emperor, executed with exquisite precision of detail. What do they say about how Shivaji's descendants saw themselves? My host knows no more about them than about the provenance of the palace. He seems increasingly ill at ease, as if disappointing an important visitor. I don't know how to reassure him, so I'm relieved when he offers to show me outside.

We step into a soothing courtyard garden of tall palms, formally arranged in brick-faced emplacements. Udein's uncle explains that before they were planted, this was where the *dasara* celebrations began. To one side are several former elephant stalls and at the back a long building with rows of close-set bars.

'Satara jail,' he explains, 'until the British built the one opposite the police station. Their parade ground is where our royal horsemen used to train.'

There's room for hundreds in this prison – captives of war, I assume, rather than common criminals. We're almost directly beneath Ajinkya Tara here. The imperturbably enduring fort seems to upbraid the sorry decline of its former owners. I'm gripped by the same melancholy I felt in the graveyard. What am I mourning? Just last night D.Y. Patil reminded me how the British propped up the princes as a counterweight to the agitation for democracy and independence. But there's something painfully sad about this man who seems to remember so little of his family's illustrious past. Does he feel it's not worth hanging on to? The princes are clearly increasingly irrelevant in the booming new India powered by men like Farrokh, the relentless klaxons from the street implacable reminders of how times have changed.

~

Despite these efforts to distract myself, all morning I've had attacks of butterflies. Now I'm too on edge for lunch, and it's a relief when Phule shows up early. Today's 4×4 is smaller, a local version of the Suzuki jeep. He explains that with the police *bandobast*, yesterday's vehicle is needed for other VIPs, and he'll have to be back by six to pick someone up from the station. He'll be both chauffeur and interpreter today, since yesterday's driver is spoken for. After Farrokh's barb, I feel a stab of conscience about diverting police resources, but if Phule, too, disapproves, it's impossible to tell through the dark shades he never removes.

My discomfort increases on the stretch of back road we take to the highway. It's twisty and treacherous, with blind bends, round which goods vehicles and buses hurtle disconcertingly. If the Pune traffic was scary, Phule's driving threatens even worse. He thinks nothing of sneaking up on the shoulder of a lorry and accompanying it into a right-hand corner, jamming his foot on squealing brakes if something's coming. I hang onto the handle above my window, retreating ever deeper into the seat. This is hardly ideal preparation for the visit ahead.

'Can we maybe put the siren on when we overtake?' I plead, after another crazy manoeuvre.

'Not necessary, sir,' he pronounces smugly. 'No one will hit a police vehicle.'

Even if they can't see it?

'Don't worry about speed, sir, fifth gear's broken.'

Fourth grinds lugubriously, as if about to follow suit. It's a relief to get onto the dual carriageway. South of Satara the landscape continues lush and fresh, quite unlike how I've imagined the interior of India from the nineteenth-century Anglo-Indian authors I've written about, who forever bemoan the dreary dun *mofussil*. Captain Meadows Taylor, H.S. Cunningham, Flora Annie Steel, as well as Kipling – so much of their writing addresses the psychological, as well as physical, challenges of living in upcountry India in the suffocating hot season. Phule tells me the monsoon season has only finished a few weeks back, and it'll be a different story by April; come June, most of what I see will indeed be scorched brown. But thanks to an extensive series of dams in this part of Maharashtra, water is much less of a problem than it used to be. Either side of us stretches some of the most expensive agricultural land in India, he goes on, blessed with this new interstate highway and a local authority which prides itself on service to the people. I wonder if that's a legacy of the influence of the Parallel Government.

It's lovelier still once we turn onto the Chafal road, the shadows of wayside jacarandas stippling our windscreen, showers of their frail purple bloom settling behind the wipers. The bases of their trunks are painted with red and white stripes, Phule explains, to signify they're government property and stop people cutting them down. He points to bare hills in the distance as if in corroboration.

'All was teak forest in British times,' he comments neutrally.

At a fork in the road shaded by an enormous banyan, Phule slows, asking if I mind him having a cigarette.

'Smoking in car not allowed. Chafal temple just close.'

I'm grateful to get out and relieve myself one last time behind a cactus hedge, where cream butterflies flicker like falling snow over a puddle. It's idyllic, but my stomach's in knots. Bill must have come down this same road when he mounted his notorious raid. Perhaps he stopped under this very tree, gathering his men beneath its vast aerial roots to give final instructions. My notes from Shinde are burning a hole in my knapsack. What am I going to ask in Chafal? Maybe no one wants to revisit the past? Has anyone even survived from that era? Is this the moment to let Phule in on my plan? What if he refuses to proceed? Above all, what if the villagers react badly to my coming? I can't stop the questions churning.

Back at the vehicle, a group has gathered to chat with the sub-inspector. I can't understand where they've materialised from. On either side, sugar cane spreads depthless and impenetrable. Only an abandoned-looking thatched hut is visible, fifty yards ahead. It sits beneath another gnarled banyan, against which a water buffalo rubs itself, chewing placidly. A spindly-legged egret picks at its ear, dazzling white except for its yellow bill. Catching sight of me, a man pulls up on his bicycle, a preposterously large sheaf of canes strapped like spears across his pannier. He's very thin, with hennaed hair and pockmarked face, shirt smeared with oil. Phule presumably explains why we're here because, propping the frame of his machine against one hip, he performs a *namaste* for my benefit.

'Welcome to Chafal,' he says in an almost indecipherable accent, 'most welcome.'

The bystanders echo him good-naturedly. Despite myself, I'm blushing furiously.

Within minutes of resuming our journey, the main stupa of the Mahadeo temple comes into view, outlined starkly against the cloudless sky. This is it. No going back. I sit up straight and take some breaths. Phule pulls into the forecourt and parks beside a bright pink wall, along the top of which orange flags flap listlessly. Here are stalls selling nostril-crinking incense, marigold garlands, coconuts and brass statues of gods, the kind we had in our living room in Africa. Most of the other visitors are elderly, males in Nehru caps, women in saris all the gayer against their menfolk's chaste white clothes. All have the demeanour of pilgrims.

Phule confers with someone and we're led up a flight of steps into the temple compound. It's breathtaking, quite the most beautiful building I've seen on my trip, clad in ivory marble, perhaps forty metres long and twenty to the top of the highest stupa. Despite its mass, it looks light as meringue, about to float free of the ground. The façade's undecorated except for the occasional relief of a god executed in the same plain style. By the side porch is a grey stone fountain, canopied with scarlet bougainvillea. Is this where the villagers were abused? I can hardly draw breath, I'm so tense. At once a youthful priest approaches, ash-smeared cheeks, orange wrap over one shoulder. He has a garland of marigolds and jasmine and Phule signals me to bow my head to receive it. The fragrance is peppery-sweet. The priest then gives me some pamphlets in Marathi, explaining its connections with Shivaji and Ramdas, his freedom-fighter guru.

Led by our guide, who rings a bell as he enters, we kick off our shoes and enter the shrine. Against the ivory walls, the three images at the far end are achingly bright under the neon strips which border their alcove. Dressed in dazzling orange and yellow, garlanded in the same fashion as I am, the trio of three-foot images stands on a plinth which brings their heads level with ours. To one side is an ugly square plastic clock, hands frozen.

'Laxmi, Siva and Ram,' Phule whispers, before preparing to do *puja*. Despite myself, I, too, entreat their intercession. As Phule continues with his prayers, I gaze up at the ceiling rose, a masterpiece of intricate concentric circles, the patterns carved so delicately they seem to have been caressed out of the marble. It's so beautiful my heartbeat slows momentarily.

When he's finished his devotions, Phule and I wander outside again. The compound is walled on three sides, the fourth open, looking onto a shallow river along which women squat, pounding clothes on laundry-stones. There's a small footbridge which looks as though it's been there for decades, next to a more recent single-lane crossing for cars. Through the canopy of trees on the far side, I catch my first glimpse of Chafal.

'I need to look around over there,' I tell Phule.

He looks bemused. 'But only thing is this temple.'

'When my father was in Satara, he conducted a big raid here. I want to see if anyone remembers it.'

I half expect him to return to the car and radio for

permission. But he simply nods and we set off across the foot-bridge. Should I take off my garland? It seems inappropriate to enter the village adorned like a god. However, I don't want to cause offence at the outset, so I keep it on.

It's two minutes to the outskirts and ten more to the centre of the village, down narrow alleys of mud-brick huts and cor-rugated-iron roofs. There's an occasional scrawl of telephone wire and electricity cable, and one or two satellite dishes. Waste runs down gutters in the middle of the lanes, where scrawny chickens paddle, watched by skeletal yellow mongrels of the kind I remember from rural Tanzania. I'm glad now of my garland to ward off the smells. By the time we've reached what seems to be the principal building in the settlement, a solid stone construction with a raised flagstoned veranda, a crowd of the idle and curious has collected behind us.

'Let me ask here in the *chavadi*,' Phule says.

He comes back out with a grave-looking man who stares at me. Thankfully, however, he doesn't seem hostile; perhaps he can't afford to be, since my guide's a policeman. The man barks an order to a youth who scampers up one of the side streets. More villagers have gathered by the time he returns, and he has some trouble boring a passage through them for Phule and me. A few minutes' walk up another alley, littered with refuse, he taps at a corrugated-iron door, awry on its hinges. I've no idea who we're going to see. But I'm praying it's not one of the surviving victims.

Indoors, it's smoky and dark. The floors are beaten earth, clothes and utensils hanging from nails in mud-rendered walls. There's a warm, musty odour of livestock. We're shown into a large, low room broken up by two rickety charpoys, each with its thin, worn bedroll, on which we're invited to sit. Soon a very old man shuffles in, leaning on a stout staff. He's tiny, unshaven, barefoot and wearing only a greyish vest and equally grimy dhoti. Behind him is an even more ancient-looking woman, stooped like a question mark.

'She asks if you want tea,' Phule translates.

'Black please, no sugar.'

Once his wife retreats, the old man mutters unhappily.

'He must put something on his head first,' Phule explains, as our host exits again.

'Who is he?'

'One of the village watchmen the night of the raid.'

I sigh with relief. I wonder what Phule's thinking. Even in the gloom, he doesn't remove his shades.

By the time tea arrives, the old man's back, almost unrecognisable beneath a gorgeous, elaborately knotted, sunflower-yellow headdress and collared shirt, a shade less grey than his vest. He takes a seat on the charpoy opposite, grasping his staff as if the years have rolled back and he's once again on guard. I feed Phule the questions, and he translates the answers.

'I remember that night. But first let me tell you what happened before. Around midnight, a car came from the direction of Patan.'

Where Bill rescued the woman tortured with cigarette butts, the one Modak washed his hands of. And where Yates reported the Mangs were on a criminal rampage.

'It was travelling very slowly with cloth over its lights to dim them. We challenged the car and two armed men got out. They told us to go to our houses and stay inside, or there'd be trouble. There was no choice. We only had *lathis*.' He bangs his stick on the ground for emphasis. 'Later, I heard shouting. It was coming from the home of the police *patil*.'

'Community guard,' Phule murmurs, 'not real police.'

'Later, when it felt safe, I went to his house. Other watchmen were already there. The women were crying. The *patil* had been beaten and tied up. His injuries were not so serious but he was in shock. One of the women said she'd heard the car leaving. Another claimed this time it was crammed with men, not just the three who'd come. I knew at once who they were. There had been rumours absconders were hiding in the village.'

'Had you searched?'

The watchman shrugs. 'They had many friends here. It was better not to inquire too deeply.'

'What happened next?'

'At about three or four in the morning, I heard more vehicles. There were so many we knew it was the police or army. They parked by the temple. In those days there was no bridge for vehicles. In minutes, there were hundreds of police in the village, running to seal the exits. They were led by Gilbert from Satara.'

Outside, the crowd's murmuring, as if the villagers can hear all this, too. I'm unbearably hot all of a sudden.

'What happened?'

It's a shattering anticlimax when the man shakes his head.

'I don't know. I was told by one sub-inspector to secure the path into the forest and allow no one in or out. I was there until dawn. I only heard shouts, carrying on the wind. I was glad to be out of the way.'

Phule and I look at each other, bemused.

'Sir, there's someone outside who saw everything,' the youth who brought us now declares.

Phule nods and I get up. But the former watchman isn't finished yet. He insists on having his photograph taken. My hands are trembling so much I can barely manage.

The alley's even more crammed than before. Everyone falls silent as we come out. I wonder if Phule, too, is nervous now. At any rate, he draws himself up to his full height as the youth beckons a distinguished-looking man towards us. He's rather younger than the watchman, a spry seventy-odd years, I guess, with thick silver hair swept back from his brow, round glasses and a scored, kindly face.

'I can tell you what happened,' he declares. 'Come with me.'

Our new guide pushes through the throng. It feels like the

Indian villagers with lathis, 1940s

entire village is following. My garland's beginning to weigh like a cross.

'This is what it was like then,' the man says. 'The whole of Chafal was forced to go down to the *chavadi*. The police held lanterns and banged on every door, searching each house. Every man between fifteen and fifty was closely examined. Many were in tears and shaking, even grown men. Imagine the impression it made on me, a ten-year-old. We talked of nothing else for weeks.'

We find ourselves once more at the *chavadi*.

'I will show you what Gilbert did.' He mounts the step onto the veranda, motioning Phule and myself to stand before him. Behind us the villagers take up position, as if about to watch a play.

'Gilbert started by saying that he had come to arrest some very bad men, six of them. He said they had committed some atrocities against two women falsely accused of being informers.'

'What atrocities?' I ask.

The man shrugs. 'He stated simply that he knew the miscreants were hiding in Chafal and they must be surrendered at once. There was complete quiet, except for children wailing. Gilbert made a constable hold a light up close to him so everyone could see clearly. Then he did this.'

I'm spellbound. The man crosses his hands either side of his hips and mimes the drawing of pistols, pointing the first two fingers of each bunched fist at Phule and me. It's like a gunfight clip from a western. Total silence descends on the audience behind me.

'He waved his weapons and said there'd be serious trouble unless the men were given up. Everyone got very frightened and someone called out that the absconders had escaped an hour or two before in a car heading for Patan. Gilbert got very angry. He sent policemen into the crowd and the men were separated from their families and examined again. Then he called the police *patil* and watchmen from the crowd and took them inside the *chavadi* with his right-hand man, an evil-looking fellow. When they came back out, this man called six names and told them to come forward. The men summoned came unwillingly, some had to be pushed. When they were assembled, Gilbert ordered them to be taken over the river to the police vehicles. We saw hurricane lamps crossing the footbridge. Later, cries came from the temple enclosure. It was obvious they were being beaten.'

'Who were the men?'

'Those who'd sheltered the absconders. Relatives.'

This is bad. Shinde's accusation is confirmed. 'Then what happened?'

'Later the men came back. They were crying and their clothes were torn. They were followed by the evil-looking man and about twenty constables.'

'Was Gilbert with them?'

'No, he stayed here and lectured us about the Prati Sarkar and how they were in league with Japan who wanted to take over India and make us slaves. That they robbed under the pretext of politics and terrorised the innocent. He kept pointing to the *patil* beside him, who was bent over his stick in pain. That they tortured their victims, even women. That it was time they were given a taste of their own medicine.'

It's too much. The tension that's built inexorably since reading Shinde's book in Mumbai University library boils over. My tears come, sudden and violent, but silently. The man looks alarmed and steps towards me. I take a deep breath. The sound of my voice takes me by surprise.

'Tell the village that I'm sorry for what my father did. But I suppose he thought he was doing his duty.'

As the man translates, Phule puts a hand on my shoulder. 'You're right. He was doing his duty.'

The villagers murmur excitedly as the man beckons me onto the stone platform. When I stumble up, he turns me so we're side-on to the audience, and takes my hands between his in a gesture of *namaste*.

'There's no reason for you to be upset,' he soothes. 'You are not your father. It was a long time ago. It's good you have come.'

The villagers start clapping, as if the show's over. But I'm overcome and stand there helplessly, fat, stupid tears trickling down my face.

'Come, we will have tea now,' the man says, leading me by one hand into the *chavadi*.

Indoors, there's one further revelation. I ask the witness whether old women and old men were abused, as Shinde claimed. He looks startled before flatly denying it.

'I would have seen. It was the six men, from the families sheltering the absconders.'

I feel part of the black burden slipping off my shoulders. 'Were they caught afterwards?'

The man shrugs. 'I don't remember. I don't think so. You

see, that night turned the villagers against the government. Chafal had been divided until then. Some had left to fight for the King-Emperor. Afterwards, everyone was for the Prati Sarkar.'

So Bill's action was entirely counterproductive.

We spend about an hour in the *chavadi*, discussing what happened to Bill in later life and how Chafal's changed over the last sixty years. Then Phule says it's time to go; he's needed at the station in an hour. I remove the garland as soon as we've said our farewells and got in the car. We're both silent on the drive home. I'm physically spent. But my mind is seething. The afternoon's provided vindication of Modak's disquiet at the consequences of the methods used against the Parallel Government; yet it's also offered a significant challenge to Shinde's account, which rested, after all, on second-hand testimony. As Nirad Chaudhuri complains, nationalist historiography was prone to inflate its claims about imperial brutality. Those who were actually there have offered a rather different narrative to the Congress worker on whose account Shinde relies so heavily.

On the other hand, I've investigated first-hand only one of the incidents alluded to in the texts I've read. What if I went elsewhere? Then I wonder if I had any right to apologise on Bill's behalf. What would he think of me doing so? Or did I let him off too lightly? How can I really understand the pressures he felt under at the time? Above all, however, I feel relief. He wasn't like Paul Scott's villainous Merrick, after all. He wasn't guilty of mindless sadism; there was some kind of rationale in his behaviour that night, unacceptably harsh as it nonetheless seems to me. Retribution in kind for the abused women. And for the beatings of alleged collaborators described so graphically in Modak's novel and elaborated on by Farrokh's manager. But I still can't understand why Bill descended to the level of his opponents. The rules are the rules, as he insisted all those years ago to François in Arusha: you can't make them up as you go along. From my perspective, sixty-four years on, it seems like a fatal error of judgement.

Back at the hotel, Phule asks me to have the concierge take a picture of us. 'For my wife,' he mutters.

At last the shades come off for a swift polish. His irises are the colour of melted butterscotch.

'We are all sons to our fathers,' he pronounces enigmatically. 'I will not forget what you did today.'

I'm sure he would have put his arms around me if we knew each other a little better. I'm intensely grateful for the approval his comment seems to express, as well as for his support during my ordeal. Without it, I doubt I would have come out of the experience relatively unscathed.

Up in my room, I place the fast-withering garland on my bedside table. I've barely lain down when I fall fast asleep and dream about Bill again. I'm at a party somewhere in London which is heaving with people. I look up to see him coming into the room, face creased in an apologetic smile, as if he's been held up in traffic. He looks as he did the year he died, hair immaculately groomed as usual, tanned, bursting with vitality. Except that he's wearing his Indian Police uniform, his leathers neat and polished, just like in his wedding photos. I barge through the throng. As I reach him, I realise I'm now older than he is. Yet he recognises me at once. He grins hugely and we hug, slapping each other on the back. When he steps back, as if to register more precisely how I've changed, I'm suddenly enraged.

'You didn't tell us you were going, you've been away so long, we've been waiting for you all this time,' I protest with childish rage.

He hugs me again. 'It's alright, old chap, I'm back now.'

Then he asks me question after question about what I've been doing with my life. He's so helplessly hungry to know everything that I reserve my own questions. I'm just getting onto explaining about my trip to India, when someone else comes into the room. He leaves the door open behind him. Impotently, I watch it swing to, knowing that when it slams I'll wake up, before I've had my turn to ask anything. When it does bang to, I sit up to find myself in pitch darkness, eyes wet again.

CHAPTER 11

Terrorism, Old and New

Everywhere *Lonely Planet* recommends in Kolhapur is full, so after a trek round the night-time city by auto-rickshaw, I end up some distance from the centre at a place which describes itself as 'modernly furnished'. I'm so tired after the visit to Chafal and the bus trip from Satara that I go straight to bed and sleep, deeply and blankly, for ten hours. After breakfast, however, I feel restored. At reception, I ask if they know of Shinde's college. I'm soon dialling from my room.

'Hello, I'd like to speak to Dr A.B. Shinde, please.'

There's a silence before a flat female voice answers. 'Shinde sahib is no more.'

'Pardon?'

'Shinde sahib died in May.'

Oh no.

'What's it about?'

'I really wanted to get hold of a copy of his book on the Parallel Government,' I stutter, 'and talk to him about its sources. And I was hoping he could introduce me to a couple of people.'

'I will tell the sahib's son. He comes at two o'clock only. You may pass then.'

I'm completely thrown by this unexpected setback. Everything depends on Bhosle now. I proceed straight to the university. It's a ten-minute taxi-ride to a spacious landscaped campus with an impressive main building in modern Saracenic style. There's another enormous statue of Shivaji galloping his horse at the end of the semicircle of front lawn. I'm taken to the second floor and shown into the History department.

'Professor Bhosle's still in Kerala,' the administrator tells me. 'His wife's unwell and she is having treatment there.'

That must be why he hasn't responded to my emails. And why he abruptly changed his plans to be in Mumbai. Still, it's hard to contain my disappointment at this second blow. 'Do you have a number for him?'

'You must ask the head.'

She leads me along the corridor and knocks at a door. Inside, seated at a long table surrounded by a dozen chairs, is a pleasant-looking individual in his sixties with gold-rimmed spectacles, an aquiline nose and a sheaf of pens in the pocket of his short-sleeved shirt. Opposite sits a younger man, handsome and very fair-skinned, in a fawn safari jacket. Both get up.

'Professor Lohor, head of department,' the older one says. 'My colleague, Dr Avanish Patil.'

We shake hands and they pore over my visiting card.

'I was hoping to see Professor Bhosle. I've come specially from London,' I plead.

Lohor picks up his phone. His colleague and I appraise each other as the silence lengthens.

'These Indian mobiles,' Lohor eventually shrugs. 'I will give you his number and you can try yourself.'

'When are you expecting him back?'

'That depends on his wife's progress.'

I'm really downcast now, unable to see past this dead end. So I'm glad to be distracted by Dr Patil's offer to show me round. Before we can get up, however, there's a knock and half a dozen white-robed figures glide into the room. They're led by a plump woman, grey hair in a bun, carrying a garish portrait of a youthful guru. My hosts now stand to perform a *namaste* and I follow suit. Once our visitors have reciprocated, they take their seats. I can't follow the conversation, but there's much gesturing from the woman and affirming grunts from her followers as they pass round pamphlets with the guru's photo on the front. At one point I hear the words 'University of Texas'. Then they rise as one and after further salutations, glide back out of the room like Banquo's ghosts. Have I dreamed it all? Lohor and Patil look unfazed, as if such interruptions are an everyday occurrence.

'What was that about Texas?' I ask as I follow Avanish outside.

'They said Texas University has provided an affidavit that their saint is "of most stable and solid mind". They want an attestation from us for the courses they run in the "science of positive thinking".'

The deadpan expression gives way to a gurgling laugh. I warm to him.

'So you're researching the nationalist movements of Maharashtra?' he asks, once he's shown me into his own office, a dark cell with a handful of dog-eared books on one shelf and a desk piled high with student papers.

'Yes. I'd been relying on Professor Bhosle for information about archives in Mumbai relating to the Parallel Government.'

Avanish's brow puckers. 'Indeed, he's writing a book on it at present. It's thirty years now since he began this work in his PhD.'

My ears prick up. 'Would that be in the library?' It might give me some leads.

'Of course. Should I take you?'

He leads me out of the department and down some flaking concrete steps to the basement of an adjoining building. The holdings seem small for an institution this size. Avanish helps me complete formalities with the chief librarian, a smiling woman in a plum sari who rubs her stomach solicitously.

'We'll have lunch afterwards,' Avanish suggests. 'Have you tried our famous Kolhapur mutton curry?'

Bhosle's thesis is soon delivered. Submitted in 1978, it's entitled 'A History of the Freedom Movement in Satara District from 1885–1947'. I skip through to the decade I'm interested in. There are several references to 'police excesses', including instances of firing on demonstrators. But look, they're all in before Bill arrived. The most controversial incident involved Hobson's predecessor, CMS Yates, producing several fatalities at a village called Vaduj. Indeed, there's only one mention of Bill that I can see. But it's disturbing enough: 'When Mr Gilbert, the Additional DSP rightly understood the threat caused by the criminals to law and order, he undertook to wipe out the existence of the criminal gangs. He shot one Mahadu Ramoshi at Kameri and arrested many of the criminals.' Criminal gangs, according to Bhosle, not the PG or their supporters. Still, it's a shock. What's a Ramoshi? Was the shooting fatal? There's no source for the incident in the bibliography. Hearsay or interviews with eyewitnesses? Frustrating. At this point, it seems Bhosle had done little of the archival work in which he's currently engaged. Most disappointingly, there's no mention of the weekly confidential reports I want.

Although doubting my chances of meeting Lad and Nayakwadi now, I keep an eye out for references to them. While Y.B Chavan and Nana Patil were the 'dictators of the movement', the two I'm after were on the executive. As D.Y. indicated, Lad was the 'field marshal' of the *tufan sena*, the armed wing of the Parallel Government, and Nayakwadi 'became increasingly convinced ... that military strength was necessary to win freedom'. Evidence of the movement's violence against civilians is hard to evaluate. At times, ironically, the PG is allied with the police in a common war against 'antisocial elements'. Thus three Mangs of 'low character' have legs amputated by PG activists for crimes of theft and arson. I remember Farrokh's acid comments about the karmic justice of Nana Patil's unsuccessful leg operation in later life.

On the other hand, Bhosle denies claims about the shoeing of collaborators: 'Laxmanshastri Joshi commented that in Satara-Sangli regions the underground workers tortured the pro-government persons by shoeing them like bulls and horses. But the statement has no foundation whatsoever.' Indeed, the thesis concludes that 'nowhere under the sun traitors were more leniently treated [*sic*]'. There's one final detail, which I wish I'd known when I went to Chafal. The principal agitator there was called Ramanand Bharati, who raised the Indian flag from Ajinkya Tara fort in Satara on Independence Day in 1947. Was this the man Bill was after, on that December night sixty-four years ago?

I've finished by the time Avanish arrives to take me for lunch. We sit at one of the open-air stalls set up along the drive to the main building.

'This place makes it same as my grandmother.'

The mutton curry certainly smells delicious, but the first mouthful feels like an iron's been passed over my tongue. I suspect it might even have floored Bill. Avanish watches anxiously and I'm afraid I've spoiled the occasion. But to my surprise, the scalding shock soon wears off and I begin to appreciate the exquisitely subtle flavours. I've never heard of some of the spices.

'You always drink lager with curry in London, no?'

'Yes, Avanish, at least ten pints and always in places with flock wallpaper.'

It takes him a moment to realise I'm joking. We compare our experience as academics. Avanish makes me feel decadent, with his sixteen hours of lectures every week and classes of 50 to 100, each student writing two essays per term.

'How do you get through all the the marking?' I ask sympathetically.

He shrugs ruefully. 'We only have two months off a year for holiday and research. No sabbaticals.'

I commiserate.

'Ah, it's difficult to be a historian here. Especially regional history. If you write in your own language you have no national audience. But there's no national audience for local history. It's very hard to get published. You need subventions from a patron. And that brings its own pressures.'

I remember Nirad Chaudhuri's laments about the difficulties of being a professional historian in India. How ever did a local boy like Shinde manage to publish *The Parallel Government*?

'Also, the state of the archives here in Kolhapur is disgraceful. Yet all the politicians live in mansions and send their children to study in America. Soon everything will be too far gone to save.'

I compare my experiences in Mumbai. 'By the way, what's a Ramoshi? And Mangs? Professor Bhosle mentions them in his PhD.'

'They're what the British called Criminal Tribes. Traditionally nomadic. These days they're called the Scheduled Tribes. In Maharashtra, Ramoshis and Mangs are the biggest groups.'

'Are they settled now?'

Avanish nods. 'We have some Ramoshi students. But they're still regarded as backward. Especially by traditionally minded Hindus.'

I then ask if he knows how I could contact Lad and Nayakwadi. He looks doubtful.

'You really need Professor Bhosle for that, now A.B.'s passed away.'

'I'm going to see his son after lunch.'

'Well, he's a possibility. But if you don't get the information you need, ring me and I'll try to make inquiries.'

I'm sorry to say goodbye, and promise to call if there's time to meet again before leaving Kolhapur. Avanish sees me to an auto-rickshaw and directs the driver where to drop me.

~

First impressions of downtown Kolhapur is that it's more 'Indian' than anywhere I've been so far – not surprisingly, perhaps, since it wasn't annexed by the British. I see few of the architectural signatures of the Raj and, once inside the surviving city walls, it's a maze of narrow streets and alleys. Kipling described the princely states as 'the dark places of the earth', but he was hardly a disinterested observer. I wonder if the city's typical of such places, and how it compared with British India. Kolhapur seems to be at least as wealthy as Satara, with none of the obvious poverty of downtown Pune. The Mahalaxmi temple in the centre of town, begun in the seventh century and vastly extended since, typifies the monumental register of public buildings. Outside it, knots of sadhus wander amongst stalls selling food, trinkets and temple offerings of marigolds and coconuts. Some are robed in saffron, some in yellow, others boast only a tatty loincloth, cheeks smeared with ash, beards matted, leaning on sticks, proffering begging bowls. A few holy men squat on the pavements, casting horoscopes or selling small bundles of leaves and twigs, traditional medicines, I assume. The noise and odours are overpowering. It's exhilarating, but I'm more interested for the moment in the weather-beaten tenement abutting the temple.

The college is busy with students running between classrooms on three sides of a rectangle compound enclosed by two-storey blocks. The gatekeeper shows me into a small office, where a portrait of a man I presume is A.B. Shinde gazes down. It's a kindly, strong-featured face with wide-set eyes, long hair curling down over faded garlands like the one I wore at Chafal. While the receptionist attempts to call Shinde's son, two teachers enter, each in jacket and tie. One's a heavily built man in his fifties, with hollow, pockmarked cheeks; the other's much younger, with a head so large it looks unsteady on his slender shoulders. Learning I'm from London University, they call for tea.

'Dr Vilas Powar,' the older man introduces himself, 'and my colleague Mr Brihaspati Shinde.'

I assume at first that this is the son. But I'm soon informed that Shinde and Patil are the Maratha equivalent of Smith and

Brown. I explain my interest in the Parallel Government, to their evident intrigue. Vilas, it transpires, did his doctorate under Bhosle and expresses regret about his mentor's wife. He knows Avanish, too, since both work on the Indian 'Mutiny' in Kolhapur.

'It spread this far south?' Remembering how it was so effectively nipped in the bud in Satara, I'm surprised.

'Indeed. There were close connections between the royal family here and those who led the insurgency in the north, Nana Sahib particularly. He'd been exiled from Pune when the Peishwas were overthrown by the British.'

The man responsible for the Cawnpore massacre and the siege of Lucknow, if I remember right: events central to the mythography of British imperialism as the innocent victim of the forces of savagery. I doubt the word 'terrorism' existed then. And Nana Sahib was also, no doubt, an inspiration to the Parallel Government.

Before my history lesson can continue, a plump-faced man with anxious eyes and an exceptionally luxuriant walrus moustache enters the room. Even though he doesn't look much older than Brihaspati, my companions rise. In one hand he has a copy of *The Parallel Government*.

'I am Mr Charunder Datta Shinde. Chairman of the college since my late father's decease.'

'I was so sorry to hear the news. I'd been looking forward greatly to meeting him.'

He opens the book. 'I would like to sign it on my father's behalf.' He studies my visiting card as he inscribes: 'To Professor Bart: with warm regards of love.' My family name doesn't seem to ring any bells. Perhaps he doesn't share his father's research interests. But that means he won't be able to help me locate Bill's weekly confidential reports, a fact he soon confirms.

Deflated again, I try to show willing while Charunder explains the history of his father's institution. It's on the site of the first school established by Shivaji. Soon a bell rings and Powar gathers up his exercise books.

'Time for classes,' the chairman announces. 'Anything else I can help you with?'

'I wondered if you could put me in touch with G.D. Lad and Naganath Nayakwadi,' I ask nervously.

He looks at me closely before smiling reassuringly. 'Let me try. They aren't far, but you'll need a car.'

Wonderful. 'I can rent one at my hotel.'

He goes into an adjoining room and returns with a notebook. 'When would you like to go?'

'Tomorrow, ideally. I'm returning to England in a week or so.'

Shinde toys with my card as he makes his calls. He nods and smiles as he speaks, though his tone's very respectful.

'That's settled. They'll both be at home tomorrow for the holiday. Mr Lad can meet you at ten. Mr Nayakwadi at two-thirty. That gives you time to talk to the field marshal and make the journey from Kundal to Walwa.'

My luck's turned again. I look inquiringly at Powar and his young colleague. 'I don't suppose either of you would be available to come and interpret?'

The younger teacher defers to Powar, who shakes his head after some consideration. 'I'm sorry. It's New Year's Day and I have family engagements.'

'I could,' his colleague offers.

The chairman nods approvingly.

'But if you're free later this afternoon,' Powar volunteers, 'I could show you some of the Mutiny sites here.'

'I'd be delighted.' It's a chance to see something of Kolhapur with a local guide. Besides, I have a long-standing interest in the uprising, and perhaps it'll also provide an opportunity to compare how Britain dealt with insurgency then and in the 1940s.

'Shall we say four?' Powar asks.

'I have an hour before my next class,' Brihaspati murmurs, 'I could walk with you.'

He tells me his name contains the Sanskrit root for Jupiter, and that he teaches English literature while researching Dalit fiction for an MA – though he's having trouble finding critical material on his chosen authors. I promise to look when I get back to London and email him anything I come across. Belying his youthful appearance, he's in fact been at the college for several years and expresses great affection for the place.

'I'm very thankful you asked me to come tomorrow. It's always been a dream to meet Mr Lad and Mr Nayakwadi.'

Our tour confirms the difference of Kolhapur to anywhere I've been until now. Put crudely, it's far more 'exotic'. Judging by people's stares, Westerners are something of a rarity. From an adjoining street comes drumming so loud and deep it makes the ground vibrate.

'One of our most famous wrestlers is getting married this evening. If you like, I can show you one training school.'

Briha leads me through a large square with impressive basalt buildings on three sides. 'The old palace,' he explains. The ground floor's now taken up with expensive-looking shops which overlook row upon row of temporary seating, facing a huge dais beneath banks of spotlights.

'For the wedding. Here in Kolhapur, wrestlers are Bollywood,' he says proudly.

So it's a surprise when the alley he steers me down issues into a courtyard with a stinking open sewer along one edge. A colonnade supports a rickety roof, under which a group of squat young men in loincloths are doing callisthenics. A couple of wrestlers, skin coated in chalk, practise moves in a sunken pit of reddish cinders.

'These *talims*, wrestling schools, were bastions of the freedom movement. All kinds of secret training went on in them.'

The perfect cover. I wonder whether the British Resident had any idea.

By the time we get back to the square, a snake charmer has set his pitch. It's no doubt corny, but I can't help stopping. He's sly-eyed, with an unkempt grey beard and grimy turban, baskets set on a threadbare mat in front of him. Responding to my interest, he raises the lid of one basket and begins to sing in a wheedling voice. A sandy-coloured snake sways up to a height of about three feet and spreads its hood. It resembles the snake Bill killed when I was a child. As soon as the man's voice fades, the snake sinks; then he resumes, making it yo-yo up and down. Soon all three baskets are uncovered and serpents rise and fall, intertwining their necks so gracefully they never seem to touch. My guide drops a five-rupee note, which seems to infuriate the snake charmer. I get out my wallet, but Briha waves it away.

'He's trying to cheat you because you're a visitor.'

I hear drummers and haut-bois players approaching from behind. Turning, I glimpse a woman with thick matted hair, a filthy sari and bare feet, whirling round and round in the middle of the musicians. I suddenly realise that the eyes in her long thin face are turned upwards, showing only the whites. Goose pimples spread over me like a rash. She spins ever faster, before suddenly collapsing on the road, jerking over and over. I look to Briha for reassurance. But he seems quite unconcerned, as do the musicians. The woman's allowed to rest a while. But soon the band increases the tempo, and a drummer hauls her upright. She doesn't seem to know where she is. Then the procession continues as before. I wonder if Bill was at first equally unnerved by such sights.

'What was that all about?'

'She's possessed by Lord Rama. Don't worry,' Briha smiles. 'We should go, I have my class. Will you say a few words?'

Judging by the similar request at Satara police station, such talks are perhaps expected of 'distinguished' visitors.

His classroom's dilapidated, with a broken window looking onto the Mahalaxmi temple and a torn cloth ceiling. Boys and girls sit separately, and the latter giggle as they stand to greet us. Briha explains who I am and, to my discomfiture, announces that I'm going to discourse on the importance of English in today's globalised world. Mindful of Avanish's complaints about the language dilemma for local scholars and writers, I rehearse Chinua Achebe's ideas about English being a world language which has to submit to many local usages. This sparks animated discussion. One student asks if I approve of Daniel Craig's recent Bond film being subtitled in Standard English for local television. That makes me laugh. Another wonders what I think of Indian English as a medium for literature. Time passes quickly, most of the conversation led by the girls. The boys look uncomfortable when Briha asks them anything until, just as the bell rings, one raises his hand. He has short centre-parted hair, a face graped with acne and a pained, intense expression.

'Sir, you are interested in European history, also?'

I nod. He reads from his exercise book.

'Did you know Napoleon was born in 1760, Hitler in 1899. The difference is 129 years.'

I shrug.

'Napoleon came to power in 1804, Hitler in 1933. The difference is 129 years. Napoleon occupied Vienna in 1809, Hitler in 1938.' I'm beginning to get the gist. 'Napoleon invaded Russia in 1812, Hitler in 1941. Napoleon was defeated in 1816, Hitler in 1945.'

His mates clap enthusiastically and I join in. Even though I've spotted mistakes, I don't want to spoil the fun.

~

Briha, Vilas and I jump in an auto-rickshaw after the class. It's a tight fit with three in the back and the motor protests tinnily. As we weave in and out of the traffic, I wonder whether I've misjudged Indian drivers. Perhaps, despite the statistics, they're the best in the world, rather than the worst. Maybe the endless horns function like bats' radar, enabling drivers to judge clearances to the millimetre. Soon we're pulling up before a set of barracks in the same style as those in Satara. In the centre of the old parade ground women are making bricks, pungent-smelling patties mixed from piles cement, cow dung and sugarcane pith.

'The revolt was instigated by the Rajah's brother, Chimasaheb, and it began right here on the night of 31 July 1857, when the 27th Native Infantry revolted.'

Step by step, Vilas takes us through the main stages of the uprising and the sites associated with them. Here's a former mission building, where some British officers escaped to, now government printing presses.

'Four fled down the Ratnagiri road, where they were eventually cut down.'

Now to the former Residency, a noble building running down to a river, where other officers and loyal troops retreated. From here a runner was dispatched through enemy lines to Satara to raise the alarm.

'It was like the siege at Lucknow, though not so long. Still, it hung in the balance until Colonel Jacob's relieving force arrived, a good week later.'

'What happened then?'

We're outside a rectangular stone enclosure with a small temple at the far end.

'The most determined rebels retreated here, the stables in those days. Inch by inch they were driven inside the temple, then up into the stupa. Lieutenant Carr's men killed them one by one. Nobody surrendered.'

I can almost see the red tunics, hear the musket-shots and the cries of the wounded. How much of the damage to the fabric dates from those days, and what do the current inhabitants know of the events? Each of the former horse-stalls now houses a whole family of squatters, according to Vilas; the communal yard a colourful jam of handcarts, bicycles, curious children, silky-haired goats, pots of herbs. Bright bouquets are drawn in chalk on every threshold. For good luck, Briha explains.

Then it's off to broad Shalini Lake, where we stop beside an ancient tree with thick branches. The base has been bricked round, distinguishing it from its neighbours. Pedalos idle on the water and on the far shore a funfair wheel turns slowly, shrieks carrying faintly to us. Over there's a huge building with a Victorian, municipal air and a Big Ben clock, which I'm informed is one of the erstwhile 'new' palaces, now a luxury hotel. Vilas pats the trunk we're standing beside.

'This was the hanging tree. All through the second half of August 1857, rebel sepoys and those who allegedly helped them were hanged in batches. They were left for the crows to pick their flesh off.'

I have an awful vision of dozens of tar-black silhouettes against the blinding sky, hands tied behind their backs, rotating slowly in the putrid breeze.

'What about the leaders?'

'You'll see.'

We jump into the auto-rickshaw and end up back at the college. But instead of going in, Vilas leads the way into the grand square where preparations for the wrestler's wedding continue apace. We stop opposite a huge gate in the old palace walls.

'Everyone above the rank of private was brought here. The British lined their artillery up, facing that opening. The whole town was forcibly assembled to watch the mutineers tied to the mouths of the cannons. Then they were blown away. According to eyewitnesses, the torsoes vaporised, but arms, legs and heads fell into the crowds.'

The public staging of these punishments seems to me as barbaric as the methods themselves. More what you'd expect from the medieval period, than from a colonial administration which was supposed to be in India to spread the humane ideals of the Enlightenment. Yet public punishment was a technique used more recently by Bill and the Parallel Government, too, to inspire fear and to cow dissenters.

'What about Chimasaheb?'

'Exiled. But because his brother immediately disowned him, Kolhapur wasn't taken over.'

'How many did the British lose?'

'One hundred and eleven. More than fifteen hundred rebels were killed or executed.'

Only a little less disproportionate than the figures coming in from Gaza. Chastening. Imperialism in the raw. Was it only because the Indian army was so tied up by the war that the British didn't unleash this sort of terror on Satara during the 1940s, as they were soon to do in Malaya, Kenya and Cyprus? My speculations are interrupted when Vilas turns to me.

'Will you talk now to our Socrates Society?'

'What's that?'

'Our weekly college debate. Last one this year, so there'll be a good turnout. It's designed to help them understand issues of the day and practise spoken English. Build confidence in public speaking.'

Although I'm tired, it seems churlish to refuse, especially since Vilas has taken such trouble over our tour. Briha's caramel eyes beseech.

'OK. What's the topic?'

'Terrorism.'

My heart sinks. 'How long?'

'Ten minutes. There'll be other speakers.'

Over tea, I frantically try to think of what to say. Maharashtra has witnessed not only the recent terror attacks in Mumbai but, earlier in the year, the Malegaon bomb outrages, directed at Muslims. Dangerous ground. I could discuss the attempted repression of the Parallel Government. Or the methods of Bill's opponents, which Bhosle's thesis described as designed 'to inspire terror in the hearts of the rulers'. All day I've been having flashbacks to Chafal. I'm not ready to discuss such things just yet. Then there's Modak's account in his memoir of the terrible behaviour of the Indian security forces in Kashmir? Equally risky in the present climate. My mind churns, unable to find the right focus.

Here we are in the assembly hall and I'm still flailing. It looks like the entire college is crammed noisily into pews facing the platform, on which the chairman and several teachers are already seated. Once again boys and girls are segregated, the latter at the front, giggling and smiling. I'm given an inflated introduction, after which a couple of staff have their say. It's shocking. The first speaker demands Pakistan be 'wiped off the map'. The second calls more euphemistically 'for the problem of Pakistan to be sorted out once and for all.' However he then goes on to decry the elaborate and costly security precautions in place for politicians and celebrities, compared with the vulnerability of the general public. Both polemics are enthusiastically received, and there's a buzz of anticipation when I stand up to speak.

The thought suddenly occurs. What about Colonel Jacob's behaviour in Kolhapur? That was surely state terrorism, designed to cow the civilian population by theatrically staged displays of retribution. But I begin by discussing the slipperiness of the term 'terrorism', citing the contradictory ways it was used in the SIB archives. I then propose that many nations suffer from terrorism today. Even Pakistan. I remind my listeners of the assassination of Benazir Bhutto and the bombing of the Marriott hotel in Islamabad in 2007. Instinct tells me I'm rapidly losing sympathy. So I switch to Colonel Jacob and the 'Mutiny', after all and from there, increasingly struggling to maintain a coherent thread, to London and the July 2005 bombings. I speculate about potential lessons from that episode, suggesting that one must be as tough on the causes of terrorism as on terrorism itself. I jump to the IRA, explaining that through the 1970s, there were bombings on the British mainland. Things got worse under Thatcher, who refused point-blank to talk to 'terrorists'. Only when Major and Blair decided to negotiate did the 'Troubles' end, even if the ensuing peace has been uneasy. The first step, I conclude, is to stop calling people you don't like terrorists, recognise them as political actors and then let politics do its business. If peace can succeed centuries of occupation and rebellion in Ireland, the same might be true in other trouble spots.

The applause is thin and lukewarm. Then it's the students' turn. Some are more nuanced than their teachers, but the mood of anger so soon after Mumbai is palpable. The debate over, teachers approach one by one to remonstrate.

'You can't call what Jacob did terrorism. It wasn't random violence against civilians. There were military rules which clearly laid out penalties for mutiny.'

'Did they include mass executions without due process, in front of civilians?' I counter, startled that locals should want to defend Jacob.

'State actors cannot be terrorists,' another objects.

'Not even when they're utterly careless about civilian life?'

A woman lecturer joins in shrilly. 'Your programme for Pakistan is not correct, sir. You cannot talk to madmen. No agreement would be credible.'

'What are the consequences of becoming ever more entrenched?'

'Mrs Thatcher was right. We have to be strong,' another interposes. 'No surrender to terrorists.'

'How do you distinguish between terrorists and freedom fighters?'

It's a relief when four girls from Briha's class come forward. Each offers me an identical deep purple rose.

'Thank you for coming to visit,' they smile.

I'm deeply touched.

Back in the hotel, I try Bhosle's number. It rings interminably. I then book the car for tomorrow's trip, feeling increasingly dispirited by my limp performance in the debate. With advance warning, I could have spoken coherently on any number of subjects for the time allotted. Why can't state actors be terrorist? What about the merciless ongoing assault on Gaza? Perhaps, after all, I should have had the courage to address the way Bill and his colleagues undermined their cause by resorting to their opponents' tactics. Or how the contemporary West's similarly tainted by recourse to extraordinary rendition, the franchising of torture to client states, the widespread abuse and killing of civilians during its military adventures in the Muslim world. Waterboarding, sensory deprivation, the postmodern analogues of thumbscrews and the rack. Then there's the multi-pronged assault on our own civil liberties in the wake of the 'war on terror', detention without trial, electronic surveillance, the proposals for secret courts, and so on. The more I think about it, the more such developments seem to have parallels with the dreadful Defence of India Rules imposed on wartime India in the name of protecting public 'security'.

Above all, the failure to address the legitimate demands of moderates like Gandhi is what gave the Parallel Government its head and, to my mind, legitimacy – though this isn't to excuse the excesses it was sometimes prone to. The same strategic mistake was made in the Amritsar massacre in the Punjab, the event in 1919 in which troops fired on a civilian protest, killing many hundreds. That, more than anything else, turned ordinary Indian opinion against the Raj and laid the foundations for its rapid demise. The British state seems to have learned little from such episodes in imperial history. The 'Bloody Sunday' shootings of peacefully protesting fellow-citizens by paratroopers in Derry in 1972 is a case in point. It led to a fourfold increase in the IRA within a matter of weeks, making a hitherto marginal organisation a central player in the latest phase of the 'Troubles,' which were thereby prolonged for three more bloody decades.

The West more broadly seems to have inherited this blindspot. For example, its refusal to support the reasonable demands of the secular PLO against unending Israeli occupation and the continuing seizure of Palestinian land since 1967 led directly to the rise of militant Hamas, democratically elected by a populace increasingly disillusioned at the impotence (and corruption) of the PLO – and hence to the current catastrophe in Gaza. But if violent repression and 'terrorism' are two sides of the same coin, and neither side escapes the mirroring effect of their close association, it's *not* a question of chicken and egg. In India and Ireland, Kashmir and Palestine, repression clearly came first. I think back to Yeravda jail and Gandhi's message of non-violence. Is his philosophy remotely tenable in a world of neo-cons and al-Qaeda?

~

Unable to find answers, I turn my attention to what reception I'm likely to get from the two nationalist leaders tomorrow. This is probably the last chance to gather material from people who knew Bill, and I need to think carefully about what to ask. Even though it's New Year's Eve, I'm too tired to think about going out. Better to sort out my questions and catch up on my sleep. I've only just got into bed when my mobile rings.

'Rajeev here. How's the intrepid traveller? Just wanted to wish you Happy New Year.'

'Great to hear you, Rajeev,' I reply, though I'd been praying it'd be Bhosle. 'Feels like weeks.' I fill him in briefly on what's been happening since we last spoke. 'Any news of Poel?'

'Any day now.'

'What are you doing this evening? Anything special?'

'At my age? I'm having a quiet evening in with the King.'

'I hope you're wearing your blue suede shoes.'

He laughs. 'By the way, I've been digging around again. Seems your father took a four-month leave from India in 1946.'

'Oh yes?' I wonder why.

'And I came up with his final transfer papers. Made a copy for you. In February 1947 he was posted from Ahmedabad to Ratnagiri. He stayed there until he left India, the exact day of Independence.'

'Heavens, Rajeev, how did you manage that?'

'Contacts,' he chuckles.

So Kiron Modak was right after all. I calculate rapidly. 'Where's Ratnagiri in relation to Kolhapur?'

'A few hours north-west by bus. From there you can catch a train back to Mumbai.'

'Let's see if Poel gets back to you. Still haven't found any of my father's confidential weekly reports.'

'You've got time, haven't you? There's one last place we can

Bill in full uniform at my parents' wedding
reception in London, December 1947

look when you get back to Mumbai. I'll push Poel as soon as I catch up with him. We go back a long way.'

'Can't thank you enough, Rajeev. You're amazing.'

'By the way, this long leave Gilbert took on half-pay, ex-India, in 1946. Is that when he married your mother?'

'No. I have their wedding certificate. It was in December 1947. They only met after he left India.' A whirlwind romance.

'Maybe a device to cover his transfer to Sindh?'

'No, the Hur rebellion was over in 1943. Before he went to Satara.'

So what was he up to in those months? Every shaft of light thrown on Bill's career in the subcontinent throws up another mystery. Like the Ramoshi in Bhosle's thesis. What had he done that Bill felt compelled to shoot him?

CHAPTER 12

Respect Between Enemies

We head north the following morning, back up the Pune-Bangaluru highway towards Kundal. First stop is G.D. Lad, former 'field marshal' of the Parallel Government. It's a beautiful first day of the year. Overnight it rained just enough to cleanse the air of dust, and it's fresh enough that we don't need air-con. Innumerable rooks tumble down the wall of rinsed pale-blue sky. Briha's smartly dressed in a cream shirt and black trousers. He's in expansive mood, head nodding slightly precariously on his neck.

'It is my son's birthday today.'

'You should have told me. We could have gone another time.'

'No matter. We're having his party this evening. I hope you'll come as our dear guest of honour?'

'As long as I don't have to make a speech,' I laugh. 'How old is he?'

'Four years only.'

A children's party in India will be another new experience. Briha tells me about the boy, the apartment he's recently bought and his career plans. Once he has the MA, he wants to do a PhD, again on contemporary Dalit literature. Right now, he's reading Mulk Raj Anand's *Untouchable* as context. I ask him how he developed this interest. For a moment he's hesitant. Then he explains that he's a Dalit himself. His grandfather was of the leather-workers' caste but managed to scrape together enough to buy a plot of land. His father added to it and saved sufficient to get Briha through school and into college. His degree completed, Briha spent several years unsuccessfully seeking a teaching job, constantly knocked back because of his origins.

'Shinde sahib gave me my chance,' he says. 'I'd written more than a hundred applications. I owe him everything.'

I warm a little to Bill's accuser.

'And you, what are you reading presently?' he eventually asks.

'About to start Amitav Ghosh's *The Glass Palace*.'

His eyes light up. 'I know it. The first part's set in Ratnagiri.'

'Really?'

'Yes, it's about the exiled king of Burma and his family.'

Is this an omen? 'I was thinking of possibly heading down there.'

We chat about contemporary Indian fiction. I find it hard to answer his questions about why exactly its English-language varieties are so popular in the West, where they often win the major literary prizes. Is this a benign legacy of empire? Or a malignant form of exoticism? Hardly anyone I can think of reads African work in English these days. And I'm a little ashamed that I know so little about the authors he's researching. Writers who stay put in India and who use Indian languages certainly get much less exposure back home, even when they do manage to get translated. Perhaps, they're the equivalent of the over-looked local historians whose obscurity Avanish bemoaned during my visit to the university yesterday.

I'm glad of the distraction. The butterflies in my stomach aren't as bad as before Chafal. Nonetheless, I'm uncertain how I'll be received. Doubtless there'll be further damaging accusations against Bill.

'We're now in old Aundh princely state,' Briha says as another junction approaches.

'So Kundal was in Aundh?'

'Just on the border.'

I wonder whether Lad cocked snooks at Bill from his sanctuary here. It's flatter than around Chafal, but the land looks just as rich. Once again, the main cash crop's sugar and we dodge intermittently round bullock carts heaped alarmingly high with canes.

Kundal's larger than Chafal, however, more of a town, with many stone buildings and tarmac roads. In the distance looms a chimney, belching smoke, which our driver says is the local sugar refinery. We're dropped at a modest school building, where the long classroom doubles up as a dormitory. I'm surprised to find it occupied, but Briha explains that these are boarders, some from so far away that they've spent the holidays here. A few sit cross-legged on tin trunks, glancing up from schoolbooks. A small group's gathered to fix a long-tailed kite in one corner, too absorbed to register our presence. We're shown through into an office and invited to sit. Several men are already there, associates and disciples of Lad, Briha informs me. Soon a vehicle pulls up outside and more people enter. Among them's a slight man in his eighties, very dark, thick white hair, alert eyes, and an unsmiling, even grim, expression, to whom everyone defers. My heart rather sinks. Briha gives Lad my card, which he glances at and passes to an assistant.

Over a scalding glass of tea, I begin my interview, asking the 'field marshal' how he became involved in the Parallel Government. Lad sighs, as if it's too complex a story to summarise easily. To start with, he speaks in English. But I can't understand his accent, nor he mine. We're soon communicating through Briha.

'When I was in fifth standard here, I began reading Lokmanya Tilak.'

The man who split the Indian National Congress in 1907 by advocating direct action against British rule. Opponents labelled his faction as 'Extremists', while describing themselves as 'Moderates'.

'He travelled a lot between Pune and his home in Ratnagiri. Once I heard him speak in Satara, when I was a boy.'

I hadn't realised Tilak came from Ratnagiri. Another sign that I should go there?

'When I went to Pune to study Ayurvedic medicine, I became more involved in politics. I was in Bombay for Gandhi's "Quit India" speech in 1942, and when he was arrested, I knew where my duty lay.'

'So you returned here?'

'Yes, nine groups were founded in different parts of Satara district and on the first of June, 1943, we raised the Indian flag in Kameri and sang the *Vande Mataram*.'

Kameri. Where Bill shot the Ramoshi.

'But things didn't come to a head until the atrocities at Vaduj in September of that year.'

The incident Bhosle referred to in his PhD thesis as a turning point in events.

'DSP Yates fired on a crowd of demonstrators, killing several and wounding many. It was followed by shootings in Islampur. After that we took up arms ourselves.'

'Did you ever attack the British directly?' The rural areas I've visited must have offered ample opportunities for ambushes.

'Yes. For example, Satara police station was raided on Christmas Day, 1944. We got away with several rifles.'

What? Bill bearded in his own den? Revenge for the raid on Chafal three weeks earlier?

'Did you know other policemen, apart from Yates?'

'There was Gilbert, who was brought in especially to lead the anti-insurgency. An Indian, too.'

'E.S. Modak?'

'Yes, Modak. And another called Pradhan. Accomplices of Gilbert.'

Was it partly to counter such perceptions that Modak wrote his memoir? Suddenly, the possibility occurs to me that Lad doesn't know who I am. Otherwise, wouldn't he say 'your father' rather than 'Gilbert', the name some people have used on this trip? Surely Shinde's son explained when he phoned to make the appointment? But Briha, following his principal's lead, addresses me as 'Professor Bart' and perhaps these people also think that's my name. Lad only glanced cursorily at my card. Maybe he doesn't associate 'Moore-Gilbert' with 'Gilbert'. Should I spell it out? But he might clam up, or sanitise what he wants to say. Exquisitely uncomfortable, I decide to let it slide.

'During that time your critics accuse you of atrocities, of being terrorists.'

Lad shakes his head vigorously before launching into a long defence of the Parallel Government. What he adds to D.Y. Patil's account is the claim that deeds of violence committed by ordinary criminals were regularly blamed on the movement.

'It suited the police and criminals alike.'

Murkier and murkier. Further, he insists that the group was first and foremost interested in social reform. In order to carry out its programme, it needed political capital.

'And so we attacked government buildings, the postal system and railways.'

I nod.

'We wanted to bring down the pyramid of oppression by undermining the base it rested on. We weren't terrorists, we were freedom fighters.'

There's silence as I continue writing notes.

'Gilbert was the terrorist in that campaign, not us,' says Lad suddenly.

My father was a terrorist? I'm winded for a moment by Lad's bald judgement. Is it one I should have arrived at myself, in the light of the debate at Briha's college and my tour of the 'Mutiny' sites in Kolhapur? I can't think of any response for the moment.

'Mind, he wasn't as bad as the others.'

The qualification is only partly gratifying. 'What do you mean?'

'Like Yates, firing on unarmed demonstrators.'

I nod. 'Did you ever encounter Gilbert?'

Lad looks at me keenly. I can't decide if he knows who I am or not.

'Only one time I met him face to face. At my marriage. He came here to Kundal on my wedding day.'

I'm bewildered. 'You invited him?'

For the first time, Lad cracks something like a smile. 'No, he was an unexpected guest.'

'What happened?'

'Word must have got to Satara I was getting married. It was the very beginning of May, 1945.'

This raid was probably Bill's last hurrah in the district. According to his service record, he was transferred on the third.

'But just as the British had their informers, so did we. Inside Satara police station. Even among the armed constabulary.'

Did Bill have any idea?

'Anyway,' Lad goes on, confirming D.Y., 'Gilbert had to get permission from the Aundh authorities to come here. So we knew he was on his way.'

'But you went ahead?'

'We, er, increased the number of guests. By the time the police buses arrived outside Kundal, nearly twelve thousand were waiting. The enemy lined up, four or five hundred of them. I was flattered to see so many. Gilbert walked in front and stopped about ten yards from the front of the crowd. I could see him clearly. He was such a big man, his face was visible above everyone's heads. He demanded I surrender. I shouted back that I wasn't going to disappoint my guests. There was cheering.'

'And then?'

'He ordered the first platoons to advance. Their rifles were at the ready. He made his demand a second time. The crowd began shouting, but no one budged. They were ten deep between him and me. I was just then ready to give myself up because I was convinced he'd give the order to fire.'

My heart's racing. 'Did he?'

'No. We stared at each other over my supporters's heads. I could see he was beginning to waver. It was something in his eyes. He was too weak or too good to fire on a wedding crowd. After a minute or two, he ordered his men to pull back. The police all got in their buses and reversed down the road. It was a great moment.'

I can't stop a sigh of relief. 'The ceremony went ahead as planned?'

Lad grimaces. 'Not quite.'

'What happened?'

'In Hindu marriages, the bridegroom must put *khum-khum* between the bride's eyebrows.'

'A red powder,' Briha explains, 'for luck.'

'I carried a dagger on my person at all times then,' Lad goes on. 'I took it from under my marriage gown. Everyone gasped and my bride looked frightened. I cut my thumb and when the blood ran, I pressed it to her brow. It was a token of the sacrifice we were prepared to make.'

I'm somewhat chilled by his tone. But desperately relieved that Bill preferred the humiliation of retreat to a bloody bid for glory. Why did he back off? Perhaps because he was leaving Satara imminently and it was no longer his quarrel. Or he understood the reaction that attacking a wedding would provoke. But I hope it was less laziness or political calculation than simple humanity.

I raise the question of the differences between life in British territory and the princely states. It seems paradoxical for revolutionaries to have sheltered amongst feudal regimes.

'You see, in Aundh the rulers were enlightened. In fact before the war they'd already decided to devolve power. It was known as the Aundh Experiment, and Gandhi endorsed it. The British never did anything like that, not until they had to. But in other places, the feudal rulers wanted to hang onto their privileges. The Nizam of Hyderabad, for instance. After we sent the British away we had to deal with him. That was a bitter struggle.' His gimlet eyes have a steely glitter. 'There was much more bloodshed than in Satara. But it was worth it,' he adds with satisfaction.

I know the Nizam ruled what was once an almost entirely Muslim principality in the middle of British India. According to Orientalist legend, he was fabulously wealthy, loved hunting and boasted an enormous harem. He elected for complete independence in 1947, which the British agreed to on the same constitutional-legal basis that allowed the Hindu Rajah of Kashmir to join India rather than Pakistan, despite its overwhelmingly Muslim population. Unwilling to sanction an independent polity in their heartland, however, the new Congress government gave the Nizam an ultimatum to join India. When it was rejected, *anschluss* followed. There was clearly one rule for the Rajah and another for the Nizam. The latter bravely – or foolishly – set his ill-equipped army to defend Hyderabad, only for it to be annihilated by Indian units battle-hardened during World War Two. Two to three hundred thousand Muslim civilians died as the Indian army and its hangers-on ran riot, including, I now understand, former members of the Parallel Government.

'There were more schools, more hospitals on average in British territory than in many princely states,' Lad goes on meditatively, 'but what's the use of such things if you are slaves?'

'Weren't the British already democratising in the 1930s? Didn't you have an Indian prime minister in Bombay Province?'

'My friend, haven't you heard about the Defence of India Rules introduced when war broke out?'

I'm suitably chastened.

When it's time to leave, Lad gestures to one of his assistants. The man comes forward with a book. It has a loud red cover of a man staring at the rising sun, chains on his wrists bursting asunder.

'My autobiography,' Lad murmurs gravely. 'Here you will find the full and true story of the movement.' He signs it in a shaky hand.

My earlier suspicions are confirmed. Like Charunder Shinde's yesterday, the dedication reads: 'To dear Professor Bart'. But despite his gift, the time he's given me and his story about Bill, I'm glad to escape. I've felt on edge, withered by his glare, from the moment he entered the room. Lad radiates disapproval. Is it because he *does* know who I am, or continuing bitterness about the Raj?

From Kundal to Walwa, where we're meeting the second surviving nationalist leader, is half an hour across more monotonous countryside, the road bisecting endless sugarcane plantations. I flick through Lad's book, the text of which is enlivened by several cartoons of the Parallel Government at work – attacking a police post, training recruits in the fields, doing social work. One shows someone being given the bastinado, hands tied behind his back, bare soles tied by a rope and raised to be thrashed.

'Justice for an oppressive moneylender,' Briha translates the surrounding Marathi script.

Is this what Bill had in mind at Chafal, when he said it was time such people were given a taste of their own medicine? But why, after two centuries of rule, hadn't the British stamped out rural usury, which kept the peasants so impoverished? I wonder, too, about the justice of Lad's claim that Bill was a terrorist. He didn't fire on the wedding crowd, thank God. And Chafal was nothing compared to what Colonel Jacob got up to in Kolhapur. However, what's uncomfortably similar is the principle: using 'shock and awe', staging public performances of summary 'justice' on victims selected on fairly arbitrary gounds, in order to cow civilians into obedience to an authoritarian foreign power. Perhaps that's one definition of 'state terrorism'?

~

When we pull up outside the community hall in Walwa, a burly man of medium height is waiting on the veranda with a broad smile. He's wearing a loose beige kurta which doesn't fully conceal chunky, varicosed calves and feet in brown socks. His thin, silvery hair is cut into an almost military short back and sides, set off by a neat Clark Gable moustache. Though he moves slowly, the former guerrilla's handshake remains strong. Perhaps he spent time as a young man in wrestling *talims* like the one I saw yesterday. In contrast to the grim-mannered Lad, he can't stop chuckling as he leads us inside the hall and motions us to sofas facing a glass-topped table. He insists we eat something and have tea first. I'm instantly at ease. Our host is one of those people who, the very first time you meet them, you feel you've known forever.

On the surrounding walls are several portraits, including Gandhi, Shivaji, Nana Patil and Lad addressing a mass rally. There are a couple of photos of Nayakwadi as a younger man. One of them arrests me. It must have been taken in his twenties and has an uncanny resemblance to Bill at that age. I examine my host carefully. Is this how my father would have looked if he'd lived as long? He was taller, but they have the same burly build and mischievous expression. A strong pang of loss catches me unawares and I warm to Nayakwadi even more. Briha, too, seems more relaxed than at Lad's. He addresses our host as 'Anna'. I assume it's an honorific, judging by my friend's awestruck demeanour. I follow suit, cracking our host into another grin. He takes my hand and squeezes it in his bearlike paw, keeping hold until an assistant serves tea and chapattis, together with a dish of the same spinach fried with garlic which Kiron Modak prepared.

I repeat many of the questions I asked Lad. Once more, I'm not sure Nayakwadi knows who I am. He doesn't speak English and presumably he doesn't read it either, since he barely glanced at my visiting card. I heard 'University of London' in Briha's introduction, but although listening out for it this time, no name at all. I decide to say nothing again. I want my host to be frank, not shelter behind the ritualised courtesies typical of most Indians I've met on my journey. Through Briha, he tells me he was born in Walwa in July 1922 and that his father was a poor farmer. His mother supported Congress, though her husband was less keen.

'He said Congress was for the elites,' Nayakwadi adds. 'I never belonged myself. I was more a communist. The people who joined Congress later,' he shakes his head sadly, 'betrayed our ideals. But in those days, you made alliances with anyone who opposed the Raj. I approved of S.C. Bhose's links with the Japanese and the formation of the Indian National Army. Anything to be free.'

'But once the Soviets entered the war, weren't communists obliged to support the struggle against fascism?'

'Mine was more a local, Indian form of communism, not the official CP kind. I simply wanted all our resources to be shared. And improve the condition of women, end the slavery of caste. You see this young man who brought your food?'

His assistant hovers.

'I knew his grandfather. He wasn't allowed water from the same well as me. Can you imagine, a neighbour you live beside all your life, but we couldn't drink or eat with him?' He squeezes my hand again. 'That is one thing you British did. By making everyone equal before the law, theoretically at least, you dealt a heavy blow to caste. But these things were by-products, not the goal of your rule.'

I glance at Briha, whose head's in danger of spinning off, so vigorously does he nod approval.

'Did you ever meet any British people when you were growing up?'

He shakes his head. 'But once in the movement I did.'

'Yates, Hobson and Gilbert?'

Nayakwadi breaks into another chuckle. 'All three, yes.

Gilbert I came into closest contact with. Twice he nearly caught me. I must say he was persistent. He caused us problems.'

It's partly gratifying to hear this. 'How did you meet?'

'The first time I was in Kameri, for a meeting with Bhauri Patel, my lieutenant. Someone must have betrayed us, for suddenly there were police outside. Patel's wife led me immediately into the women's quarters, where I put on a sari. I was much slimmer then,' he guffaws. 'The police ordered everyone into the yard while they searched the house. They had to be very careful about touching women, so I stayed in the middle of the group and pulled the edge of the sari across my face and prayed no one would notice. No one did,' he concludes with a rumbling laugh.

This man is fun. 'And the other time?'

'I was at another friend's in Eitwade. It was after dark. Again, Gilbert suddenly arrived. Nobody heard him coming.'

Is this the incident recorded in Modak's *No Place*, when 'Bill' walked for two miles in his stockings?

'I couldn't play the same trick again, there weren't any women around. Instead I ran into the courtyard at the back. There was a very high wall, no possibility of escape. Only the well and a banyan tree. I knew I'd be caught if I climbed into its branches, so I jumped over the side of the well. Just in time, because suddenly I heard a great grunt and someone landing in the courtyard from the other side. Gilbert had come round the back and somehow got over the wall.'

'Didn't he hear the splash?'

Tears of laughter squeeze out of Nayakwadi's eyes. 'I'd climbed down the roots. It was a very old tree and they'd broken through the side of the well. I worked my way well inside them and held my breath. I could see a torch playing over the branches and then this shadow reached over the well. The light shone on the water. I was close enough to Gilbert to hear him breathing. Then he cursed and the light disappeared. I stayed down there, hanging in the roots, while the house was searched. I heard a constable saying, "He can't just have disappeared, the sahib was covering the back."'

Nayakwadi calls for more tea. 'Ah, I enjoyed my duels with Gilbert,' he sighs.

I'm touched by his tone. Respect, even affection, for Bill from one of his most redoubtable opponents.

'What do you think of the Raj now?' I ask.

'All in the past. I feel no bitterness.'

'And India today?'

For the first time, Nayakwadi's expression clouds. 'India today?' He shakes his head, before decrying the chronic corruption, incompetence and self-serving of the political elites.

'The ordinary man suffers badly, in terms of education, health and justice. Here in Walwa is better, because we established a sugar co-operative to give the farmers a fair price. The profits go to improving everyone's lives, not just the few. This community centre' – he gestures round the room – 'was paid for by us. And the school. Dalits, Muslims, Christians, all are welcome. But many in the surrounding villages still have no electricity, despite the dams their taxes pay for. And there are so many landless still. These are the real battles facing India.' He shakes his head. 'Not this stupid warmongering with Pakistan.'

'What do you mean?'

'All engineered by the capitalist classes. If there was no poverty, people wouldn't care which country they lived in, what gods others believed in.'

I wish Nayakwadi had been at the lecture yesterday. He radiates such moral authority. And so much humour and warmth. I could get very attached to him.

'How do you see the struggle of the Parallel Government now?'

'We need another one,' he answers straight away, with a mischievous grin.

I feel obliged to ask him, too, about the accusations of atrocities against his movement.

'Well, mistakes were made,' Nayakwadi acknowledges. 'Some people were wrongly accused, unjustly persecuted. But it was a war, and sometimes decisions had to be made very hurriedly. It doesn't detract from the good that was done. Especially if you can admit your mistakes afterwards and say sorry.'

I'm deeply moved by the meeting. I feel I've heard wisdom, distilled by decades of experience, of learning, of action and of self-interrogation. Nayakwadi strikes me as a man of luminous integrity, with the kind of values I most admire. What a shame he and Bill were on opposite sides. Even more so that Bill couldn't make this journey with me. Still, Nayakwadi's half-admiring, almost affectionate account of his opponent is something solid to counter-balance the trip to Chafal. Especially as there've been no allegations of the kind Shinde and Lad made.

When we get back in the car, I thank Briha for his patient interpreting. 'By the way, we kept calling him "Anna". What does it mean?'

'Father,' he responds. 'But less formal.'

Daddy, daddy, daddy, I mutter under my breath.

~

Kanishka's party is a soothing distraction to round off a tumultuous day. Briha drops me at the hotel to change and while waiting for him to return, I buy a bag of bright-dyed candies for his boy from the shop next door. The flat's in a modern three-storey block, ten minutes away on the back of Briha's Honda. There are already quite a few people, though I'm disconcerted to find all the men are in the front room and the women in the kitchen. Class appears to make no difference to the gender segregation I've encountered throughout my trip. Briha takes me through to meet his wife, a very shy, pretty woman who hands me a plate of dal, rice and vegetable curry, with an iced bun and a piece of cake wedged incongruously either side. My host then proudly points out the recently completed terrace off the kitchen, where one or two men are smoking, before leading me back to the living room. In one corner a video plays. His wedding, Briha explains. But their little boy holds centre stage today, seated against a bolster, dressed like a miniature maharajah, surrounded by friends. He wails when he catches sight of me.

'It's your colour,' Briha chuckles, 'he's not used.'

While his mother comforts the boy, Briha insists on tying a long-tailed cinnamon-coloured Kolhapur turban on my head and everyone applauds and wants photographs. I'm sure it looks ludicrous with cut-offs and sandals. Then the blessing takes place. Trays of food are circled round Kanishka's head, and he's offered spoonfuls while guests throw rice over him. Self-possession restored, the boy's as gracious as a little prince. Then everyone sings 'Happy Birthday', followed – to the same tune – by 'May God Bless You', before Briha cuts a cake, garishly decorated with miniature funfair fixtures made of icing. It's heartening. In modern India, some dalits, at least, are entering the middle classes. Things have moved on from their predicament under the Raj, described so poignantly in Anand's *Untouchable* or Nayakwadi's story about his helper's grandfather.

Later, I chat with a couple of Briha's colleagues who were at yesterday's debate on terrorism, some civil servants and IT types. One approaches with hands full of sodas, inviting me to help myself.

'Many Marathis in London, *yaar*?' he grins.

'Don't know I've ever met one. Plenty of Gujaratis and Sikhs and Tamils.'

'Those types are everywhere. Especially here in Maharashtra,' he adds in an aggrieved tone. 'Traders. We Marathis are soldiers and artists and administrators. Gujaratis and Sikhs, they will always cheat you. As for Tamils ...' I'm afraid he's going to spit. 'Never trust one. They will eat the food off your table in the evening and stab you in the back the following morning.'

Remembering ASP Shinde's comments in Satara police station about the problem of local chauvinism towards those from other parts of India, I escape to the terrace. It's shaded by a gigantic jackfruit tree, stars blinking through its leaves. I lean against a concrete pillar and gaze at them, thinking about Nayakwadi's closing remarks. Did Bill ever acknowledge his mistakes or feel remorse about the past?

At his father's call, the boy makes his way down from the roof of the four-storey block of flats where they're living in Dar es Salaam. It looks onto Selandar Bridge, which divides the older part of the city from Msasani Peninsula and Oyster Bay, where the new African ministers and diplomats live. The boy never wanted to live in a city, but he's enjoying it now. From here it's an easy walk either to the beach or the Italian ice-cream parlour and bookshop off Independence Avenue. And the flat roof's the perfect place to practise football on his own, when he can't bribe Lindsay to play in goal, the parapet walls perfect for angled passes and thunderous shots. His father's promised a kick-around after the fancy-dress party at the Gymkhana Club.

The boy's got his Shaka, King of the Zulus, outfit ready in his bag, with lion-claw necklace and zebra-skin armband, though he's had to make do with a Maasai spear, stabbing sword and short shield. Since discovering King Solomon's Mines, *he's become obsessed by all things Zulu. Everyone else is going in some kind of British army uniform, Marine Commandos, Guards, SAS. The boy's worried about his raffia skirt. Will everyone laugh?*

'Look, old chap, Shaka didn't racket round in a jockstrap or shorts,' his father reassured him that morning. 'Let them have a taste of your assegai *if anyone gives you gyp.'*

RESPECT BETWEEN ENEMIES

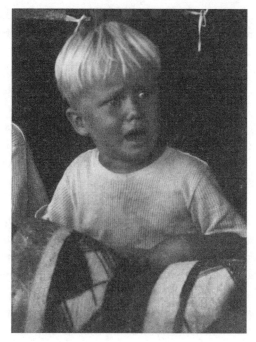

The author preparing for a fancy-dress party c. 1958

He's already on the stairs as the boy reaches the landing, juggling a tennis ball in one hand.

'Come on, I've got your stuff. Want some water?' He offers the Gordon's Gin bottle, sweating with condensation from the fridge.

When he's finished drinking, the boy leaps down the stairs, two and three at a time. 'Race you.'

'Hey, that's not fair, I'm carrying everything.'

The boy goes back up, but his father shoos him away with a laugh.

'Careful on the second floor.'

The tiling's being relaid and there's only rough cement for the moment. He's already tripped once and grazed his elbow.

Placing the boy's holdall and his sports bags on the seat behind, his father settles behind the wheel.

'Did you remember Neil's goggles?' the boy asks. 'The Jenkins are going snorkelling off South Beach tomorrow.'

There's an impatient sigh. 'We're late.'

'I promised, dad.'

'Well,' his father replies, singling out the right key on his fob, 'run back up, there's a good chap.'

The boy leaps back up the stairs almost as quickly as he descended. He loves the way his golden body feels. He never seems to tire, however hot it gets, however long he plays football. He wants to play for the Gymkhana Club when he's older, like his father. Perhaps in a few years they'll turn out together. Goalkeepers last longer than outfield players, he knows that, and his father's still fit as a flea.

He opens the door to the flat quietly as he can. His mother takes a nap in the late afternoon. So it's a surprise to find her in the kitchen. To his horror, she's crying, misery scored in a deep line between her eyebrows. The boy freezes. She says nothing as she turns, tears running silently down her face.

'Mummy, what is it? What's the matter?'

She steps forward quickly and hugs him. It's not something she often does, so the boy knows this must be serious. Behind his back he can hear her sniffling into the paper tissue she always carries. Despite himself, he hates the way she does that. Why can't she use a proper handkerchief like other mothers?

'It's nothing. What did you come back for?'

'Daddy forgot Neil's goggles.'

'Better get them then.'

Unsure what to do, the boy finally breaks away and darts into the bathroom. By the time he returns, his mother's wiping her eyes.

'You sure you're OK, mummy?'

'Yes,' she sighs, to his guilty relief, 'run along now or you'll miss the party. I stitched up the raffia skirt for you.'

'Alright, old chap?' his father says as his son slams the passenger door of the Land Rover.

The boy stares straight ahead. 'Mummy's crying,' he eventually mutters. Will his father cancel the outing now?

'What?'

His son nods.

'Stay here.'

His father's gone more than half an hour. The boy tries to understand what's going on. He's hardly ever seen his mother cry. Last time was several years back, when he nearly dashed his brains out with a stone-hammer which bounced up like a rubber ball from the rock half-buried in the drive in Manyoni. He'd been helping the masons build the new veranda. The blow stunned him for several minutes and removed a perfect square inch of skin above his eyebrow. Like the mark below his left knee, where he fell from a tree, he's now proud of the scar.

What can it be? Ever since he saw his father kissing Viva Balson, the boy's kept a wary eye out. But that was ages ago. The boy still sees Eric and Viva when they drop off or collect their kids from school. But so far as he knows, his father hasn't seen the Balsons since they left the Ngorongoro Crater.

Eventually, his father returns, looking thoughtful. When he gets into the driver's seat, he doesn't say anything for a while. Then he turns to the boy as if suddenly remembering he's there.

'What is it, dad?'

To his alarm, his father leans forward to rest his forehead on the steering wheel. For a moment, his shoulders heave. The boy repeats the question. When no answer comes, he slides across the seat and puts a hand on his father's arm. There's another shudder before his father looks up again.

'Have to try harder,' he whispers.

'What do you mean?'

'It's difficult for mummy now. Ames has gone to school in England. I'm at the office all day, and you and Lindsay are away at St Michael's most of the time. And no Kimwaga to help.'

There isn't room in the flat. It's the only black mark against Dar es Salaam, that and the fact they can't keep dogs. Tunney and Dempsey have stayed behind in Tabora until his father knows how long they'll be in Dar es Salaam. The Emperor Haile Selassie has offered his father a five-year contract to open the first national parks in Ethiopia and everything's up in the air.

'That woman who comes is useless. Mummy has to do it all again herself. She spends too much time on her own.'

'Why doesn't she come to the Club?'

'She doesn't want to.'

'Should we try to help more?'

His father smiles gratefully.

He says nothing as they drive into town. At the entrance to the Gymkhana Club the boy sees his friends milling around, inspecting each other's uniforms. His father suddenly turns to him.

'Look, old chap, I'll just drop you at the party if you don't mind. I'm going to head home now. We'll have a kick-around another time.'

'Shall I come back, too?'

'No, everyone's waiting for you. I'll pick you up later.'

A hand powerful as a bear's squeezes the boy's for a moment before reaching back for the bag containing the fancy-dress outfit.

'Bayete, Nkozi,' he salutes as the boy turns back on the veranda of the Club.

CHAPTER 13

Like Father, Like Son

'Poel will be here in the next couple of days,' Rajeev affirms, during his early morning catch-up call. 'He'll see what he can do, once he's back in the office. You've time to visit Ratnagiri, then. Nice place, like Goa fifty years ago. I think you deserve a little break, no? Gather your strength before Mumbai?'

It makes sense. A chance to see another of Bill's postings, the last before he left India. There simply isn't time to get up to Nasik or Ahmedabad this trip. And since I've missed Bhosle, it's unlikely I'll be able to clarify whether Bill was ever in Sindh.

There's no 'Volvo' from Kolhapur, so it's the local country bus, hot and sticky, people packed in the aisle and a strong whiff of poultry from the coop cradled by the woman across from me. To begin with, I'm diverted by my neighbour, an eighty-year-old veteran of the Mahratta Light Infantry. He's on a pilgrimage to the great temple at Ganpatipule, north of Ratnagiri – preparation, as he puts it, 'for going upstairs'. His mischievous tales about the mishaps of military life have me in stitches. Until, that is, the bus begins its descent to the Konkan littoral; with steepling crags and plunging ravines to either side, the constant squeal of brakes prevents conversation. We lurch against each other as the driver spins his wheel like a ship's captain, one way then the other, to the vehement klaxons of lorries coming the other way and the clucks of scrabbling chickens. The veteran places a finger in each ear and closes his eyes with an anxious expression, as if we're headed 'upstairs' sooner than planned.

Finally we reach the safety of the coastal plain, where it's much sultrier, air hazy and saline as we approach the ocean. The landscape's also very different from up on the Deccan plateau, orchards of cashew and areca palm, mango, banana and endless emerald paddy fields. On this final leg we're shown a video, perhaps as a reward for our fortitude. It's an irritatingly enjoyable Bollywood musical in which an over-loud song with the punchline 'I've got your number' is endlessly repeated by actors seemingly trained at the Benny Hill Academy of Innuendo. The attendant squeezes jovially through the press in the aisle, offering an acidic cologne which my neighbour slaps gratefully on his hands and neck, as if purifying himself for his pilgrimage. Will this next stage of my own quest provide further enlightenment? And will there be expiation? After Chafal and the nationalist leaders, I sense my trip may be beginning to wind down. If only I can get to hear Bill's own voice before I leave India. Everything depends on Poel, unless by some miracle some of his confidential weeklies have been preserved in Ratnagiri.

The long drive, change in climate and recent days of intense emotion have sapped me. I decide to stay holed up for the rest of the day, chilling and reading Ghosh's *The Glass Palace*. It's a joy to shower and then relax into a well-written novel which deals with the last half-century of the Raj. I'm surprised by what I read. Like me, Ghosh came here to Ratnagiri to do research. Perhaps he stayed at this very hotel, given its proximity to King Thibaw's palace. As Briha intimated, the early parts of the text reconstruct the fate of the exiled Burmese royal family in Ratnagiri at the turn of the twentieth century. Exile seems to have been the Raj's favourite punishment for royal opponents. But Thibaw's story is darker even than those of Pratapsinh of Satara or Chimasaheb of Kolhapur.

At his accession, Burma was the richest country in Asia; as his reign wore on, Western merchants cast increasingly covetous eyes on its resources, notably teak and mahogany. The king granted a concession to a British company to log 30,000 trees a year. When he discovered it was extracting more than twice that number, he levied a fine. The company officials complained to the Indian authorities, which launched a military expedition. Thibaw was punished not only by the annexation of his kingdom but with removal thousands of miles away, to this far side of the Indian land mass. Even when the royal couple died, the British wouldn't allow repatriation of their bodies, in case they became a focus of unrest. Apparently the tombs stand forlorn somewhere in town. It's a sad, cruel story, Imperialism in the raw again, vividly realised in this semi-fictional form.

~

After a good night's sleep, I head for the local police station. It's quite different to the one in Satara, a low, cream rectangular building in bungalow style. In the centre of the moth-eaten lawn is an old cannon, painted blue, and along its borders are crimson bougainvillea bushes and dwarf fan palms. In the soupy coastal air, the atmosphere's altogether sleepier, too. Although it's already nine o'clock, neither the DSP nor his deputy has arrived for work. I wander outside for half an hour, trying to get a feel for this part of town. Opposite the station is a deserted murram parade ground, much like those I've seen before. But it's too hot and humid to probe further away than the nearby dual carriageway which thrusts down into the heart of Ratnagiri. However, not even its fumes can entirely subdue the sickly, fishy smell which, a helpful passer-by explains, emanates from the town's canneries, its main industry. Below, modern Ratnagiri spreads along the shore, an occasional minaret slicing through the humid haze. My chance companion tells me that nearly half the population's Muslim, very unusual in southern Maharashtra.

By the time I get back to the station, my quarry's been sighted and I'm shown in to Deputy Superintendent Athanaker's office. Like his colleagues in Satara, he's fascinated by my photos of Bill in India and delighted to learn that I'm the son of the last British IP officer in charge here. Bill's tenure isn't recorded on the name boards, however. Unlike in Satara, here they go back only to Independence. Why the difference? Through the window, I see people rise suddenly from seats on the veranda and salute. The DSP's arrived, followed by several men in white and blue uniforms. Athanakar leaves the office for a moment.

'Mr Indore will be pleased to see you,' he announces on his return.

It feels like a council of war is taking place in Bill's old office, painted a satin cream which looks slimy under the neon strip lighting. An ugly air-con unit hisses in one corner. Athanakar introduces me, hands over my card and tells Indore why I'm here. The DSP's about fifty, dark jowly complexion, flashing gold tooth and dark stains under the arms of his uniform shirt. I shake everyone's hand and am asked to wait at the back of the room, where tea's brought to me. The visitors speak animatedly, often interrupting each other. The conversation switches between English and Marathi, or perhaps Hindi, and I gather the visitors are from Customs and Excise and the Coastguard.

'We're discussing maritime defence in the light of the Mumbai terror,' Indore explains when the meeting breaks up. 'Explosives used in previous attacks during the 1990s came through Ratnagiri, and we're investigating whether the same may have happened this time.'

It's hard to imagine such a sleepy-seeming place being a nerve centre of terrorist planning. I mention the wartime arrangements for coastal defence against the Japanese which I came across in the SIB archives.

'I should like to see those files,' Indore responds thoughtfully. 'We're in the process of reorganising our arrangements now. Perhaps we can learn something from the British,' he adds sincerely. He asks about Bill's time in Ratnagiri and I explain my mission.

'I wondered if I could consult copies of his weekly confidential reports and the station Part IVs?'

After some consideration, Indore shakes his head. 'Part IVs, OK. But not the others, even if we can find them. Confidential, as the name says.'

'I saw them at Satara,' I plead disingenuously.

He looks shocked. 'At Satara? But that is most irregular.'

I flash my most winning smile. 'I've come all the way from London.'

He reflects a moment. 'Very well,' he nods, 'please come back the day after tomorrow. I'll see what I can do.'

'Most kind,' I respond as I get up. 'Also, any chance you could find some constables from that time?'

He agrees to make inquiries, though he doesn't hold out great hopes. 'What are your immediate plans in Ratnagiri?'

'First I thought I'd try to find out where my father lived.'

Indore grins amiably. 'That's easy. It's my house now. Further along this road. Please to look around the grounds. But you can't go in. My wife and daughter are at home. Shall I send someone with you?'

'If it's not too much trouble.'

Indore barks into an intercom.

'You know the history of Ratnagiri? About Thibaw?'

I nod. 'I thought I might visit his palace this afternoon. It's round the corner from my hotel.'

'The DSP's house was where the king stayed when he first came here.'

I'm delighted by the coincidence. A constable knocks and enters, saluting smartly.

'He will take you.'

It's not quite what Satara laid on, but I'm grateful nonetheless. The officer takes me into the yard and summons me onto the back of a large motorbike. He doesn't bother with a helmet, or think to offer me one, and soon we're racing along the narrow road away from the police station. I cling anxiously to his waist, trying to remember whether I'm supposed to lean into, or away from, bends. I swear his knee brushes the tarmac as we tear round a last sharp curve and into a long drive shaded by mangoes and palms. At last a speed bump forces my escort to slow and we skid to a stop as a sentry walks out of his hut. So this is where Bill spent his final months in India. It's calm and quiet behind the stone perimeter wall, the last stretch of drive to the house lined with tubs of generously flowering oleander and hibiscus. What a relief this must have been after the aggravations of Satara and Ahmedabad. We dismount and I wander off to look around.

If not exactly fit for a king, it seems more than adequate for a DSP: another large, red-tiled bungalow built into the shallow fall of the hillside. The sloping grounds are bare now, except for a few enormous tamarinds and peepuls, with glossy heart-shaped leaves. Through them I glimpse downtown Ratnagiri and patches of sapphire sea. Easy to imagine Bill taking tiffin and lime-juice soda on the terrace, where passion-fruit smothers a rickety pergola. Perhaps in those traffic-free days he could even hear the waves at night, as he tried to decide whether to stay on in India after Independence.

I'm hoping the DSP's wife will open a window and invite me in for a cool drink. But the windows stare back blankly. Since I can't see indoors, I don't linger, and ask to be dropped back at the hotel. At a loss what to do until Thibaw's palace opens, I settle on tackling the postcards I've accumulated. If I don't hurry up, I'll beat them back home. The post office isn't far, a lovely colonial building in the same style as the police station and Bill's quarters, with deep projecting eaves. When I'm done, I notice the large modern building opposite. Someone tells me it's the Tilak Memorial Library, partly endowed by his family; and that it has one of the best reference sections outside Mumbai and Pune. Remembering the formative influence of Tilak on Lad and Nayakwadi, I wander over.

It's high-ceilinged and cool, with elegant furniture and few readers. The librarian registers me, tells me a little about the history of the institution and strongly recommends a visit to Tilak's house in the centre of town. Happily, he suggests I consult the *Bombay Gazette* to get a feel for the situation in Ratnagiri when Bill was there. More luck. British bureaucracy was nothing if not self-reflexive. There are hundreds of tomes in gold-brown bindings, six or seven massive volumes for each year. Every administrative directive is recorded, it seems, from bannings of major political organisations to regulation of *tonga* fares. Everything's so clearly tabulated, I can navigate easily. I see orders for the arrest of members of the Parallel Government, including Naganath Nayakwadi. I also find the proclamation of the award of Bill's Indian Police Medal. The date, 16 June 1945, suggests it must indeed have been for 'meritorious service' in Satara, which he left weeks earlier. Every posting and transfer in the entire civil administration seems to be recorded here. But I can find no mention of Bill's secondment to Sindh. Where on earth did Professor Bhosle get his information?

A couple of things strike me as I flick through the pages. First, the British authorities seem to have consistently identified Muslims as neutral in their struggles with mainstream Indian nationalism, at least in Bombay Province. The collective fines imposed on villages sheltering dissidents consistently exempt them, as well as Christians and members of 'the backward classes'. I suddenly realise that I've met no Muslims amongst all the police officers encountered on my trip. Do the roots of contemporary discrimination against them in Indian public life go back to their perceived role as favourites of the British? I also wonder whether it was here, in religiously mixed Ratnagiri, that Bill developed his penchant for Muslim employees in Africa: Hamisi Sekana, his chief game scout, Daoudi and Salim Salendwa who accompanied us on the Ugalla River safari and, above all, my beloved childhood minder, Kimwaga Hamisi Farahani.

Second is how imperturbably the juggernaut of the Raj continued, up to the very end. In early August 1947, for example, one district magistrate is 'pleased to lift the current prohibitions on processions and the firing of fireworks' for 14–15 August, as if after Independence Day everything will simply revert to the status quo. The order could come straight out of a Kipling satire of imperial bureaucracy. Ratnagiri seems to have been largely calm during the six months of Bill's jurisdiction. There are occasional outbursts of communalist feeling, leading to bans on gatherings over a certain size. But most administrative directives relate to mundane matters such as cloth rationing, prices of essential foodstuffs and traffic control. I get the sense that Bill might even have felt bored here. After the turbulence of Satara and Kolhapur, I wonder if I won't soon feel becalmed myself in this dozy place. Still, it's only for a couple of days, and perhaps there'll be the chance of some swimming.

~

After a late lunch I get ready to visit Thibaw's palace, where the king moved from Bill's cottage. As I leave the hotel, I'm hailed by a young man leaning against a bright red scooter. He has a sallow moon-face, wide-set eyes and, almost unprecedented amongst the men I've seen so far, no moustache.

'Excuse me, sir, two minutes?'

'Yes?'

'I am studying Hospitality BA and need to practise my English. Where are you going just now, sir?'

'To Thibaw's palace.'

'I will take you, sir. Perhaps we can talk together? My name's Keitan. But also Ronny, yo.'

I'm confused, but it seems more than a fair exchange. To my relief, Keitan – as I settle on calling him – has two helmets, and we're soon chuntering along a road with magnificent views across Ratnagiri Bay. Over his shoulder, my new acquaintance tells me a little about himself. He's the only son of Brahmin parents and his dearest wish is to get work overseas. Can I possibly help? When I tell him I'm only an academic, so my capacities in that regard are minimal, he gives a resigned shrug.

'Then you can helpfully correct my accent?'

As I tell him why I'm in Ratnagiri, he repeats some of the words to practise his pronunciation. We'll have to work on his v's and w's.

Thibaw's 'palace' is an enormous brick pile set on a bluff overlooking the estuary. It's seemingly inspired by the stodgiest kind of northern British municipal architecture, and was completed shortly before World War One. It looks like it's been coated in a treacly anti-rust paint, perhaps to protect against the monsoons and coastal damp. The couple of acres of grounds are being refurbished, though the old water features are clogged with sand and broken bricks, a few baby palms struggling to survive in drums.

The mysterious house in Ratnagiri

The interior's largely empty, except for one room filled with lovely eighth-century stone sculptures excavated nearby. The only vestiges of the royal tenancy are two red velvet divans, a dark-varnished portrait of the king, his desk and bath, carved from a single block of caramel marble. After Thibaw's death, our guide says, the building was used as a local government facility, but has since been vacant for several years. There's a miniature durbar room, echoing with doves lodged in the wonderful carved teak beams. Imported from Burma, no doubt. We're told that Thibaw's daughter was so distraught at being confined under virtual house arrest that she eventually eloped with the carriage driver who delivered supplies from Ratnagiri. Her descendants live somewhere in town today.

The guide then takes us out onto the first-floor balcony, which has a jaw-dropping vista onto a wide brown river which quickly broadens out further into the estuary. It's studded with fishing boats and outriggers, some sliding towards the ocean beneath a modern road bridge set on soaring pillars. In the distance are magnificent headlands, one crowned with what looks like another of Shivaji's forts, the same style as Ajinkya Tara. I wonder what Thibaw felt as he paced this balcony, year after year, decade after decade, his once-vast domains now brutally truncated to the acre or so of grounds below. How he must have been drawn to the unbounded sea in front, tantalisingly out of reach, the forbidden highway home.

'This dirty country,' Keitan complains, wiping off some dog shit he's stepped in as we prepare to get back on the scooter. He seems very upset. 'It would be better if you British came back to rule us.'

It seems rather a large jump, especially after the stories we've just heard. 'British politicians are hardly squeaky-clean.' I describe some of the recent scandals.

Keitan looks startled. 'But here, 24 per cent of federal parliamentarians have criminal charges outstanding. They just pay the judges to postpone their cases year after year. Some are accused of murder, extortion, drugs.'

He launches into a bitter denunciation of Ratnagiri, the lack of job opportunities, the social conservatism. He's not as articulate as Nayakwadi, but equally impassioned. I'm painfully struck by Keitan's rose-tinted ideas about life in the West. More than anything, he seems lonely, his eyes swimming with vulnerability. I imagine he spends a lot of time hanging about outside hotels frequented by foreigners.

'Come on, let's go and get some tea.'

Keitan's very particular about his diet. No black tea, no coffee, no alcohol. Only certain kinds of fruit, and those only on specific days. I infer that his parents are strictly orthodox and that's really what he's chafing against. We sit in the little playground across the road from Thibaw's palace, where he tells me more about his course and his pen pals in New Zealand and Uzbekistan. I've got one eye on the shoreline far below us which extends in a shallow curve to the colossal bridge, after which it's caster-sugar sand. I get out the photos of Bill in India, one of which has always puzzled me. It's of an attractive thatched bungalow, surrounded by palms, the veranda screened with rattan punkah fans, a beach falling away in the foreground. In Aunt Pat's album, there was no caption.

'Do you think you could help me find this house?' I point past the bridge. 'I think that might be the beach it's on. It's the old part of Ratnagiri, yes?' I don't hold out any great hopes, but at worst it's a chance to do something vaguely touristy. Perhaps, I add, I'll find a nice spot for a swim.

To my surprise, Keitan looks uncomfortable. 'We cannot go down into Bangladesh.'

'Bangladesh? What are you talking about?'

'That's what we call the Muslim area. Down below. All the way up from the bridge, to Ratnagiri jetty.'

It floats like a pencil in the far distance.

'You can't be serious, Keitan. Come on, I'll be with you.' I have all the confidence born of three weeks in India without the remotest hint of concern about my personal safety.

He looks uncertainly at the low sun above the sea, before nodding. 'But we must be off the beach by dark. And I won't take my scooter down there.'

I wonder whether I'm being pushy. But I want to explore contemporary Muslim India, if only for the fag-end of one afternoon. Keitan reaches for his helmet.

'Let's go, then. I will park on the bridge and we can walk down.'

I linger a moment once Keitan's chained his scooter to the railings. From this height, the panorama's awesome. Early indications are that the sunset will be spectacular, the water already taking on an opal sheen, the hazy sky turning oyster. Far below, the river meets the incoming tide in a turbulent series of brown flourishes. An incoming fishing smack labours against the current, buffeted by the frothing confluence.

'You should see it during monsoon,' Keitan observes, 'the water's ten feet higher.' He sighs. 'I'd like to hang-glide from up here.'

What? I can't imagine anything more scary.

'Do you know they used to have flying machines in ancient times in India?'

'You mean like hang-gliders?'

'No,' he says solemnly. 'With engines powered by mercury.'

I'm flummoxed. Keitan's eyes ache with sincerity.

'That is correct. With mercury, only. Yo, it says so in the Vedas.'

He doesn't seem to want to pursue the topic, and turns instead towards the steps raking down the side of the bridge.

It's many steep flights to the bottom. At ground level, the coastal road peels inland and an imposing series of colonial buildings, hidden by a dense canopy of foliage from where we were standing on the bridge, comes into view.

'What's that?' I ask.

Keitan shrugs. 'I think some school?'

It looks far too grand. Intrigued, I set off up the drive. Outside the first building, a group of youths is gathered. They're mid-teens, judging by their shorts and the faint down on their upper lips. They examine us intently, before one says something which makes the others laugh. Keitan seems uncomfortable, so, taking him by the arm, I stride past the onlookers into the edifice. He's right. It is – or was – some kind of school, a technical institute, judging by the ancient lathes huddled along one wall. A man comes forward, dressed in overalls. He's not particularly friendly, and somewhat cursorily explains that it's indeed an industrial training college, founded by the British.

'Sorry if we've intruded,' I say, 'it looked like your students were on a break.'

He seems mollified and suggests we continue to the main campus, where we can get further information on the history of the college. I'm not that interested and suggest that we head for the beach now. Keitan nods, with an odd look of relief.

Outside, the group of youths has swelled. There are maybe fifteen now, white shirts or vests tucked into their khaki shorts. Some instinct puts me on guard. One of them, an undernourished lad with a thicker fuzz of moustache than the rest and pinched, pockmarked cheeks calls out something I don't understand which Keitan seems unwilling to translate. I'm not sure the lad understands me, either, when I say we're just looking around. But he smiles ambiguously as he mutters.

'Gazza,' is the only word I register in his response.

Imagining he's referring to Paul Gascoigne, the eccentric former England soccer idol, I grin back, tapping one forefinger against the side of my head. The thin smile fades. Keitan pulls me away and I follow, puzzled and reluctant. Others in the group jostle forward and again I hear the word 'Gazza'. The tone's clearly menacing now. Perhaps they're Tottenham supporters, insulted by my disrespect to their one-time hero. Whatever, it's definitely time to go.

Keitan remains tight-lipped as we make our way to the shoreline, and his hands seem to be shaking. However, I feel relaxed again by the time we cross a building site with cone-shaped piles of stones, pallets of brick and steel rods scattered like spillikins. The site's deserted, but it looks as if an old breakwater is in the process of being refurbished. We pass through the yard and onto the sand. From here, the bridge looks very high, the noise of traffic indistinct. The first part of the beach is blinding white sand, stretching up to a line of scrub, along what looks like a shallow ditch voiding into the sea. About a mile away is the jetty. I pause for a moment, to get out the photo of the bungalow I'm looking for.

'You OK, Keitan? What were those boys saying?'

He's bug-eyed with tension. 'I told you. This is Bangladesh. They're angry.'

'What about?'

'Gaza. A full-scale land invasion began this morning. Many civilians have been killed.'

I'm mortified. Perhaps the youths thought I was mocking their co-religionists while Israeli F-16s continue to brave the slingshots of Palestinian youths to dump more white phosphorus bombs to cover their tanks and infantry.

Just as we resume our walk, a plume of sand fans out prettily six feet in front of us, like some bird landing heavily. When the next stone whistles overhead, however, Keitan grabs me.

'Run!'

I do so until we reach the brake of scrub ahead. Jumping across the ditch and crouching behind a bush, I look back the way we've come. About a dozen lads from the Technical Institute are bent over, selecting missiles from the piles of builders' material. Two or three are already advancing down the beach. Perhaps it's the policeman's genes which take over.

'Wait a minute,' I tell Keitan as he prepares to make another crouching run down the beach.

Letting the youths advance a few paces, I jump out from our hiding place and rush at them, yelling at the top of my voice. The vanguards spin round instantly and race back towards their comrades. When they're halfway there, I turn again and toil back towards Keitan, lungs burning so much I can hardly suck in breath.

'Come on, let's go.'

The next half hour's a nightmare. I'm shaking like a leaf and pouring with sweat by the time we slow to a walk. It's frustration and fear and panic. And, to my consternation, white-hot anger, too. Behind us the beach is empty. Keitan's adamant that we can't cut inland to the road. It's curtained behind scrub and bushes.

'They may be coming up that way,' he insists.

So we stick to the water's edge, a thousand of the most disgusting yards I've ever trudged. This is the original flush toilet, in use aeons before Thomas Crapper patented his invention. Every few yards, piles of more or less desiccated turds wait for the sea to carry them off. The wilful tide, however, has simply returned many, higher on the beach. It's like a minefield, the stink almost vomit-making. To make matters worse, every so often someone steps out of the thicket screening the road and strides purposefully towards us. Each apparition makes me jump. But they're dressed in lungis, not shorts, thank heavens. Picking their way expertly through the waste, they find a patch of pristine sand, hitch up their robes, squat down and deposit their mess, all the while gazing nonchalantly as we pass.

When we reach the jetty, Keitan's relief is palpable. 'Is all Hindu now,' he mutters, climbing up a gangway onto the pavement, 'no more Bangladesh.'

'I'm really sorry, Keitan, I should have listened.'

He shrugs. 'I didn't say anything at the school because I hoped they might think I was a Muslim, too, who had brought you. They were saying bad things from the moment we arrived.'

I explain the mistake I made, but he doesn't seem to understand about Gazza and Tottenham.

'Should I go to the police, do you think?' I explain my connections with DSP Indore.

Keitan looks alarmed. 'They will question me. Why I took you there.'

'But it was me who made you go.'

My escort looks unconvinced. 'If they come, they will beat every youth they find. They won't care about who was involved or not.'

I don't care, either. I just want them punished. Keitan's beseeching look pulls me up. No, I don't want that. Not after Chafal. Nor do I want my unwilling guide to be further harassed. Or to waste hours driving round in a squad car or, more likely, on the back of a terrifying motorbike, trying to identify the perpetrators.

Across the invisible boundary we've just traversed, it's another world. The sun's a vivid saffron balloon, sagging just above the sea, which is now the mobile silver of a fish's belly. The beach beyond the jetty is busy with families enjoying the early-evening breeze. There are camel-rides and impromptu games of cricket. Girls wander past, sipping at candyfloss. No one, however, is in the water, not even paddling. Little wonder. We flop into chairs at a tea-house on the front and I begin to relax a little, even managing a bitter half-smile at the irony of being presumed guilty by association with the 'enemy' in 'the war on terror'.

Over refreshments, Keitan asks about my plans.

'Think I'll just relax tomorrow. Read a bit. And you?'

His round face deflates. 'Family business. Would you like to see Ganpatipule the day after? There's a wonderful temple.'

Presumably the one my fellow-passenger on the bus from Kolhapur was headed to.

'I have to go back to the police station to see if they've found any documents for me.'

'The beach is very clean. And good for swimming.'

It's an enticing prospect. 'Don't you have to study?'

Keitan shrugs. 'I will be practising my English with you. It's about fifty minutes on the scooter. You can see some of the country.'

Go with the flow. 'I'd love to.'

He makes to high-five me. 'Yo, Professor, right on,' he declaims, in a terrible American accent.

We catch an auto-rickshaw back to the bridge, where Keitan fires up his scooter and drops me at the hotel. Much of it's candlelit. No reading until the electricity 'load-shedding' is over. I eat a delicious spicy kingfish curry. Later, in the bar, I find myself talking to a Chinese-Malayan man who's working at a shipbuilder's further down the coast. David Khoo's on his second two-year contract, but says he's unlikely to renew. He has silky black hair and an ageless face.

'This country's too frustrating. You know, the local police wanted a fat whack to confirm my residency permit last time. I already paid in Mumbai. Had to phone my embassy, get them to fix it. I suppose it's not their fault. Even a commissioner only earns 100,000 rupees a month. That's 2,000 dollars. Yet every assistant deputy superintendent sends their kids to college overseas.' He sips his drink thoughtfully. 'Look around. What do you see?'

I say it's hard to make out anything through the thick cigarette fug of the bar.

'Right. But alcohol permit rooms are non-smoking by law. How do you think they get round that?' He sighs as he rubs two fingers against his thumb. 'India could be like China, if they got it together. But they're so divided.'

I think of the invisible line between 'Bangladesh' and the Hindu beach, the ethnic sniping at Briha's party.

'And the infrastructure,' he says, shaking his head in

exasperation. 'Most of the money goes straight into the pockets of the politicians. You know how long it took to get my business cards from Mumbai? Seventy days, man. It's 390 kilometres or something. If the postman walked here with them, it wouldn't take that long.'

Sounds as if I'll be home before my postcards after all.

'What are you doing tomorrow?' he smiles. 'I go fishing every Sunday with a friend, if you want to come along. We know a few nice places. We leave about midday.'

'Sounds perfect.' It's something I haven't done since my African childhood.

Back in my room, I lie sweatily on the bed, staring at reflections of candlelight in the blank television screen, trying to summon the energy to write my daily log. What a day it's been. Never a dull moment in India. I smile at my earlier premonitions of boredom in Ratnagiri. Then I think about Bill. I've had a tiny taste today of what he must often have faced, especially during his time in Ahmedabad, as Partition approached and communalist tensions spilled over. Facing down adult rioters armed with stones, home-made bombs and bottles of acid isn't something I can envisage myself doing. Only some perverse instinct made me run at the boys. Attack as the best form of defence. Perhaps circumstances sometimes goaded Bill into the same animal reflex of rage? Didn't I want the malefactors punished, just as I did the poacher during the Ugalla River safari? It feels less easy than ever to pass judgement on him, calibrate the behaviour of a father who was less than half my present age. Not least because my reaction this afternoon now makes me feel directly implicated in what he did. How would I have behaved if I'd got hold of one of the lads? And what if I hadn't surprised them, or they'd stood their ground? To my chagrin, I start trembling again.

CHAPTER 14

An Act of Restitution

I spend Sunday morning reading *The Glass Palace*. Affecting though Ghosh's account of Thibaw is, what really resonates with me comes later, as we follow the fortunes of an Indian officer in the army of the Raj, in the period contemporaneous with Bill. He finds himself in Singapore, participating in the doomed rearguard action against the Japanese. Once made prisoners of war, many of his men swap sides and join the Indian National Army, led by S.C. Bhose, the exiled 'Extremist' whom Naganath Nayakwadi so admired. After heartfelt conflict over what to do, and despite deep reservations about Japan's true intentions, the officer throws in his lot with the forces aiming to liberate India from British rule. The fateful decision leads him eventually to a miserable death.

In the 'Author's Notes', Ghosh confesses that this part of the narrative is based on his own father's experience, although Lt. Colonel Ghosh was 'among those "loyal" Indians who found themselves across the lines from the "traitors" of the Indian National Army'. While writing his book, Ghosh clearly found himself – like me – caught between loyalty to his beloved father and recognition that the imperial cause the latter fought for was essentially indefensible: witness the barbarous treatment of Thibaw. Like me, too, Ghosh interviewed some of the rebel leaders his father fought against. He also clearly admires some of them although, equally clearly, he has qualms about aspects of the way they prosecuted their cause.

Putting the book down, I feel a surging sense of liberation. I'm not alone in the kind of dilemmas and challenges this trip has thrown up. Moreover, I'm particularly struck that Ghosh seeks neither to judge nor to condemn, but to understand the complexity of the particular problems and pressures of wartime which his characterrs face. Shades of Gandhi in Yeravda jail. Above all, he emphasizes the possibilities of reconciliation between former antagonists, through empathy with both sides. I think back to Chafal. If the villagers are prepared to forgive Bill, there's no need to beat myself up further about what happened there. If Nayakwadi can acknowledge that mistakes were made by both parties to the conflict and draw a line under the past – without forgetting its lessons – I see no reason to contradict him.

Suddenly, my quest to find Bill's confidential weekly reports, to hear his version of events, seems much less pressing. Haven't I learned what I need about his role in 1940s Indian history? And understood better why he sometimes behaved as he did, even if it was wrong affronting all my postcolonial principles? I'll see Bill differently from now on. I suddenly realise that my dream of meeting him again at the party perhaps symbolises the idea that we're equals at last. And the anger I so belatedly expressed at his 'deserting' me, which I was unable to vent at the time because of the circumstances of his death, is entirely consistent with the deep and loving relationship we had. Further, I'm beginning to realise that my memories of Bill are more complex and dynamic than seemed the case while they sat undisturbed in my mental archive. I can now see in them nuances and shades invisible under the sunny glare of nostalgia, or beneath the frozen gaze of grief. As a result of my coming to India, Bill's been resurrected, but as a much more fully human being than the outsize figure in the immobile tableaux of aberrated mourning and childhood mythology.

The rest of the day has a holiday feel. I buy some beers for the picnic and after a brief stop at a cannery to pick up ice, set off with David Khoo for an afternoon's fishing. We're joined by a Polish colleague of David's, dressed in parakeet-bright Lycra, as if for the Tour de France. He fixes his skeletal racing machine on the roof rack, explaining that he finds cycling the coastal roads a perfect way to 'decompress' before another hectic week at the shipyard. Lukas has vivid ginger hair and alabaster skin and despite his swallowtail shades and slathers of suncream, long-distance cycling doesn't seem wise in this sweltering heat. He's the only other Westerner I've seen in Ratnagiri, and I wonder what the rural folk think when this vision whirls by in a Joan Miró splash.

A few miles north, we stop by an inlet. Lukas sets off at an alarming sprint up the adjoining headland, leaving David and me in the shade of the bridge. After setting up camp stools, the driver settles himself to doze amongst cooling-boxes ready for the catch. Sipping my beer, I watch David bait his line and cast into the tidal stream, fringed on the other side by flat-topped mangroves. I'm no expert, but I can't think the middle of a white-hot day is the right time for fish. After lunch and a snooze, at last I get my swim. The water's bracing where the gentle current meets the sea, and I let myself be carried towards the breakers which mark the ocean's beginning. It's exhilarating to bodysurf the bouncing white-caps or dive to examine shells on the sea floor, before another playful wave nudges me back towards the bridge. It's good to be a proper tourist in India at last.

That night, pleasantly worn out by swimming, I fall asleep at once, into a second dream about Bill. I'm in a small plane, something I've avoided pretty much all my life. Weirder still, I'm flying it. For some reason I can't turn my head. But I'm intensely aware of a large, oppressive presence beside me, made more threatening because it's getting dark. The engine cuts out suddenly and I know we only have seconds before we crash-land. I do a reasonable job of wrestling the rudder to hit the field rushing towards us at the correct angle. It's bumpy and before I can slow the plane sufficiently, we hit a ridge and it flips violently onto its nose. I bang my head and lose consciousness for a moment.

When I come to, we're tilting slowly and my companion's been thrown onto my side of the cockpit. His weight is such that I can barely move. Worse, I smell smoke. With a super-human shove, I wrest myself from under him, punch out the windscreen, crawl through it and drop to the ground. I begin to run away over sticky ploughed furrows. I'm barely fifty metres clear when the plane explodes, the fireball rising slow and graceful as a hot-air balloon, turning the landscape orange. As the plane disintegrates from the force of the blast, I wake, the image so intense that I'm shielding my eyes. Shaken up, I spend the rest of the night trying to work out what it all means. By dawn, I think I'm there. What a relief. It wasn't Bill I left to his fate, but the brooding burden of his loss that I've cast off at last. It's taken four decades and a trip to the other side of the world to get here.

~

I'm still smiling foolishly to myself when the waiter brings over the paper at breakfast. Inside, there's an item about the hundred most influential institutions in the development of modern India. All the armed services are cited, and there are honourable mentions for various educational, wildlife, even fashion, institutes. However, today's Indian Police Service is notably absent from the list. Remembering David Khoo's denunciations, I wonder whether this reflects its degeneration from the IP of Bill's time, or is the outcome of tendencies present in its predecessor's ethos and practices. It's saddening that the modern force, which has been so good to me, enjoys such low esteem.

I get a further taste of how today's police is regarded by ordinary Indians when I set off to photograph Bill's old residence. To my surprise, Keitan's already waiting outside the hotel, polishing the chrome on his scooter. He's wearing a Nirvana t-shirt today, and embroidered jeans.

'Yo, Professor, just wanted to confirm a time to meet later.'

'How about after lunch, to be on the safe side? Want to join me?'

He smiles deprecatingly. 'I only eat food prepared at home.'

'Too bad. Could you give me a lift?' It's so hot that I began sweating the moment I left the lobby. 'I need to go to the DSP's house to take some pictures.'

Keitan looks as uncomfortable as when I suggested going to 'Bangladesh'.

'OK, jump on,' he eventually offers.

However, he pulls up a hundred yards short of the entrance to the bungalow.

'I can't drop you there,' he says. 'They may ask questions.'

'What do you mean?'

'Why I'm with a foreigner. How we know each other and everything.'

Is he just being wacky again? But I'm all too aware of the consequences of having pressed him to enter 'Bangladesh'.

'They may think I've requested you to take photos to pass on to robbers or a terror cell. Please, if anyone asks, you met me on a trip last year.'

I'm flabbergasted. 'OK. You head off. See you at the hotel at two?'

'But how will you get back?'

'If it gets too hot, I'll jump in an auto-rickshaw.'

The sentry waves me though with barely a glance at my card. Because I'm white? No sign of Indore's police car, and the bungalow has the same blank look as on my previous visit. Once I've got my photos, I wander back to the station. The DSP's busy in his office. I wait on the veranda for half an hour before being shown in. Marble-patterned ledgers, like those I saw in Satara, sit piled on his desk.

'Part IVs for that time,' he smiles. 'Please to examine them at the back of the room. You may make notes.'

'Any luck with the weekly confidentials?'

He shakes his head. 'My records man says he recently burned the ones from just ten years ago.'

I'm almost blasé now. It's the ones from Satara I really wanted. At least I'll hear Bill's voice in the station summaries. But it's not to be. I spend an hour on them, while civilian supplicants come and go. After Keitan's comments, I half expect them to retire backwards out of the room, bowing like petitioners to the Rajahs. But Indore conducts himself in genial fashion and there's a fair amount of laughter. It's bizarre. Nothing signed by Bill. In fact, there are no entries for 1947 under any of the headings. They stop the year before and resume in 1948. Perhaps, if Bill was appointed in February and stayed only six months, he wouldn't have been there to do the reports at the appropriate time, end of year? Or could he not be bothered, knowing he'd soon be leaving? He was never much of a desk-wallah.

'I almost forgot,' the DSP says, with a glitter of gold tooth, when I return the ledgers. 'We've found an old constable for you. From traffic.'

Traffic? How disappointing. Nonetheless, since Indore's gone to the trouble, I smile enthusiastically.

'Can you come back at six this evening?' he asks wearily. 'We need to send someone to get him and I have so much to do today.'

~

When Keitan turns up on his scooter after lunch, I'm feeling buoyant. I've accomplished pretty much everything possible in Ratnagiri, and can now relax with a good conscience. We breeze through seaside villages like in a *masala* road movie, past shoals of tiny fishes spread out to dry under nets on the verges, like silver quilts in the bright sunlight. Herons prance up and down, shaking their heads indignantly at being denied access to this harvest. The houses are mainly thatch, shaded by mangoes, jackfruit and clumps of banana. Vividly painted outriggers bob on the sea beyond. Occasionally the road skips inland through rice paddies, an occasional water buffalo wallowing in a canal.

It's even more delightful when we arrive at Ganpatipule. As Rajeev said, this must be what Goa was like in the old days, miles of pristine beach with icing-sugar sand, huge blue skies and almost no Western tourists. I can't wait to get in the water. But, stupidly, I left my swimsuit to dry in the hotel. Keitan rebuffs my inquiry:

'No underclothes, there are ladies.'

Stripping down to my cut-offs, I run to the ocean and flop in with a huge splash. When I surface, I see Keitan sitting on the beach, baseball cap now pulled down backwards. Behind him, a line of pilgrims snakes towards the temple. The *mandir*'s similar in style to the one at Chafal, but deep cinnamon-pink in colour. Can't tell if it's paint or marble. Worshippers who've completed their devotions gather in festive family groups on the beach, umbrellas up against the sun, arranging picnics. Some perform ablutions in the shallow surf.

'Only Muslims know how to swim,' Keitan comments wistfully when I rejoin him. 'All the fishermen are Muslim. We Hindus have no swimming pools to learn in.'

I lie back on my shirt, hair caked with salt, at peace. Is this how Bill felt as his time in India closed? It's barely three weeks since I arrived at Mumbai airport, but it feels like months. How did he get his head round going 'home' after so many years in this extraordinary place? How will I feel in a few days' time, plunged back into the greyness of a northern winter? As if reading my thoughts, Keitan props himself on one elbow.

'Did aliens build Heathrow?'

I'm thrown. Does he mean migrant labour?

'From spaceships?' he clarifies earnestly. 'I read it in a book.'

'What book?'

'Danikow. Eric von Danikow.'

Isn't it Daniken? I remember the name vaguely from my random adolescent reading. My older brother was an avid sci-fi fan, the walls of his London squat lined with everyone from Asimov to Zamyatin.

'I don't think so, Keitan. Probably built by Irishmen.'

Keitan examines me with a pained expression, as if I'm being satirical.

After lingering over what I expect will be my last swim in India, we look round the temple and village. I'm more interested in the latter today, particularly the stalls selling two of my favourite African childhood treats – fresh coconut juice and jaggery, dark crumbly blocks of the first unrefined pressings of sugarcane. Keitan tells me that according to traditional medicine, the latter's something to avoid. I ignore his warning. But what I hope will be a Proustian moment is spoiled when it slips from my fingers onto the sand. So I content myself with sipping from the freshly lopped coconut gourd. Keitan declines that, too, opting instead for what looks like a persimmon from the bag of fruit he's brought along.

'Shall we go back a different way?' he asks when I complain I'm starting to burn. Despite the awning we're under, the sun's rays cook like a microwave.

'Why not?' Go with the flow.

'There's another route. Less buses.'

The lush coastal strip yields for a while to scrubby, eroded hills. But once we enter the river-fed valleys further inland, everything's green again, orchards of sweet lime and fields of *jowar* and sugar. Unlike round Satara, the cane here is deep reddish-yellow.

'Would you like to see how it's cut?' Keitan asks, as we slow by a culvert. The harvest's in progress, the remaining crop pushed back some distance from the road in shallow curves. At intervals, cutters work away with machetes. Some look barely adolescent and still younger children strip the stalks of leaves, before carrying them in bundles towards carts, where white oxen lie prostrate beside them. Birds criss-cross overhead, swooping for insects put to flight by the tumbling canes. As we dismount, a plump man in a suit comes out of a hut towards us. He's the landowner, he explains, pointing to his 4×4 further down the road. We chat for a while about yields. But I'm more interested in the workers. He explains they're itinerant labourers, mostly from Aurangabad, hundreds of kilometres to the north-east. I ask if we can go watch how it's done.

We tramp across a crackling mulch of cane-leaf and approach a very dark old man, head wrapped in a sweaty turban to protect against the sun. Either side of him are a woman and a very pretty girl of about twelve, squatting to swing their machetes, while a small boy flits between them, gathering felled canes. The man straightens up with a broad smile.

'He asks if you want to try,' Keitan interprets.

I take the machete and attempt a couple of swings. It's heavy, very difficult to make a clean cut. I'm quickly reduced to hacking randomly. The man adjusts my stance and explains how to balance the cleaver so it lands at the right angle. Still, it's exhausting, doubled down at the base of the canes, and I'm quickly pouring with sweat.

'How long's your day?' I ask through Keitan, relieved to hand back the machete.

'Ten hours,' the cutter answers deferentially, before pointing to the woman. 'Nine for my wife.'

Wife? I assumed he was her father. Now I see his eyes are youthful. It's hard labour and poverty which have scored those lines around them.

'What do you get paid?'

'One hundred rupees for me. Seventy for women. Fifty for the children.'

'Per day?'

He nods. I'm shocked: £1.20 for the man, 60p for the kids. I spent more than that on the coconut water and wasted jaggery.

'He says they work as labourers for eight months of the year, all over Maharashtra, then go back to Aurangabad.'

'Don't the children attend school?'

'He says they can't afford it. They have just enough if the four of them work as a team.'

'And if one gets sick?'

The man shrugs. It's heartbreaking. The girl has such intelligent eyes, so much grace.

Keitan follows my gaze. 'She'll be married off in a couple of years, to another labourer. Like her mother was. And her mother before her,' he sighs.

My conscience stabs. 'I'd like to do something for the children. There must be a school. It can't cost much.'

The man's looking at us inquiringly. Keitan takes me to one side.

'It's impossible. They need their labour. Do you know how much such a girl's dowry costs?'

I shrug, spirits dissipating rapidly.

'Between twenty and forty thousand rupees.'

'But that'll take them their whole lives to find.'

'That's where the moneylenders come in.'

No wonder the Parallel Government targeted such people. Or that Nayakwadi asserted that the movement's needed again.

I thank the family for giving us their time. It feels a feebly inadequate gesture, but I ask Keitan to give them some money, which they accept with graceful, dignified smiles. They then *namaste* and return to their cutting. As we head to the scooter, I notice a mess of tattered cloches on the other side of the verge, like an abandoned allotment. A woman squats, fanning a brazier.

'This is their camp,' Keitan explains.

I don't think I've ever seen anything so wretched. Flimsy bits of plastic, laid over bent branches held in place with rusty wire, each barely big enough for one person. Faded saris dry on an improvised clothesline, while sugarcane pith blows between the ragged rows of see-through shelters, impersonal as coffins.

I'm feeling thoroughly chastened when we resume our journey. Keitan, too, seems thoughtful.

'The worst thing,' he says, 'is how hard it is to escape such a life.'

Though Brahmin-born and so pernickety about his diet, he's as impatient as Nayakwadi with traditional distinctions.

'Not touching other castes, not eating with them, that's disappearing,' he shouts over his shoulder. Then he taps the side of his helmet. 'But it's in here that's important. Ninety-nine per cent of people still marry within their own caste. Not even that. Their own sub-caste.'

'How can anyone tell your caste?'

'Names. Colour of your skin. Sometimes your features. Now do you understand why I want to go abroad?'

I nod.

'It was a bad thing when you British left.'

I don't have the energy to argue. But it makes me reconsider Briha's good fortune in escaping his Dalit background. Perhaps he's an exception, after all.

We arrive back in Ratnagiri's bustling port area, where a night-fleet's in the process of leaving. With time to spare before my appointment with Indore, Keitan suggests we visit the market and Tilak's home. It's hectic in the narrow alleys and despite some unease after the stoning incident, I'm glad to get off the scooter and walk. With every inch of pavement taken up by produce for sale, we have to dodge through the vehicles which somehow growl their way through the maze. I wonder if Thibaw's great-grandchildren live somewhere nearby, and look out for the Burmese royal peacock emblem above the doors of the mean-looking houses. Keitan calls me down a passage where the stink of fish is gut-churning. Tilak's house is grand, with terracotta tiles and shallow-pitched, low-spreading eaves. To one side of the front yard stands a tarnished metal relief, perhaps ten feet long and six high, with scenes of Tilak's life and dealings with other nationalist leaders, all presided over by Shivaji. Did Bill ever come here, to one of the spiritual birthplaces of the Parallel Government? Perhaps he took the opportunity to reflect on his experiences in Satara and consider why Indian independence had become an inexorable necessity.

We stop for refreshments at a tea shop, one side of which is given up to internet booths. I'm not in the mood to check my emails, but Keitan says he wants to send me a message to ensure we're connected before I leave Ratnagiri. After finishing my drink, I wander up to pay. Beneath the glass counter, a pile of photocopies catches my eye. They're an excerpt from T.B. Macaulay's address to the British parliament on 2 February 1835, with an indistinct photo of the speaker in later life. Before becoming a famous Victorian poet, Macaulay had been in charge of the East India Company's educational policy:

> I have travelled the length and breadth of India and I have not seen one person who is a beggar, who is a thief. Such wealth I have seen in this country, such high moral values, people of such calibre, that I do not think we would ever conquer this country, unless we break the very backbone of this nation, which is her spiritual and cultural heritage. I propose that we replace her old and ancient education system, her culture, for if the Indians think that all that is foreign and English is good and greater than their own, they will lose their self-esteem, their native self-culture and they will become what we want them, a truly dominated nation.

I imagine an enraged Tilak comparing Macaulay's description with wretched lives of the kind led by the migrant labourers we met this afternoon. I buy a copy. When Keitan's finished in his booth, I press it on him.

~

Once again, I have to wait for Indore at the police station. A couple of seats along the veranda I notice a wizened, cloudy-eyed old man in a crocheted prayer cap. What's he saying? When I shrug, he continues to stare disconcertingly, muttering under his breath. I'm tired and do my best to ignore him. So I'm surprised when Indore's attendant eventually beckons both of us to follow. There's much courtly bowing and smacking his chest with an open hand from the old man when we enter. The DSP sounds as if he's reassuring him.

'This is the traffic man we found,' he announces when my fellow visitor's at last been been persuaded to sit, an honour which he appears shy of.

'Mr Dawood says he was trying to say hello outside.'

I twist awkwardly to shake hands with the man, apologising for my rudeness. His opaque pupils sink into the creases of his smile. Indore translates in a slightly bored tone. Perhaps he's eager to get home after his long day.

'I was in traffic,' the man confirms several times, as if I might be hard of hearing.

'How did you know my father?'

'I saw him often in his car. The back was made of planks.'

So Bill still had his 'Woodie' in Ratnagiri. Still, this doesn't seem very promising. And even less so when Dawood proceeds to explain at length how much better-regulated traffic was in those days. There was only the tiny bus station and the ferry to deal with. Time enough to stop bicycles travelling without lights at night. Indore chuckles.

'Ratnagiri was much smaller,' the DSP reminds him gently.

The veteran doesn't seem to have heard. 'He was a big man, Gilbert. Very smart,' he suddenly pronounces.

My ears prick up. 'Did you ever talk to him?'

Dawood shakes his head. '"Yes sir, no sir," mostly.'

'Can you remember any stories about him?'

My informant considers long and hard. He seems on the point of giving up when a memory suddenly comes. 'A great fisherman. He was always out with his rod when he could find time.'

Memories of trout-fishing camps in the Southern Highlands of Tanganyika come flooding back.

'Once he left some crabs with me. In the control post at the crossroads. He said he wouldn't be long. Even though their claws were tied up, I didn't like them scraping around my feet. I stepped down onto the road to direct the traffic. He laughed at me when he came back.'

Why did Bill leave the crabs? 'Anything else?'

'He was a very strong swimmer.'

'Oh?'

'One day he saved a woman from the sea. Near the ferry terminal. I wasn't on duty. Head constable told me.'

'What, exactly?'

'That a woman fell from the ferry and Gilbert jumped into the water.'

'He saved her?'

Dawood nods. 'But her husband was very angry.'

What?

'To have his wife touched by another man.'

'Perhaps the husband pushed her in,' Indore intervenes, with another gold-toothed chuckle.

'Where did this happen?'

'The ferry. Where the big bridge is now.'

He can remember nothing else. But it doesn't matter. I'm so pleased to hear a final positive testimonial to Bill from a contemporary with no particular vested interests. We chat for a while about the man's later career and life in retirement before it's time to go. When we shake hands, Dawood mutters something which makes the DSP shake his head.

'What did he say?'

'I told him you were a doctor. He wants to know if you are good with eyes.'

I mime my apologies. On the way out, the thought suddenly occurs to me: at last I've encountered a Muslim police officer. Are they, like Dawood, simply relics of the past?

Before returning to the hotel, I ask the ever-patient Keitan, who's parked discreetly down the road, if we can pop back to the estuary bridge for a moment.

'As long as it's not to Bangladesh,' he grins.

On the way, he chaffs me about my obsessive interest in Raj sites and architecture. I wonder if he read the Macaulay excerpt while waiting.

'Look, there's a tree probably planted by the British,' he teases, 'certainly that house was built by *sahib-log*, maybe those pavement stones were walked on by the viceroy.'

We park up halfway across the arc. It's a beautiful evening; the sun's set but it continues to illuminate the horizon, while the lamps of the fishing fleet bob like fairy lights. Ratnagiri means 'mountain of jewels' in Marathi, but 'sea of jewels' feels more appropriate at this moment. The beach where we were stoned is empty even of toileteers, and looks idyllic at this distance. Below, broiling cross-currents are creamily visible. In *The Glass Palace*, this is the site of a suicide. Discovering that his wife no longer loves him, the first Indian collector of Ratnagiri launches the scull he's brought back from Cambridge. Racing downriver, he disappears just here, where the fresh water smashes into the salty tide. Neither he nor his craft are recovered.

As with defusing the Mills bomb in Nasik, it must have taken some courage for Bill to plunge into that cauldron to rescue the woman. I wonder whether the pair was pulled back onto the ferry or if Bill dragged her all the way to the old jetty, now clearly visible from this side of the building site, where our assailants armed themselves yesterday. Perhaps on the very beach where we were nearly stoned, her husband remonstrated with him, his half-drowned wife struggling, uncertain as a pupa, to right herself in her sodden saris. I'd like to think it was restitution, an attempt at balancing the books before he quit India. Otherwise, why take the risk when he was about to leave, his whole life in front of him?

But perhaps, after all, it was simply reflex, instilled by long training.

The boy can't understand it. Snippets of his life speed like a film through his mind, right up to just a few minutes ago, when he was talking with Mrs Ambrose and Jacqueline as they relaxed in sunloungers beside the pool at the Tabora Club.

'*Don't know how to swim?*' *Mrs Ambrose asked incredulously, after her daughter went inside to get another Fanta.*

The boy had reddened. It's impossible to swim in the upcountry rivers and lakes where they've been posted up to now. If it isn't crocodiles, it's bilharzia, borne by snails which deposit eggs in the urethra. At school it's said they can only be dislodged by means of a very fine wire brush with copper hairs. But he'd felt ashamed, nonetheless, because everyone his age here – girls, too – runs and dives into the water with such abandon.

He'd give anything to be able to do bombs off the boards like the teenagers, so confident in their supple bodies. The boy can't bring himself even to go in the shallow end, for fear he'll be challenged to a race. He pretends to prefer sunbathing and mocking the girls. But he was ecstatic that Jacqueline left before her mother asked the question. She's that pretty, snake of hair down to her waist, cabled for swimming but brushed out now she's finished her dip. Lately he's been getting a sugary, sinking feeling when he slyly watches her, pretending to squint because of the sun.

'*It's easy,*' *Mrs Ambrose had assured him.* '*Just run and take a big jump. Once in, you'll know what to do. It's natural.*'

More than anything, he'd wanted to impress Jacqueline, make the straw drop from her mouth.

He sees himself now, as if from above, in slow motion, through the fluid pressing into every opening with a transparent stifling silkiness, preparing to make his approach from the far end of the pool. Past joins present almost as soon as he hits the water. How long has he been thrashing like this, lungs burning at first, now glutinous and soggy, as he tries to touch bottom long enough to hurl himself violently up again. Once or twice he's surfaced long enough for an almighty cough and gasp of air, but mainly it's more mouthfuls of water. Each time, the world grows more bleary and indistinct. Liquid gravity is winning him.

Then, from nowhere, the Ambrose girl's suddenly next to him. She pushes him up and he catches another choking breath. But the boy's so tired now, he just wants to hang on, anything for a rest. He puts both hands round her neck, hoping she'll swim them both into the sunlight. For an age they struggle, limbs intertwined in an intimacy he could scarcely have dared hope for. He knows she's shouting something from her water-gagged mouth, but the element's too thick to hear. Suddenly she's spent, too. Her head drops back and the efforts to free his grip weaken, her long hair drifting like weed. How beautiful it would be, her hands all over him, if only her brown eyes didn't goggle so.

When he's about to surrender to the sweet languid feeling in his limbs, just as the light starts to drain out of the water, there's an underwater eruption, as if one of the larger lads is doing a bomb. A vast shape throws deeper shadow over them. The boy feels his hands torn from Jacqueline. A moment later, there's sun on his face and he's half aware of his chest being scraped over the tiled edge of the pool. Shouting comes from far away, half drowned by the sound of vomiting. Once on his back he feels, rather than hears, his name being called. His face is turned to one side, supported in his father's hands, while someone pumps brutally on his chest. It continues to pour, the water, retched out of his nose and mouth and eyes, tasting of bile and chlorine and foulness, his sides racked with cramps as he tries to yield more.

As his vision comes into focus again, the boy sees his

father's tennis shoes still bleeding water. For once the voice above him's thin and uncertain.

'Thought I'd lost you there, old chap. One minute more.'
He folds his son up to his chest and rocks him.

Although the boy can't see his father's grey eyes, he can taste salt on his cheeks, feel the thick arms trembling. As he continues to be rocked, he's transfixed by the sight of Jacqueline Ambrose. Her swimsuit's pulled down off her shoulders. There are angry weals on her neck, above the lovely swellings on her upper chest. Her mother cries helplessly as a friend comforts the girl. Jacqueline stares blankly at the boy before sitting up on one elbow and pulling her straps up. He wants to say he hasn't been looking. But he feels too peaceful to care. He doesn't mind how long he stays like this, buoyed in his father's arms, sun slowly fluffing up his flattened hair.

'You stupid woman, you bloody stupid woman,' the boy's father suddenly yells after the retreating Mrs Ambrose.

Her daughter, hair once more in its pigtail, glances back tearfully. Club members look on, sympathetic but astonished. After all, the boy's father's a byword for gallantry.

CHAPTER 15

Two Farewells

My last morning in India, I return to Rajeev's flat to find him in trainers, fleece tracksuit pants and striped hoody, Elvis once more warbling from the corner of his day room. He looks pumped-up.

'Aren't you cold?' he asks, staring at my bare arms. 'People are freezing to death up in Lucknow. They say it's minus five in London.'

My heart sinks. 'Well, I'm going to make the most of it. Been running?'

'I like to do a fast walk at five-thirty in the morning,' he explains. 'Clears the head and gives me time to think. And the air's OK to breathe at that time.' He offers tea. 'Did you bring that Shinde book?' he asks, when it comes.

I get *The Parallel Government* out of my bag and pass it over. He leafs through the opening pages.

'I thought so. I asked around about this fellow after you left. You see, this is a kind of semi-official publication. The foreword was written by Y.B. Chavan himself and, look here,' his finger stabs the page, 'Shinde acknowledges receiving "a sumptuous publication grant" from the chief minister's office.'

I recall Avanish Patil's mournful comments at Kolhapur University about how patronage is essential these days in order to get local history published in India.

'Listen, my friend.' Rajeev reads from the foreword: 'Chavan claims that "Police excesses on men, women and children are ... narrated factually." Of course he'd say that, given he was one of the leaders of the Patri Sarkar. I don't suppose Shinde felt able to question some of the behaviour of the movement in the way you told me Nayakwadi was.'

I demur. True, Shinde perhaps ought to have gone to Chafal to check the account given by the Congress worker on which he relied so heavily. Equally, he interviewed only those engaged on the nationalist side: no equivalent police testimony's adduced, other than excerpts from the elusive confidential weekly reports. But there's no reason to doubt that he used his sources in good faith. Besides, there's Modak's evidence, too, even if aspects of it now seem questionable. Rajeev's surprised I wish to defend him.

'Well,' he shrugs, 'I suppose everyone tells the stories they need to. None of us can really be objective.'

He gets up and goes to his desk. To my astonishment, it's littered with what look like 1950s comics and trash-mags. Except for one blue folder.

'This is what I dug up while you were away.'

Extraordinary. Original typewritten orders relating to Bill's later career. The first's from N.A.P. Smith, the inspector-general of police and is dated 16 January 1944: 'Mr Moore-Gilbert, who is officiating as DSP, Nasik, until Mr Price's return on 23-1-1944, should thereafter be appointed as an additional ASP in the Belgaum district. The purposes of this appointment are in a sense confidential and have been outlined in a separate letter addressed to the Adviser. But it can be broadly stated that it is intended through Mr Moore-Gilbert to effect an improvement in the training of the armed police operating against the Radderhati Berad and other gangs in the Belgaum area.'

'What's the Radderhati Berad?'

Rajeev shrugs. 'Probably some outfit like the Patri Sarkar.'

So Bill was never supposed to go to Satara? I wonder what place he'd have in history had his original secondment proceeded as planned. Perhaps all controversy would have been avoided. Then again, had he gone to Belgaum, Bhosle might never have emailed me and I'd have had no reason to come to India. There'd have been no need to track down Modak, I'd never have been passed onto Dhun Nanavatty, visited Chafal, or been put in touch with the old nationalist leaders and constables. I wouldn't have met Briha, Keitan or Rajeev. I'd know no more about my father than I did before I came here. I'd have learned a lot less about myself, too, my investments in my childhood memories, my adult values.

That directive's immediately countermanded by another, stamped 'Home Department' and dated two days later. It's also signed by Smith: 'I suggest that Mr Moore-Gilbert should be appointed as Additional Asst. Supdt. of Police, of the Satara District and not in the Belgaum District. This recommendation is made as the result of discussion I have had today with the District Magistrate, Satara, and the D.I.G.P. [Deputy Inspector-General of Police], C.I.D. Conditions in the Satara District have deteriorated sensibly in the last three or four weeks and I consider, therefore, that Mr Moore-Gilbert should go first to Satara and be diverted later if necessary to Belgaum.'

There are further orders, from the 'Political and Services Department'. The first confirms Bill's appointment as 'officer on special duty' in Ahmedabad after the period of long leave 'ex-India' he took in 1946. There's no clue here as to where he went, but I'm beginning to suspect he used it to make his first visit to Tanganyika, to visit my grandparents and see if he could make a life there. I can't imagine he'd have taken my mother and the young son from her first marriage somewhere so far away, just on spec.

A couple of documents signed by Bill himself relate to his time in Ahmedabad. One requests funds for a temporary shorthand typist to assist him in the preparation of a Home Guards Training Manual. A subsequent report states that he's succeeded in engaging someone. But Bill adds a postscript: 'In this connection, please communicate directly with the D.S.

Portrait of Bill, months before he died

[District Superintendent] Police, Ahmedabad as I have relinquished charge as S.P. [Superintendent of Police] Special duty and am proceeding to Ratnagiri.' There's one final order, dated July 1947: 'Mr SM. Moore-Gilbert, I.P., Dist. Supt. Police, Ratnagiri, is granted leave ex-India on average pay for eight months followed by leave on half average pay for one year, three months and twenty-eight days from 15 August, 1947, preparatory to retirement.'

Did Bill only make up his mind at the last moment to leave, the very day of Indian Independence? Whatever, it seems a very generous redundancy package, ample to get married and buy a stake in my grandparents' coffee farm.

'Could I get a photocopy of these documents?' The ones with Bill's signature would be precious.

Rajeev looks uneasy. 'They're not supposed to have been taken from the archives. A friend did it for me.'

How on earth did he arrange that? Evidently I'm not hiding my disappointment well.

'Alright then, but we'll have to do it in my special place,' Rajeev says. 'It's on the way.'

'Where are we going?'

'I want to try one last place to see if we can find those confidential weekly reports. Bring Shinde.'

'Has Poel come up with anything?'

My host shakes his head apologetically as he gets up. 'I'll explain later.'

I gather my things.

'Before we go, have a look at these.'

He leads me to the desk. The comics are indeed vintage, mainly American ones with heroes like John Steel, Robot Archie and Rick Random, the lurid colours now respectably dulled by age.

'I used to buy them as a kid. They were smuggled into India. Morally corrupting and all that. Glad I looked after them. Worth a lot of money now. I might need to cash them in for my retirement.'

Elvis, comics. What other surprises does Rajeev have up his sleeve in our last hours together?

'When do you retire?'

Rajeev laughs ruefully. 'Four months, three weeks and a day.'

~

We head East from Rajeev's flat. I'm going to badly miss this bustle and spectacle, the warm milling crowds. India, or Maharashtra at least, has got right under my skin. I can't believe it took me so long to get here. What must Bill have felt on his last day in Bombay Province, after nearly nine years of service? Perhaps, like me, he was bereft, even if the adventure of Africa was beckoning. How did he spend his final hours? With friends? Arm-in-arm with one of the 'girl-friends' in Aunt Pat's photo album? Packing and last-minute shopping for the curios which found their way into my childhood home in Tanganyika? Perhaps he strolled in civvies, before enjoying a final curry with Bombay Duck, trying – like me – to make sense of his time here. The closeness I felt to Bill during my first tentative explorations of Mumbai surges up again and I miss him piercingly.

In the cramped photocopy shop tucked away up an alley, the proprietor behaves as if he's receiving a distinguished visitor. Rajeev disappears after him into a back room, returning a few minutes later with two manila envelopes.

'Make sure you don't leave it anywhere,' he mutters, handing me mine.

I put it carefully away in my knapsack and we set off again, in the direction of the old Victoria railway terminus and Crawford Market. After fifteen minutes, however, we veer south-east. There are signs for Cama Hospital and we turn up a nondescript lane which skirts its perimeter.

'Want to show you something,' Rajeev says.

We stop at a junction, where the roads are barely wide enough for two vehicles to pass. It's a shabby and unremarkable site, a temporary-looking tea stall set up next to a back entrance to the hospital.

'This is where they killed poor Kamte, whose grandfather was Moore-Gilbert's colleague. Those bloody bearded bandits. They just want to go backwards. Serves them right what's going on in Gaza.'

He's visibly upset, so I don't ask if he's seen the latest television pictures.

'They hid behind that gate after they attacked the hospital. When the police vehicle stopped at this junction, they shot Kamte and his colleagues in cold blood. One constable survived by playing dead. They dragged the bodies out and drove off on their rampage downtown.'

I remember the images of the boxy black-and-white vehicle, like the one I was lent in Satara, careering southwards, pedestrians throwing themselves to the ground as the only Mumbai attacker to survive sprayed sub-machine-gun fire out of the passenger window.

'I'm very sorry, Rajeev,' I mutter, patting him on the shoulder.

'Why was Kamte allowed to bleed to death just a hundred yards from the hospital?' Face working, he leads me on.

Soon we're passing through a rather more imposing gate, into an annexe of what Rajeev explains is the headquarters of the City police, the senior branch of the Maharashtra force, and of the Bombay service before it. We're nodded through with barely a glance. Either he's known, or security's ridiculously lax, especially given the recent attacks. We enter a modern three-storey building, where Rajeev chats to the duty sergeant.

'Special Branch number two,' Rajeev informs me. 'The City lot have their own archives, separate from the State police where you went before. It's a long shot.'

We're shown into a clammy ground-floor room where the windows are wide open onto a courtyard. A slight man with a scholarly air and bullfrog cheeks stands up to greet Rajeev effusively.

'My friend from London University I was telling you about.'

After the compulsory tea, Rajeev shows him Shinde's book. The archivist skims the footnotes and bibliography.

'I'll have to consult. Of course, there's the issue of permission.'

'I've phoned Ramanandan,' Rajeev reassures him. 'So has Mr Poel.'

'Who's Ramanandan?' I ask.

'Assistant commissioner, City. Poel's counterpart. A lot of intelligence was collated here in those days, since City was senior.'

While the archivist leaves the room to confer with colleagues, we chat about the frustrations I've encountered hunting down the confidential reports.

'Yes. And no wonder all the "Terrorism" files were missing when you went to look,' Rajeev nods lugubriously. 'Poel and

I, we made some inquiries. Seems the whole lot were taken by someone inside the force.'

'What?'

'Apparently he wanted to write a history of the Patri Sarkar. He disagreed with some interpretations of the police role in events.'

'Did he do so?'

Rajeev shakes his head. 'He died before finishing.'

'So where are the files?'

My friend grimaces. 'I suspect they're with his widow. She lives in Pune, apparently. Someone's going to contact her.'

Too late for me, I think ruefully. It's criminal that such a precious historical resource might be mouldering in some monsoon-damp basement.

'And many of the other files you looked at have been tampered with as well. After Independence, some of that stuff would have been dynamite. It could have ruined a few careers, especially the material on police informants and collaborators.'

'Please to follow,' the librarian invites us when he returns. 'We need to go into the main holdings.'

It's an extraordinary room, the size of a tennis court, no windows, like a bank strongroom. Floor-to-ceiling shelves are stocked with metal canisters, like ammunition boxes, all with handwritten labels. These records would seem to have a better chance of being preserved than most I've seen.

'Right back to the earliest days,' the librarian affirms.

The entire archive of the Bombay City police. What stories must be hidden here. Yet very few scholars come these days, our guide tells us. There's little interest in the history of the security services during the Raj. We find ourselves at a desk where a young man in Gandhi glasses is studying Shinde's book, glancing intermittently across at a computer screen. He looks doubtful.

'I've checked the references on the pages you marked. I'm afraid they're not in this building. Even though some of them have Special Branch file numbers. If you've already looked in State Police HQ, there's only one other place they might be.'

Rajeev and I glance at each other. 'Home Department at Mantrale,' we intone simultaneously.

'Sorry,' my friend murmurs.

But I smile. The possibility of hearing Bill's voice and understanding his perspective on events has kept me going through some tough times on this journey. Since Ratnagiri, however, I've been increasingly comfortable that mysteries remain. They might be reason to come back to India sometime, get to the Home Department archives in Nasik and Ahmedabad, see some of the friends I've made again. I'm already beginning to miss them.

Back in the office, I chat with the chief archivist about his treasures, while Rajeev goes to relieve himself. My curiosity eventually gets the better of me.

'How come Mr Divekar has access here? No one's asked any questions,' I venture.

The librarian seems surprised that I don't know. 'Well, he worked at State Police Headquarters for eighteen years.'

What? No wonder Rajeev was able to turn up the documents we've just photocopied.

'Anyway, these raw people can get in anywhere.'

Raw? Something rings a bell. An acronym in the newspapers? But before I can ask, my friend returns, with another docket which he's studying intently.

'Here,' Rajeev says when he's finished, 'you might be interested in this.'

I can't believe my eyes: the confidential internal police report on the Mumbai attacks. I'm amazed to see that the death toll's put at 123, when in the newspapers the lowest figure is in the 170s, sometimes much higher. Who's been inflating the figures and why? Who'll write the true history of the Mumbai attacks, I wonder, recalling the problems with

Shinde's 'official' account of the Parallel Government. Will this document, too, disappear from the records or be tampered with?

~

After lunch in the canteen, we walk the streets. I don't care how tired I get because I can always sleep on the plane. I want to squeeze the pips from these last few hours. Finding ourselves outside St Xavier's school where, in Kipling's novel, Kim was educated, I insist Rajeev poses for a farewell photograph. He seems oddly shy to start with, as though I've proposed something indiscreet, but finally agrees. We then catch an auto-rickshaw to the Ballard estate, the model suburb built by the British during World War One on land reclaimed from the newly excavated Alexandra docks. It's a beautifully regular quarter, spacious and uncluttered after so much of Mumbai, the buildings uniform and in good repair. This would have been the last Bill saw of the city before embarking on his final voyage home. We pause at the war memorial, topped with Georgian gas-lamps and decorated with reliefs of lions. One facet pays homage to the port workers who volunteered for the ill-fated campaign against the German forces in Tanganyika in 1917. I'm delighted by this adventitious link to my childhood. Then it's a farewell tea at the Britannia café, run by an acquaintance of Rajeev's.

'I'm tired,' he suddenly announces, walrus moustache drooping lugubriously, as we sip tea and eat tiny, over-sweet cakes.

'Shall we head back?'

'No, I mean really tired. I'm getting old.'

'Nonsense, it's getting up at five in the morning to exercise. No wonder you feel whacked.'

'Still,' he smiles, 'another day closer to retirement. Then I'll do what you're doing. Research. I can't wait. You saw all those boxes in Special Branch?' He rubs his hands. 'It's that – or something on the history of comics.'

I laugh. His mobile goes. Again, the bizarre wait until it rings off and Rajeev texts back. My question can't be stifled any longer.

'Rajeev, what's "raw"? I've seen it in the papers,' I hazard, somewhat ashamed of my dissembling.

'Roar?'

'R-A-W.'

He looks at me quizzically. 'Oh, you mean Research and Analysis Wing,' he says at last. 'Something like your MI6.'

Bill was right. Things are often not quite what they seem in India. It all falls into place. This is why Rajeev was able to see the intercepts warning of the Mumbai attacks. And how his ubiquitous contacts were able to dig up so much useful information for me. And his bizarre way with his phone. That day in Elphinstone archives, I couldn't have fallen on anyone more useful for my quest. I smile at the irony of photographing Rajeev outside St Xavier's, for the school was Kim's springboard towards the imperial secret service. But Rajeev looks more like my idea of Kipling's Lama, with his wise yet unworldly expression.

'I'd never even have got going on this trip, if it hadn't been for you. I'd have probably ended up fried on a beach in Goa.'

'Nonsense, dear man. Wish I could have helped more. It's been worth it?'

I nod sagely. 'Can't believe how much I've learned. And what luck I've had.'

'That's the joy of research, isn't it? The serendipity. But if you don't seize your breaks, you're wasting your time, no? I thought when I first saw you, here's someone like me, who wants to find things out. I told you once that you'd have made a good detective. Like your father.'

We embrace at Flora Fountain on the old Hornby Road, surrounded by the monumental buildings of the Raj. It seems so long ago that I was making my way to Elphinstone for the first time. With a strong pang of loss, I watch Rajeev cross the street, shoulders hunched, looking restlessly left and right as he dodges vehicles, until he disappears into the crowds on the pavement opposite. There's nothing for it but to head back to the hotel and pack. It seems to take only minutes to settle up, make the return drive to the airport and check in. All the while I review what's happened during the last few weeks. Leaving aside the first two or three years of my life, which are almost devoid of memories, I knew Bill for barely eight or nine years. By coming to India I've doubled the extent of my knowledge of his life. It's a gift I could never have anticipated. And what I've discovered hasn't tarnished my childhood memories. By setting them in motion once again, in a nuanced and complex interaction with a previously unknown Bill, my trip has made them even more precious. To extend J.M. Barrie's metaphor, December roses can have a richer and more subtle scent than their summer forerunners.

When the engines open to full throttle for take-off, I take a last look out of the window. The lights of the Dharavi slums recede like glow-worms, before they're hidden behind the terminal building. As we draw abreast of it, I see tiny figures on the roof. They're armed. The bumpy tarmac drops seamlessly away and soon we're banking westwards towards the greeny-lilac afterglow of the sunset.

They're late for the airport. His father's waiting in the passage, wearing a dark blue Aertex shirt, khaki shorts and white knee-length stockings, hair impeccably Brylcreemed after his shower. But despite the encouraging smiles, his grey eyes are full of concern. The boy swivels one last look round his room, taking in the yellow football in the corner, leather flaking from the thrashing it gets up on the flat roof. There's a brand-new one waiting for him in England, courtesy of his grandmother in Norfolk. He sees the blistered flip-flops by the bed, the tat-tered raffia Zulu skirt on the hook, the Dan Dare annuals on the bedside table, Tunney's lead curled carefully on the windowsill. He's got everything for the journey, his royal blue and cream BOAC sports bag with Rider Haggard's Nada the Lily, his sandwiches and the short-sleeved Fair Isle sweater, like his father's, which his mother knitted for the night-flight and the cool days of an English spring.

He feels for his Airfix box, checking it's protected by the pullover. It contains the Lancaster bomber which he wheedled as a final farewell present. 18s/6d, it says on the front, but they paid forty East African shillings. He feels a little ashamed. But he doesn't want to be looked down on in the Modelling Club when he arrives at junior school. He feels in his pocket for the English ten-bob note his parents have provided to buy tuck and the Humbrol camouflage paints to decorate the plane. Then he tightens the elephant-hair bangle which Kimwaga's sent down from Tabora.

'He says he's sorry he can't come himself,' his father had announced the previous day, 'his little girl's unwell. But he wants you to have this,' he added, adjusting the bracelet to go over the boy's wrist. 'It's to keep off the evil eye, Kimwaga says.'

As the Land Rover crosses Selander Bridge, the boy stares out to sea. It's low tide and the muddy creek's draining fast, scoring crazy channels in the sand as it races reefwards. In the distance, white triangles of dhow sail show against the cloudy ivory and grey of the late afternoon sky. Almost every day now, for the past four weeks, he's been down on the beach. Even this morning there was one last swim. He hasn't been able to stop since at last learning how at the Gymkhana Club. He wanted to travel with Dar brine on him, to prolong the connection as long as possible; but his mother insisted the boy shower, or he'd itch all the way to London.

London. All of a sudden, the enormity sinks in. The boy fiddles furiously with the elephant-hair bangle. Yet he's been so looking forward so to the East African Airways flight

*which starts in Dar and calls at Zanzibar before its final des-
tination, Nairobi. There, they'll change onto the much bigger
BOAC plane. Will it still be the Bristol Britannia, the 'whis-
pering giant', for the long haul to Europe via Khartoum and
Benghazi? Or one of the new VC-10s, more impressive, but
which skip some of the stops where desert winds blow? Either
way, it means another stamp in his Junior Jet Club logbook,
giving him enough for a visit to the pilot's cabin on his flight
home. And there'll be peppermint creams. Every unaccompa-
nied child has them showered on him by the crew.*

*Now, at the last minute, the boy doesn't want any of it.
When will he see the dogs again, and Kimwaga, who's looking
after them back in Tabora during this temporary assignment
in Dar, where his father's the acting chief game warden? He
yearns for his minder's encouraging smile and woodsmoke
smell. Will Kimwaga be willing to move with them to Addis
Ababa, in eighteen months' time? What about all his friends
from St Michael's, some of whom live here in the capital? In
his suitcase is the paper napkin they all signed, offering their
good wishes, that last night in the refectory. Even beastly
Brother Rayner gave him a pat on the head. A handful of
his comrades has already left for England and others will be
going in the autumn, to schools with gritty-sounding names
like Stonyhurst and Ratcliffe College.*

*'Make sure you write every Sunday, won't you,' his father
smiles uncertainly, 'and we'll write every week as well. We'll
keep you up to speed with all the news about Kimwaga's baby.
And Tunney and Dempsey. You'll have Ames if you feel home-
sick. Barney's in Cambridge and he'll take you out from time
to time for a slap-up tea. He's getting a big red sports car now,
a 1935 MG. Much more stylish than a DKW.'*

*And there's more advice on how to conduct himself in his
early days at an English school. There'll be one other pupil
joining this summer term, his mother's found out, so he won't
be the only new boy.*

'*You'll soon be pals,*' *his father reassures him.*

And his family? When will he see them again? The summer term only lasts a couple of months, and then he'll spend the early part of the holidays with his grandparents in Cornwall before coming home in August. Cornwall. His heart sinks. He was there the previous year, endless blank days while his grandfather smoked cigarettes and watched racing all afternoon on the black-and-white television. Nothing like the coffee farm on the edge of the Rift Valley near Mbeya. Walks with his grandmother were the only distraction, but it rained so much that they sometimes couldn't get out for days, their only visitor the grocer's boy clunking up the lane from Constantine on his bicycle. Eventually, the boy complained of feeling ill. What else could explain the deadening sense of colourlessness? When his grandmother took him to the doctor, the man fussed and tested and asked question after question. He'd once lived in Kenya and talked fondly of life there. Slowly the boy could feel himself reviving. Eventually the doctor turned to his grandmother.

'*Madam, the problem's simple. The boy's not ill. He's bored. Very, very bored.*'

And that was how he discovered boredom. Cornwall, boredom, horse racing. Horse racing, boredom, Cornwall. Forever associated now. He prays school will be different.

August. It seems – what's that word his old headmaster Father McCarthy loves? – aeons away. He can barely remember the previous one, so packed are the days out here. The boy feels his lip's betraying wobble. But he mustn't cry. Shaka didn't blub when he was exiled. But why didn't he ask to carry on at St Michael's until he was thirteen? Why was he so keen to take the entrance exams early? It's the weight of expectation, he senses that dimly. He has to be as good as the brothers who've preceded him. If only he hadn't gone along with it. Then there'd be more trips, like the one to the Ugalla River, fishing holidays in the Southern Highlands, or nights camping in the wide bowl of the Ngorongoro Crater, hyenas howling hungrily nearby.

On the platform steps behind the wing of the Dakota, the boy turns back. He's not far below the level of his parents, who stand with other well-wishers on the flat roof of the tiny airport building. It's only fifty yards but he knows the chasm can't be bridged. Too late to go back and melt one last time into the cuddles he's just received, enjoy the whispers of encouragement from his mother, his father tousling his head, saying he expects 100 runs before the end of May. He has one arm now round his wife's waist. She's wearing a busy floral print dress and scrunches her habitual tissue in one hand. For once the boy doesn't mind. His younger brother's making faces, screwing his nose up, half-mocking, half-comradely.

The world turns watery as the steward calls him into the cabin, the interior hot and sticky despite the ceiling fans, gyrating elliptically. His canvas bucket seat is on the same side as the terminal. Unfortunately, there's a large man next to the window. He, too, must have people on the rooftop, because he keeps leaning forward and blocking the view, fatty folds of neck bunching as he twists his crew-cut head. The boy catches glimpses of his family but despite his frantic waving, they can't seem to tell where he is. For a moment the clouds part and the sunset seems to be sucked into his father's pupils, like the orange-red blur of a Polaroid flash. He raises a hand to shield his eyes against the glare and they disappear in shadow.

On the Typeface

This book is set in Sabon, a narrow Garamond-style book face designed in 1968 by the German typographer Jan Tschichold. Tschichold had been a leading voice of sans-serif modernist typography, particularly after the publication of his *Die neue Typographie* in 1928. As a result, the Nazis charged him with 'cultural Bolshevism' and forced him to flee Germany for Switzerland.

Tschichold soon renounced modernism – comparing its stringent tenets to the 'teachings of National Socialism and fascism' – and extolled the qualities of classical typography, exemplified in his design for Sabon, which he based on the Romain S. Augustin de Garamond in the 1592 Egenolff-Berner specimen sheet.

Sabon is named after the sixteenth-century French typefounder Jacques Sabon, a pupil of Claude Garamond and proprietor of the Egenolff foundry.